Sharon Koman

D0072490

EXILES *from* EDEN

A NORTON PROFESSIONAL BOOK

EXILES *from* EDEN

PSYCHOTHERAPY
from an
EVOLUTIONARY PERSPECTIVE

Kalman Glantz, Ph.D.
John Pearce, M.D.

W·W· Norton & Company · *New York* · *London*

"Never Borrow Money," p. 37, appears courtesy of Ann Landers, Los Angeles Times Syndicate, and appeared in the *Boston Globe*.

Copyright © 1989 by Kalman Glantz and John Pearce

All rights reserved.

Published simultaneously in Canada by Penguin Books Canada Ltd., 2801 John Street, Markham, Ontario L3R 1B4.

Printed in the United States of America.

First Edition

Library of Congress Cataloging-in-Publication Data

Glantz, Kalman.
   Exiles from Eden : psychotherapy from an evolutionary perspective
   / Kalman Glantz. John Pearce. — 1st ed.
      p.   cm.
   Bibliography: p.
   Includes index.
   1. Psychotherapy. 2. Human evolution. 3. Genetic psychology.
I. Pearce, John K., 1935- . II. Title.
RC480.5.G54 1989
616.89′14—dc19

ISBN 0-393-70073-9

W. W. Norton & Company, Inc., 500 Fifth Avenue, New York, N.Y. 10110
W. W. Norton & Company Ltd., 37 Great Russell Street, London WC1B 3NU

1 2 3 4 5 6 7 8 9 0

To Gary Bernhard
sine quo non

and

Gladys and Kenneth Pearce
who passed 90 in style

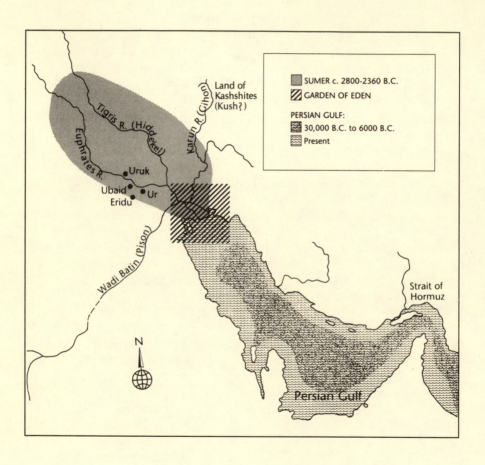

Land of
Kashshites
(Kush?)

SUMER c. 2800-2360 B.C.

GARDEN OF EDEN

PERSIAN GULF:

30,000 B.C. to 6000 B.C.

Present

Tigris R. (Hiddekel)

Karun R. (Gihon)

Euphrates R.

Uruk

Ubaid   Ur
Eridu

Wadi Batin (Pison)

N

Strait of
Hormuz

Persian Gulf

Eden

ARCHAEOLOGIST JURIS ZARINS thinks he has discovered Eden. He believes it now lies under the Persian Gulf, downstream from the ancient civilizations that flowed along the banks of the Tigris and the Euphrates. It was from those civilizations that the Israelites took the story of the Garden of Eden.

Satellite photos have revealed many of the features that are found in the Biblical description of the "garden." For example, the Bible says that the garden was watered by four rivers, the Tigris, the Euphrates, the Pison and the Gihon. This was a mystery. The Tigris and Euphrates are known, but no one could find two other rivers in the region. The new photos reveal the bed of a fossil river, the Batin, and the bed of a seasonal stream (a *wadi*), the Karun, coming into the delta of the two living rivers. The Hebrew story says that the Gihon was located in the "land of Kush," which has long been identified as Ethiopia. That would make the geography purely mythological. However, Biblical scholar Ephraim Speiser has suggested that the word Kush refers to the land of the Kashshites, a people who conquered Mesopotamia in about 1500 B.C. The Kashshites were contemporaries of the Israelites, and they were in just the right place.

That this area should now be under the sea could shed light on another myth common to this region—the great flood of the Noah's ark story. Consider this: the Sumerians always claimed that their ancestors "came out of the sea." Zarins believed that they did, having retreated northward from the encroaching waters of the Gulf.

Eden was not paradise. It was just a place—a place where human beings lived the way all humans lived before the rise of civilization. Zarins believes that the area had been inhabited by simple foraging peoples—people who lived by hunting and gathering. The descendants of these people were, in his view, the creators of the great agricultural civilizations that arose upstream, in the fertile river valleys. Thus the myth of the garden would seem to be a cultural memory of a time when humans lived simpler lives, free of the arduous labor of the fields, but exposed to the dangers of life in the wild.

We are all exiles from Eden. We have been exiled to civilization, to a brave new world whose glories are rivaled only by its problems. This book is about some of the problems.

Contents

ix

Acknowledgments

MANY PEOPLE HAVE contributed to this book, beginning with the scientists whose ideas appear throughout these pages. We are grateful to them for the inspiration they have given us.

We would like to thank most especially those who have given of their time and expertise to help make this a better work. Leda Cosmides, John Tooby and Jim Weinrich each read a version of the text and sharpened its theoretical focus considerably. Irven DeVore and David Pilbeam helped us to eliminate assorted errors from Chapter 2. Robert Hinde made many suggestions for the improvement of Chapters 4 and 5. Bob Goisman and Amos Naor gave us excellent suggestions on Chapter 12. Robert F. Bales, Chris Beels, Judy Cormier, Helene Deguise-Lopez, Len and Martha Friedman, and David McGill read various drafts of the book and provided us with helpful feedback. Bob Brodsky and Toni Treadway read early drafts, listened enthusiastically to the ideas as they were worked out, and made very helpful comments about style. Bob McAndrews and Bill McKelvie provided insight and encouragement when portions of the material were being prepared for submission as a dissertation to the Union Graduate School. Jill Rierdan suggested the title. Susan Barrows did more than edit the book, she frightened us into many improvements. Finally, special thanks are due to Lorraine Fine Glantz, who read endless drafts, forced us to clarify many passages and ferreted out innumerable typos, and to Susy Pearce, who cheerfully put up with having Sundays and holidays peppered with evolutionary psychology.

I

EVOLUTION

and

HUMAN BEHAVIOR

CHAPTER 1

Overview

It would indeed be the ultimate tragedy if the history of
the human race proved to be nothing more noble than
the story of an ape playing with a box of matches on a
petrol dump.
— David Ormsby-Gore

THIS IS THE STORY OF AN ONGOING ADVENTURE. One of us was studying
evolutionary biology while being trained as a psychotherapist. To his surprise, he began to find in the biology a more promising foundation for the
practice of psychotherapy than that provided by traditional theories of psychotherapy. He wanted to share his excitement with others. In the process,
he enlisted the collaboration of a second author with a wider background in
psychiatry and psychotherapy. Jointly, we are attempting to share our dis-
coveries with our readers.

Our hope is to begin to place the practice of psychotherapy on a firm
theoretical basis — the science of evolutionary biology. The reasons for doing
so are several. The first is to promote the unity of scientific understanding.
Evolutionary biology is a discipline that is surging ahead, reshaping our
basic understanding of human beings. It underlies such practical enterprises
as the gene factories that are beginning to dot the landscapes of business and
academia. It is the unifying factor in the study of all animal and plant
behavior. If we can bring psychotherapy theory into harmony with this
powerful new way of thinking, we will have brought together things that
rightly belong together. Second, in evolutionary biology we think we have
found a basis for the unification of psychotherapy. Evolution provides the
most general possible perspective from which to look at humans. From this
vantage point, it should be possible to sort out why different psychothera-

pies—dynamic, behavioral, systems, hypnotherapy, etc.—work, and how they can fit together.

This is hardly the first time that biology has been brought to bear on psychotherapy. Freud, after all, has rightly been called a "biologist of the mind." He drew heavily on the biology and Darwinism that were current in his time. But since biology has progressed, an updating is necessary.

Is this simply a theoretical exercise? We don't think so. Beliefs about human nature subtly influence everyone. A new theory, when digested, will bring about changes in practice. Therapists will notice new things and will see familiar things in a new perspective.

There is another need to ground psychotherapy in biology, one which is particularly acute at this time. Psychotherapy has come under attack from some biologists, especially those who study the brain. The brain is the organ of behavior, writes Nancy Andreasen, author of *The Broken Brain*. According to her, if something is wrong with a person's behavior, find out what is wrong with that person's brain and treat it. Talking about the problem won't do any good.

This attitude has of course been fostered by the spectacular successes of biological psychiatry (psychopharmacology): lithium for manic-depression, neuroleptics for the symptoms of schizophrenia, tricyclics and MAOIs for the control of depression, anxiety, and panic, etc. These drugs have indeed created a revolution in psychiatry, and other useful medications will no doubt be discovered. But psychopharmacology is only one aspect of neuroscience, and a fairly narrow one at that. We took a broader view. We undertook to study the evolution (history) of the brain, the social context in which it has to function, and the tasks it has to perform. This historical approach has convinced us that psychotherapy, *while not a cure for major mental illness or organic disorders*, will prove to be the treatment of choice for much of the psychological distress now seen in clinical practice. Most psychotherapists are probably persuaded of this already, but will perhaps be reassured to know that there is a strong biological rationale for their position.

A note on our method. In this book, the findings of evolutionary biology are described but not closely argued. The arguments, widely available in other sources, are terribly technical, and would weigh down our text. We have not tried to "prove" what the evolutionary biologists have put forward, but rather to apply their findings to psychotherapy. From those unfamiliar with biology, we ask therefore a temporary suspension of disbelief. We hope that readers who are intrigued but skeptical will want to look at the basic science more closely. We recommend that they consult David Barash's excellent book, *The Whisperings Within*.

Themes of the Book, in a Nutshell

The human species has a beginning. It evolved from ancestral species approximately 100,000 years ago. It inherited many of its characteristics from those ancestors — *Homo erectus*, *Homo habilis*, and the australopithecines (the famous Lucy and her kind). By 30,000 years ago, it was decorating the walls of caves with great works of art and making numerical notations on bone and stone surfaces. The skill and artistic sensibility manifest in these paintings clearly identifies the makers as completely developed humans. If the cave painters were alive today, we would not be able to tell them from ourselves. Indeed, they *are* us. Our species has not changed genetically since that time, despite the enormous cultural and technological changes that have occurred.

How do biologists know this? Because we are today one species. People from all races can mate and produce offspring. People of all races have essentially the same abilities. Surface traits like hair or eye color are variable, but there are no essential differences between Asians, Europeans, and Africans, or between the people of the cities and the people of the most remote jungle settings. Genetically, we are all the same, despite having lived apart for thousands of years. All biologists agree that this means that we are descended from people who were, genetically, the same. Stephen Jay Gould, the eminent Harvard paleontologist, made the point forcefully in his March, 1988 column in *Natural History*: "[We should not be] . . . surprised that the passage of 30,000 years has yielded no perceptible change in human cognition. This geological moment is but a very small segment, by anyone's . . . standard, in the life of most species."

The early humans — and their immediate ancestor, *Homo erectus* — lived for hundreds of thousands of years as nomads who foraged for food in small bands made up of closely related individuals who depended on each other for survival. Food had to be gotten every day. Predators were a constant threat. A slight mistake could mean death. That way of life was shared by most humans until a mere 10 or 12 thousand years ago, when humans discovered how seeds grow and began to practice agriculture.

We have a window into that way of life. Until recently, a few peoples still lived exclusively by hunting and gathering: the !Kung (Bushmen) of the Kalahari, the Aborigines of Australia, the BaMbuti (Pygmies) of the Congo forest, the Inuit (Eskimo), some Native American (Indian) peoples, and a few others. Scientific understanding of early humans is drawn from eyewitness accounts of these peoples as well as from the archaeological record. We have used this material and only this material to construct our picture of early human social organization.[1] Furthermore, we have tried to confine our generalizations to traits which were common to all these peoples, despite the sharply contrasting environments in which they lived. The common traits are the ones most likely to have come down from the earliest humans.

Note that no society which developed agriculture or herding can be used to illuminate our ancestral way of life. Thus we do not derive any lessons from the Masai, the Arapesh, the Trobriand Islanders, the Navajo, and the other staples of classical cultural anthropology. These peoples all have been marked by the agro-cultural revolution. Like modern American civilization, they represent themselves, and nothing more.

We want to emphasize in particular that we do not consider the Yanomamo, immortalized by Napoleon Chagnon in *The Fierce People*, to be close approximations of the hunter-gatherer lifestyle. True, the Yanomamo and other similarly warlike peoples of South America do hunt, but they also use slash and burn agriculture. To us, the evidence overwhelmingly indicates that slash and burn agriculture is a cultural innovation which is generally accompanied by another cultural innovation: ritualized warfare. This is true not only in South America, but also among the peoples of New Guinea, where killing for revenge is also a way of life. For a description, see Mervyn Meggitt's aptly-titled book, *Blood Is Their Argument*.

We have also excluded the Kwakiutl and other Native American peoples of the Northwest Coast of America. While they were indeed pre-agricultural, they don't really qualify as hunter-gatherers because they were no longer nomadic; they had permanent settlements. They lived in an area so rich that they could harvest the bounty of the land almost as if they were farming it. Their major economic problem was disposing of their surpluses, which they did in elaborate rituals such as the *potlatch*. It isn't surprising that they developed many of the institutions of modern life, such as art, permanent settlements, institutionalized waste, inequality, and social stratification.

Only the hunter-gatherers who survived into historical times as true nomads can be expected to provide us with some idea of what life was like in humanity's original, or natural, environment. The natural environment is the one in which our species evolved. In it, our specifically human comple-

---

[1]To what extent contemporary hunter-gatherers reflect the way of life of our ancestors is a subject that is hotly debated in anthropological circles. For example, it is becoming clear that at least some BaMbuti (Pygmy) peoples have lived in association with nearby agriculturists for centuries (Bailey and Peacock, in press). This raises the possibility that their social organization has undergone some modifications. Nevertheless, the hunter-gatherers who were actually observed by anthropologists are without doubt the best source of information available about early humans, and nothing better is likely to appear, so we have to go with it.

ment of genes took on their present form, and the human brain came into being. That brain was shaped by the evolutionary processes of mutation and natural selection to help a weak primate species compete with other, stronger animals in the grasslands of Africa, under harsh and demanding conditions.

Our mode of survival, as we learn from the study of evolution, was coordination, cooperation and exchange. Men, the hunters, exchanged food with women, the gatherers. Men, and often women, coordinated their efforts on the hunt; women gathered food, reared children, built shelters and performed other tasks requiring a high degree of cooperation. The human brain expanded and developed new complexity while coping with the demands of this extremely rich social life.

Our physical and social environments have changed drastically since that time. Fewer and fewer people around the world live or grow up in extended families, surrounded by supportive adults. Few of us have to face predators and forage for food on a daily basis. In myriad ways, the onrush of progress in science and technology has radically transformed the world. And not just some of the world. Not just Europe and North America. Ways of life have changed for almost all human beings.

The environment has changed; the genes have stayed the same. This brings us to a problem. If our ancestors were adapted to the hunting and gathering environment, and we are like our ancestors, then we, like them, are "adapted" to that environment. That is to say, we are predisposed to behave in ways which would serve us well in that original environment. We have genes that evolved to help us survive in that environment. Those genes are not necessarily helpful in the one we live in now.

The result, we maintain, is a mismatch between genes and environment. This mismatch is responsible for creating much of the psychological distress that psychotherapists are called upon to treat. It would not make much sense to treat people suffering from this mismatch with psychoactive drugs (although it might help relieve some symptoms). Only by helping people to understand themselves and learn to match their behavior to the current environment can fundamental improvement be expected to occur. This is why we say that in the current environment there are fundamental biological reasons why the need for psychotherapy is widespread.

Perhaps the most obvious example of the price we pay for a changed environment is the inappropriate triggering of the fight-or-flight response. When faced with a threat, humans, like other animals, respond with a series of physiological changes that prepare the organism for quick physical action. So long as the threats emanated from wild animals and similar external dangers, the fight-or-flight response served us well. We were better able to run or defend ourselves. Furthermore, actual running or fighting helped the body to get rid of (metabolize) the chemicals that prepared it for action. But today, we face threats of a different sort, threats, for example, to our status on the job—a boss who doesn't like our work, or a colleague who is out to beat us to the next rung on the ladder. A physical response would not be appropriate. But the body responds with fight-or-flight arousal, and we sit in a hormonal stew that ultimately damages our health.

An awareness of what the natural environment was like makes it possible to think about things in a new way. To illustrate this point, we want to recount a story. At the time of writing, one of us had recently become a father. His wife, an expert on children, told him to walk with the infant to make him stop crying. Not surprisingly, it worked. "Why do you think walking makes him stop crying?" asked the father. "The pediatrician told me walking simulated the rocking a baby experiences *in utero*." The father was unimpressed with this explanation. After a period of reflection, he had a thought: If a child cried while being carried around in a band, it might signal the presence of the band to prey or to predators. Children with a tendency to cry while being carried might endanger the survival of the band. Or parents might be forced (by fear, or by other band members) to abandon such children. Hence children with a tendency to cry while being walked would tend not to survive and the genes predisposing to such behavior would tend to die out.

Great idea, the father thought. But can it be proved? Hardly. It's a plausible idea. It helps to explain the observable data. It fits in with what is known about the genetics of behavior and about the transmission of traits from generation to generation. In short, it makes sense. But it can't be proved.

Some months after we wrote this paragraph, we came across the following lines in Bruce Chatwin's book about the Australian Aborigines:

> We looked up to see a procession of women and children on their way back from foraging. The babies swayed peacefully in the folds of their mother's dresses.
> "You never hear them cry," Marian said, "as long as the mother keeps moving."

So, we are proposing a way of thinking that accounts for the obvious facts of everyday life. We hope that the reader will find this perspective both novel and useful.

Let's look at the outline of the book. Chapter 2 contrasts the natural environment with the modern one. In Chapter 3 we present some data concerning the biological basis of human social life. We discovered, for instance, that the evidence indicates that humans are not totally selfish, as

Freud had argued, or irredeemably competitive, as the Social Darwinists once believed. Rather, we have strong genetic predispositions to help others. In the natural environment these predispositions apparently helped us to survive; they induced people to weave a web of obligation that created a mutual support system—a seamless web of community. In modern society, particularly mass society, our predispositions to help others often go unrewarded. We believe this creates psychological problems for many people.

In Chapters 4 and 5 we examine child-rearing practices among hunter-gatherers and contrast them with those prevalent in the contemporary Western world. We conclude that various widely accepted contemporary child-rearing practices may be far from ideal for human children. We think we can explain why, even with the best intentions, parents often fail to raise happy children.

Here again, genes and environment interact. The evidence seems to indicate that children are born with a need for child-rearing of a certain type. Just as they need food and vitamins, so they need certain parenting practices, including some that are generally unavailable today (e.g., frequent contact with many supportive adults, a danger-free home zone contrasting with a dangerous environment, relatively prolonged nursing, and nag-free, go-at-your-own-pace learning). We think that our analysis helps to explain many of the problems of adults in today's world.

In Chapters 6, 7, 8, 9 and 10 we discuss sex and gender. We will provide some explanations for such common phenomena as sexual jealousy, and look at some differences in the way men and women make love, express emotion, set priorities, and relate to one another.

Sex and gender are problems for civilized humans. Many religions and moral systems single out sexual activity for criticism. Contemporary women's liberation sometimes seems to deny the existence of gender distinctions. Like many before us, we feel that attacks on gender set the mind against the body. We think that the appreciation of gender has a lot to offer both sexes.

In Chapter 11 we look at the brain from an evolutionary perspective. Here we challenge most directly the exaggerated claims of biological psychiatry. We rely heavily on the neurobiological finding that the brain creates "models" of the environment. Some models are created utterly outside of awareness, such as the visual models the brain creates out of signals from the retina. Some are cognitive models, such as a person's expectations about the behavior of strangers.

The model-forming capacity in animals evolved because it enhanced survival and reproduction. In the language of evolutionary biology, the ability to build models was adaptive. Models must provide the organism with correct information about the environment—how to elude predators, find food, and recognize potential mates. An individual whose model doesn't do that will be less likely to survive long enough to pass along its genes.

In humans, the cerebral cortex plays an extremely important role in the model-making process. The creative power of the cortex is a two-edged sword. It makes it possible for humans to generate models of magnificent complexity, but also makes it possible to form models that are self-defeating and/or destructive to others. The Nazi conception of the world is an example of what this power can do.

We think that outside the natural environment the models that individuals create are less likely to be adaptive. The social scene is too complex and stressful for many people to master. Social support is often unobtainable. Frequently, survival can be achieved only through the sacrifice of important values. Natural ways of behaving don't produce the desired ends. People become confused and generate false ideas about self and other.

In a confusing environment, a perfectly good brain can generate a perfectly terrible model. And this model will not be improved by drug therapy (although drugs can certainly improve, temporarily at least, the outlook of people with emotional disorders). Hence the need for psychotherapy.

In Chapter 12 we look at the field of psychotherapy from the perspective we have developed. We argue as follows: Although none of the existing "schools" provides a comprehensive framework for therapeutic interventions, most schools suggest interventions that do fit into a broad biological approach. The biological framework can be used by those who believe in exploration and by those who believe in conditioning, by individual as well as systems-oriented therapists, by practitioners of body-oriented and expressive approaches as well as by those who rely exclusively on verbal procedures. We provide support for those who believe that the best psychotherapists use many different kinds of interventions.

The last three chapters are devoted to transcripts of case material. In many of these, we talk to patients about some of the subjects we discuss in this book—the original environment, life in a band, model-building, gender-based behavior, etc. We have chosen to present such exchanges for a couple of reasons: to provide additional examples of the use of these concepts, and to demonstrate that the concepts can help clients understand themselves and their environment. Not all clients can benefit from this kind of information exchange, but those who have the ability should be given the opportunity.

On the other hand, we do not want to give the impression that the explicit use of theoretical concepts drawn from biology constitutes the essence of the therapy we are proposing. The principal aim of this book is to suggest to the therapist new ways of conceptualizing psychological problems.

Throughout, we have asked ourselves some basic questions: What happens when a creature with old genes has to live in a completely new type of society? What are the problems? What are possible solutions that a person might try out? We humans are fond of easy, novel solutions. But as many traditional peoples have found out to their sorrow, new solutions often result in the destruction of traditional social organizations — societies that worked. Undoubtedly, our species' superior intellectual creativity and behavioral flexibility have gotten us where we are today, but where we are today has both advantages and disadvantages. We have, on the one hand, achieved extraordinary wealth, and have produced new and delicious ways of living. But on the other hand, we have horrendous social problems and we may be on our way to destroying the planet. The intelligence and flexibility of our species must be intelligently managed. We think it can be gently guided by biological wisdom.

Among most pre-industrial peoples, the elders and the shamans were wise in the way of the tribal ancestors. As therapists, we must draw on the entire history of the human race to protect ourselves from the ethnocentrism of our own cultural backgrounds. A good therapist must be wise in the ways of the species.

CHAPTER 2

Psychotherapy and the Natural Environment

Something there is that doesn't love a wall.
— Robert Frost

ONE OF THE NICE THINGS about the study of evolution is that it dissolves the old nature/nurture debate that has so long plagued the social sciences. Genes and environment turn out to be two sides of the same coin. Over the long term, genes are shaped (chosen) by the environment. They can best be described as instructions for coping with environments. Good instructions survive. Bad ones are eliminated by natural selection. But "good" and "bad" depend entirely on prevailing conditions.

The shaping of genes by the environment occurs on many levels, from individual to species. If an individual organism isn't equipped with genes that prepare it to cope with the environment it is born into, the organism will not survive and won't leave any offspring, i.e., any copies of its genes. For example, if the seeds of a tree fall on the wrong kind of soil, they won't germinate — even if the seed's genes are perfectly normal. Similarly, genes coding for a perfectly good camel will not succeed if the camel is somehow born into the arctic environment.

On a larger scale, if environmental conditions change, organisms with perfectly good genes will die out. This is what happened to the dinosaurs. When the climate on earth changed, the genes that coded for the marvelous array of creatures we call dinosaurs suddenly became obsolete. Dinosaur genes just didn't produce organisms that could survive. Genes that coded for

12

mammals were better suited to the new conditions, and thus our distant ancestors got their start.

Through this interaction with the environment, genes construct organs, like eyes, that help in the struggle for survival. In the process, genes construct organisms with a tendency to behave in certain ways. The genes that code for behavior are not separate or different from the ones that code for anatomical structures. Behavior and anatomy are linked. The behaviors, like the organs, are suited to specific conditions. For example, some genes construct organisms with a tendency to freeze in the face of danger; these organisms always have markings that make them hard to see in their natural environment. In a different environment, the same markings might make them stand out, which would turn freezing into a self-destructive behavior.

Ultimately, genes do something else: they create needs which can be satisfied only by particular environments. Fish genes create organisms that need water. Monkey genes create organisms that need mothers to teach them how to behave. Human genes make organisms that need adults around in order to learn how to talk.

In this chapter, we look at human evolution to see how our natural environment shaped our genes, and how, in turn, our genes shaped our behavior and our needs. We hope that this will throw some light on how people today behave and on why they suffer from psychological distress.

The Hunting and Gathering Environment

Our species—*Homo sapiens*—came into existence sometime between 300,000 and 100,000 years ago. (That's kind of fuzzy, but it will have to do until more and better bones are found.) For almost all of that time, most of us lived in small nomadic bands, constructed only temporary shelters to shield us from the elements, and foraged for our food without growing it. The males in these bands hunted big animals when they could. The females gathered plant food and killed small animals. Everybody probably scavenged.

The hunter-gatherer way of life was no utopia. Life was short, much shorter than the span we take for granted now. There was danger on all sides. There was little protection from extremes of temperature. Hard physical exertion was often necessary. People had little privacy. They had no way to get away from each other's idiosyncrasies. Quarrels could explode at any time. Fear of the supernatural probably played a significant role in their lives.

Few if any modern humans would want to live the way these ancestors lived. But to understand human nature, one has to become acquainted with the hunter-gatherer way of life. Our genes were formed during the period we lived as hunter-gatherers, so it is not surprising that when one begins to look at that way of life, many of the most confusing features of human behavior begin to make sense.

Despised traits like greed, envy, jealousy, aggression, and love of gossip turn out to serve vital social functions. What we often label as our "lower" impulses reveal themselves as essential components of the social order. Self-interest and competitiveness serve to ensure that we are enthusiastic about going out and getting our food. Greed and envy serve to motivate us to maintain equality in a context in which sharing means survival. The tendency to enjoy conformity makes it possible for aggressive, potentially violent males to work together on common tasks. The love of gossip helps to maintain group pressures that in turn support order. So does the fear of retaliation by friends and relatives. Guilt and shame motivate people to meet obligations and thereby create reliable support networks.

Outside the nomadic foraging band, the human emotional system does not function in the same way. Once the powerful human brain creates greater levels of social complexity, the delicate balance characteristic of hunter-gatherer life begins to disintegrate. Many of the more negative aspects of the human personality are released to form social institutions of which we are less than proud.

The ultimate blow to the hunter-gatherer way of life was delivered by the invention of agriculture, a mere 12,000 to 10,000 years ago. As agriculture forced humans to reshape their lives in response to new necessities, the coherence of the social system started to break down. In the presence of agricultural surpluses, greed could lead to antisocial hoarding, something that was impossible for nomadic peoples, who can't possess more than they can carry. Guilt, gossip and aggression lost their functions, as other institutions — police, military, etc. — took on the task of maintaining order. The old emotions came into conflict with new institutions such as church and state and ultimately became sins or deplorable weaknesses.

But the old emotions did not go away. Greed, envy and all the rest remained a part of us. The amount of time we spent hunting and gathering dwarfs the amount of time we have been farmers and keepers of domesticated animals. Our genes have not had time to change — to adapt themselves to the new technologies. Old genes, new environment. The potential for conflict is great.

We believe that one consequence was the emergence of a characteristic feature of the civilized human: grandiose fantasies about the "higher" nature of man combined with chronic disappointment about the impossibility of ever living up to these God-like ideals. This characteristic way of thinking helps, in vulnerable people, to set the stage for the splitting of the self into two parts: an idealized self and the "bad" self, with the latter being the part that does not fit the current cultural ideal.

The Hunting-Gathering Band

Much of what is known about the way of life of our ancestors comes from observations of contemporary hunter-gatherer peoples. To understand how the last 12,000–10,000 years have affected us, the reader needs to have some familiarity the way of life of these peoples. We have provided a brief description in the following section. Readers who want more information may consult one of many excellent ethnographies. Among the most readable are Colin Turnbull's *The Forest People*, Marjorie Shostak's *Nisa: The Life and Words of a !Kung Woman*, Elizabeth Marshall Thomas' *The Harmless People*, Farley Mowat's *People of the Deer*, and Richard Gould's *Yiwara: Foragers of the Australian Desert*. (Note, however, that the way of life of these peoples was probably not characteristic of *all* our ancestors. See the box entitled "The Emergence of Cultural Complexity" for a discussion of this issue.)

The social organization of a contemporary hunting and gathering band is a miracle of dynamic balance. Freedom and conformity, self-reliance and cooperation, generosity and envy, sharing and greed, love and anger — all are bound together like particles in an atom. Every problematic impulse can be observed, every "deplorable" trait is there, and yet it all works: the band swirls through desert and jungle in a tiny tornado of communication and support.

There is no one single explanation for this acrobatic triumph of sociality. The band is a product of long years of evolution, an integrated system. Perhaps, though, two major forces or "glues" can be identified: kinship and the immediacy of threats to survival.

The members of a band are closely related. Helping someone means helping a relative or someone married to a relative. Cheating means cheating a relative. Not working means letting relatives down. And because there is no stored surplus on which the group can draw, each individual has to pull his or her own weight. Drones, malingerers, and sociopaths can't be tolerated; they endanger everyone else. As a result, self-interest and the good of the community are very difficult to separate. Since no one can survive alone, everyone has to obey the rules, more or less. In turn, the rules of the social order are the rules that enable each individual to survive.

Order is achieved through tradition and conformity. No courts, judges, or prisons are necessary. No one wants to be ostracized from the circle of

Here and there, the intelligence of humans probably began to transform the social environment long before agriculture was invented, and perhaps as early as 26,000 years ago. There is increasing evidence that some early human groups founded relatively permanent settlements and lived in them for much of the year. Differences in the amount of decoration found on buried bodies may indicate that there was social inequality. The Natufians, a hunting and gathering people that inhabited Israel from perhaps 14,000 years ago, had storage sites antedating agriculture. The Natufians were apparently storing wild grains. So, many of the features that are characteristic of modern society may have been "invented" more than once. Readers interested in this topic may consult *Prehistoric Hunter-Gatherers: The Emergence of Cultural Complexity*, a conference volume edited by Douglas Price of the University of Wisconsin and James Brown of Northwestern University.

We have some indication of what a hunter-gatherer society based on abundance might look like. The Kwakiutl and other Native American peoples of the Northwest Coast of America were pre-agricultural, but they lived in an area blessed with enormous resources. There are salmon runs and seals, shellfish galore, and forests full of game and other delicacies. Indeed, the area is so rich that the main economic problem of these groups was to dispose of their surpluses. In one of their main rituals, the *potlatch*, vast quantities of goods are given away, and even destroyed. The ritual enhances the status of the donors while helping to ensure that the less fortunate have sufficient supplies.

In addition to waste, the Northwest Coast cultures had developed relatively rigid social stratification, inequality, competitiveness, and slavery. Apparently, that is what you get when you combine abundance and intelligence. The human emotional system, crafted for survival in a harsh environment, is simply not adapted to extreme wealth, however much we crave it.

The evidence seems to indicate that any time a group of humans can find a source of resources stable and abundant enough to support a relatively high population density, it will form a more complex society, with many of the negative features of modern society. Human nature being what it is, only the rigors of the nomadic, foraging lifestyle seem to produce a more benevolent, egalitarian way of life.

The power of abundance to change behavior for the worse is not limited to the human species. When Jane Goodall first began to study chimpanzees, she set bunches of bananas out for them, to entice them out of hiding. You might think that the sudden appearance of all those bananas would bring out the best in chimpanzees. On the contrary, fighting and aggressive displays increased dramatically. This is a painful lesson, but one which ought not be ignored.

talking, giving, and sharing. The major methods of "law enforcement" turn out to be gossip and ridicule, activities that we now indulge in only covertly and with guilt. The obvious joy that humans take in the seemingly "base" act of laughing at others turns out to play an essential role in maintaining social cohesion.

People in the band conform, but not against their better judgment, as we often have to do. They seem to feed on their participation in the life of the group. They flow towards it, just as they huddle together physically when there is no obvious need to do so. They are tuned in to each other in a way that we only dimly understand.

Within the framework of the social norms there is considerable freedom. There are rules about marriage, of course, but these rules are often honored in the breach. Adultery does sometimes lead to violence between males, and killing is known to occur, but there is no systematic attempt to control the sexual activity of women. Infidelity is not officially accepted but neither is preventing it an obsession. Nisa, Marjorie Shostak's irrepressible !Kung informant, refers slyly to her husband as "the one in the hut" and to her lover as "the one in the bush."

The system produces virtual equality. Since there are no means of storing wealth — no grains and no money — there are no rich people. Besides, in nomadic bands, possessions have to be carried, making ownership more trouble than it is worth. As a result, everyone is a worker, and no one can live off the labor of another. Each couple has to find food and create shelter for every single day.

Equality, however, is not an ideal, or even, as far as we can tell, a concept. It is a byproduct of the system, a condition that is maintained by keen self-interest. Everyone watches closely as food is distributed. Those who feel that they have been shortchanged protest vociferously. The details of the rules that govern food-sharing differ from culture to culture, but whatever the rules, observant eyes make sure that no one cheats. Everywhere, each individual watches closely whenever edibles are handed around. If someone has an especially good tool, a bow or a spear, the chances are that others will become envious. Someone may ask to borrow it and may keep it indefinitely. The possessors of coveted objects are often relieved to be rid of them, for the envy of others makes them uncomfortable.

The hunting-gathering system is based on the division of labor by sex: men hunt, women gather. This way of dividing up the chores is imposed by the child-bearing and child-rearing functions of the women. Pregnancy is long and has high metabolic requirements. Lack of food or an excessive expenditure of energy can interfere with conception or damage the fetus. Carrying children while chasing giraffes or while waiting hours for a seal to poke its nose through the arctic ice is not practical. The biological need for specialization is compelling.

On the other hand, the economic contribution of both men and women is essential to survival. Game provides most of the protein, but, at least in some societies, more than half of the calories are provided by foods the women gather. Where gathering is not feasible, as in the arctic among the Eskimo, women make indispensable contributions in the areas of tool making, preparation of clothing, and construction of shelter. As a result, the role of each sex is roughly equal in importance, even without taking into account the contribution of women in the area of child-bearing and childcare.

Specialization by sex has two major functions. It forces men and women to share, and it keeps them from having to compete. Each gender is occupied with its own affairs, and each has to contribute to the welfare of the other.

The significance of the hunter-gatherer data

Modern humans are not genetically different from ancient hunter-gatherers. The impulses and predispositions that characterized them characterize us as well. To understand how the modern environment affects people today, we must first understand the relationship between human behavior and the hunting-gathering environment.

In both body and mind, the human species was quite literally shaped by the social and physical environment of hunting and gathering. In the transition from a primary reliance on plant food to the hunting and gathering life, bodies were reshaped and brains were expanded. We became what we are because we could not survive in a demanding environment without a lot of help from relatives and friends. *It is therefore impossible to separate the process by which we became human beings from the process by which we became hunter-gatherers*. We can understand this best if we look back to the way we were before we became fully human.

Back to the Womb of the Species: A Brief Outline of Human Evolution

The animals who started down the road that led to humankind were four-legged primates with small brains who subsisted largely on fruits and leaves. These distant ancestors—the dryopithecines—may have eaten meat occasionally, like chimpanzees, but they did not hunt systematically and almost certainly did not share food with one another. They lived in groups, but each individual had to forage for itself. Even the young were on their own once they were weaned.

We have inherited many of their characteristics. We share with them such physical traits as the general plan of the body, all the principal organs, and the major structures of the brain. We also owe to them the fact that male and female humans are different in size and shape (sexually dimorphic). Finally, we inherited such behavioral characteristics as the fight-or-flight response, the male specializations for defense, and the tendency to maintain personal space and prerogative through bluff and aggressive displays.

However, we are also different from them, socially as well as physically. And the social differences are more important by far.

Except in the case of the rare monogamous species, if any such existed on our ancestral line, fatherhood as we know it almost certainly did not exist among them. Males did not directly provision the females or the young with food or other resources. An infant's survival depended almost totally on its mother's ability and willingness to look after it properly. The males probably helped to find sources of food, and in some species would defend the group from predators. But that was the extent of their "fathering." The males lived lives of their own, somewhat apart from the females and their offspring. They were almost certainly polygynous. They would mate with any available female, provided of course that they weren't prevented from doing so by a more dominant male.

Ancestral primate females were subject to *estrus* (heat), which is to say that they became sexually receptive only on a monthly or seasonal basis. For the most part, females subject to *estrus* do not tolerate sexual advances by a male when they are not in heat. Human females, in contrast, are sexually receptive throughout the month and year, a trait that facilitates prolonged relationships between males and females.

Males and females probably had separate status hierarchies, which means that the success of a mother probably depended, at least in part, on her position in the female hierarchy: high-ranking mothers generally produced more offspring that would survive to maturity than did other females.

There was little if any coordinated, cooperative action involving groups of males. In male-male relationships, aggressive displays figured prominently. Bluffing and threatening served to establish dominance hierarchies which in turn helped to maintain order within the group. However, bluffing and threatening sometimes failed, so actual fighting was not uncommon.

It is true that males also related to each other in other ways. One of the most important male-male activities was grooming. Indeed, grooming can possibly be seen as a forerunner of friendship. Grooming also had what might be called "political" significance. Bouts of grooming played a role in establishing and expressing dominance, and therefore in the reduction of violent conflict.

One has to be careful about overgeneralizing. If we can judge by what we see in some living species that probably resemble our distant ancestors, the latter may have had some traits that foreshadowed those we consider uniquely human. For example, as University of Michigan anthropologist Barbara Smuts has shown, male and female olive baboons establish "friendships," long-term relationships based on companionship and mutual grooming. These relationships are not pair-bonds, because they are not based primarily on sex—although "friends" do occasionally copulate with each other. Pygmy chimps (*Pan paniscus*), perhaps our closest living relatives, resemble us in another way. Although the females are subject to estrus (heat), they engage in sexual activity throughout all phases of their cycle.

However, grooming, baboon friendship, and chimp sexual receptivity do not add up to human social organization. The societies of those animals are still quite far from the intense male-male cooperation and the permanent male-female cohabitation that characterize human society. We can be fairly sure, therefore, that our distant ancestors also did not have societies like ours. To get to where we are now, the traits of these creatures had to be modified substantially.

We have some information about the series of steps that led to the emergence of the typically human form of social organization, but many details remain to be clarified. What follows is only a broad outline.

The first step for which we have some data was taken by the australopithecines, a primate group that first appeared in the fossil record some five million years ago. The australopithecines are generally considered to be the first creatures showing markedly human characteristics (hominids). They lived mainly on the ground. They walked upright, and they had bigger brains (for their body weight) than any earlier primate.

The famous Lucy was an australopithecine. She belonged to the species most experts now believe was our ancestor—*Australopithecus afarensis*, the most slender (gracile) of the australopithecines. But Lucy and her like were quite unlike modern humans in their behavior. According to anthropologist David Pilbeam, *A. afarensis* may still have used trees for a variety of purposes. Males had more than one mate. Infants were probably born with about the same body and brain size as those of present-day apes, so they would not have caused great difficulties at birth. They were probably no more of a burden to their mothers than are the infants of apes.

Members of the species might possibly have used tools, such as digging sticks and stones for cracking open nuts. After all, chimps crack nuts with stones and use twigs to catch termites. Nevertheless, tools did not play a particularly significant role in the lives of the australopithecines.

Pilbeam does not believe that there was any major division of labor between the sexes in the form of differential food-gathering. There may have been some, however. Among chimps, females, and only females, use tools to crack open nuts. Indeed, male chimps have been observed bringing nuts over to females to have them cracked, much like men asking women to prepare them a dinner. Still, these separate tasks have little or no impact on the structure of chimp society, and there is no reason to believe that the effect was any greater among the australopithecines.

Finally, there was little or no food-sharing. *A. afarensis* fed mostly on vegetable matter. Its males did not hunt. There would have been little reason to share food. All in all, says Pilbeam, it was more like an odd ape than a human being.

The next ancestral species to appear was *Homo habilis*, the first species in the genus Homo. The brain of *Homo habilis* shows some increase over that of the australopithecines (to about 750 cubic centimeters for the males), but the real innovation of the members of this species seems to lie in the fact that they ate more meat. They have left their tool marks on the bones of dead animals. Were they hunters? The case is still open. Many scholars feel that they scavenged more than they hunted. Did they share food? No one really knows yet.

The penultimate step was taken about 1.5 million years ago, when *Homo erectus*, our direct ancestor, first appeared on the African veldt. *Homo erectus* was an unusual creature. It had a bigger brain (950 cubic centimeters for the males) than any of its predecessors, and it hunted. Furthermore, the archaeological record seems to indicate that the hunters brought food back to a home base, something they would do only if they intended to share it with others. This would imply that some degree of division of labor had come into being, with the males specializing in hunting and the females in gathering.

If food sharing was taking place, the basis of reciprocity had been established. What anthropologist Helen Fisher (1983) has called a "contract" between the sexes was coming into being.

These transformations may indicate that the males of the species were changing. They were probably relying somewhat less on threat displays, bluffing and other dominance-oriented behaviors. They were developing the ability to cooperate with each other and to form lasting relationships with females. Socially, they were getting closer to the behavior characteristic of contemporary hunter-gatherer groups.

If this reconstruction is correct, one conclusion seems inescapable: *our ancestors were hunting and gathering before they were fully human.* We inherited significant elements of our social organization from another species. If Freud had known this, he wouldn't have imagined a revolt of the brothers against the father in order to explain the existence of the family.

As mentioned before, modern man—*Homo sapiens*—came into being sometime between 300,000 and 100,000 years ago. Our species was fully formed long before agriculture was invented. By 70,000 years ago, ancient hunting and gathering peoples had laid flowers in graves. No later than 30,000 years ago, they were scrutinizing the movement of the heavenly bodies, using language freely, inscribing notational computations on stones, antlers and bones, and painting great works of art on the walls of deep caves.

The surviving hunter-gatherer peoples are their descendants—and so are we. The BaMbuti, the Inuit, the !Kung, and the Australian Aborigines are brother and sister to us. The few thousand years during which we had no contact with them has not significantly modified the DNA that resides in our cells. Our thoughts have soared beyond them, but our emotions have not. Their passions and pettiness mirror our own. Their predispositions and ours are identical. We are linked by our genes; we are separated by our cultures.

If we want to understand human behavior, we have to understand the hunting and gathering way of life. John Bowlby, the first psychiatrist to apply ethological principles to the study of children, called that way of life "the environment of evolutionary adaptedness." We call it "the natural environment." The human species can't go back, but neither can it afford to forget.

The hunter-gatherer band provided a framework which was particularly suited to the genetically-mediated emotional needs of human beings. The band provided essential social nutrients: identity, support, people who need you, a sense of purpose, and a context in which all the various emotions have an important role to play. Because the band was self-contained, its members rarely ran into conflicts of interest. Because it was made up of relatives, conflict between self-interest and social interest was minimized. Because the band had a clear, unmistakable mission—to survive—its members knew why they existed. Because roles were clearly defined, people knew what they had to do. Because there was a clear, unmistakable threat from the environment, people didn't sit around wondering why they were on earth, and what to do with their lives. In other words, the hunter-gatherer lifestyle promoted integration of all phases of life.

Agriculture put a virtual end to that way of life. Here is what the Bible has to say about the transition:

THE PROCESS OF EVOLUTION

Some explanation may be helpful here for readers who are not familiar with the process involved in the creation of new species. Again, the important point is that behavior changes as well as anatomy and physiology. A chimp can figure out problems that would stump a howler monkey. A human can remember and return a favor years later, something no other animal can do. How does that happen? How does a behavioral repertoire get incorporated in the genes of a new species? The answer is that behavioral capabilities are not fundamentally different from anatomical capabilities. They are selected in the same way—by the effects of changes in the coding of the genetic material. These genetic changes lead in turn to anatomical changes, including changes in the layout and chemistry of the brain. These create changes in the way individuals tend to behave.

Anatomical and behavioral changes are caused by mutations which produce random genetic changes in either sperm or egg; these changes are either eliminated or retained by the process of natural selection. Most such modifications are destructive; they either kill the cell, prevent conception, cause spontaneous abortion, or lead to early death. But a few, very few, are beneficial. The beneficial modifications enable individuals carrying them to survive better or reproduce better than individuals carrying the unmodified genes. Some genetic changes are *selected* by the environment while others are rejected.

Animal breeders help this process along by allowing only animals with desirable anatomical or behavioral traits to reproduce. As everyone knows, artificial or guided selection of this kind has led to the development of docile cows that give more milk and dogs which can be trained to bite only strangers. In the future, the techniques of genetic engineering will further enhance our species' ability to modify the genes of other creatures.

When beneficial modifications become established in a population, especially if that population is geographically cut off from those who carry the old genes, a new species may arise. If the new species has substantial survival advantages, it may eventually spread widely, and may even replace the older species.

To return to humans: We came into being through modifications that enabled us to survive better in a hunting and gathering environment. Hence, our genes predispose us to get along in a hunting and gathering band. The behavioral traits that we possess were adaptive during the period when our species evolved into its current form.

Because you have . . . eaten of the tree
of which I commanded you "Do not eat of it"
cursed is the ground because of you;
in toil you shall eat of it all the days of your life;
thorns and thistles it shall bring forth to you;
and you shall eat the grasses of the field.
In the sweat of your face
you shall eat bread. . . .

God's curse? That we will become farmers. . . .

Modern Industrial Society

We believe that this analysis begins to provide a basis for an understanding of how society affects individual functioning. The hunter-gatherer model allows us to ask ourselves how far any society, at any stage of development, has diverged from the one to which we are genetically adapted. Such an analysis does not of course tell us that any given society is better or worse than another; that is ultimately a question of values. But the model does provide one framework for thinking about values. We have drawn conclusions based on this model, some obvious, some speculative. We want to emphasize that the more speculative conclusions are our own. Someone else using the same information might see things differently. We understand that the available facts are open to more than one interpretation.

At least one conclusion does seem inescapable. Industrial societies have moved very far indeed from the environment in which we evolved. One can recognize in them the basic traits of human social life, but only in the same way that one can recognize oneself in the funhouse mirror of a carnival. Very few of us really belong to something that we can call a band. We have been growing up with fathers who go off to work somewhere, and are, hence, absent. We are now growing up with absent mothers as well. We exist in the midst of strangers. We don't belong, from birth, to a group of supportive relatives who can provide us with an unshakeable sense of who we are. We have to manufacture our identity out of bits and pieces, cut from a vast patchwork of cultures and history.

Modern societies are all composed of many separate parts, and the parts are not well integrated. As sociologist Daniel Bell has pointed out in *The Cultural Contradictions of Capitalism*, the religious, social and economic realms operate according to different rules, celebrate different values. People must play many roles and so find their allegiances divided. Furthermore, the requirements of specialization force them to narrow their self-concept and put aside essential parts of themselves. To find a safe haven, people must frequently find a place for themselves under the protective wings of massive institutions. Of necessity, they must abandon control of their destiny to strangers.

Modern societies teach people to strive for excellence rather than find comfort in adequacy. This striving produces psychopathology as well as progress. Unachievable goals, fostered by the idea of unlimited human potential, lead to failure and self-rejection. Neither poverty nor wealth seems to provide protection from psychological distress. The poor suffer, but the rich do too, in other ways. Frank Pittman, an Atlanta-based family psychiatrist, has described the misery of rich kids for whom no achievement seems to matter. Nothing counts as a real success because they *have* everything. They fritter their energy away grooming and dressing exquisitely, waiting around for the time when they have grown up enough to inherit the right to take on tasks that are worthy of them, like running their parents' businesses.

One element of our modern dilemma is simply abundance. It exacerbates inequality, producing envy among the poor and guilt among the rich. Abundance can rob its possessors of the identity gained by providing for oneself and one's relatives, and it can leave the appetite so jaded that motivation is impaired. An individual with a surplus needs no more from others, and the basis of reciprocity is destroyed. "I don't need friends," says the rich man, "I have money." Hence, the rich may be isolated by their wealth. This does not apply only to those who are literally rich. The solidarity of the working class tends to disappear as soon as unions achieve high salaries for their members. It is difficult to combine a large economic surplus with good social relationships and mental health (although we would all like to try . . .).

The nature of contemporary stress

The nature of the stressors modern humans must cope with has changed dramatically. Once we had to cope primarily with environmental emergencies that required a direct physical response. Today, we are subject to subtle, chronic psychological stressors for which there is often no appropriate response, physical or otherwise. The boss frowns when we walk by his office. Should we say something and reveal our insecurity? Or ignore it and risk continuing to displease him? Is he frowning at us? Should we ask?

Other stressors are generated entirely within ourselves, by our ideas about how the world works, and particularly by unreasonable expectations about ourselves. The authors are as subject to this as anyone else. Will this book be up to our hopelessly high standards? Will it sell? Will anyone actually read it? Will our colleagues be annoyed? Will evolutionary biologists tell us we got it all wrong? Our anxiety about meeting standards makes us uneasy. We feel small and vulnerable. Insecure, we procrastinate, putting off the day of reckoning when it is sent off to the publisher, while we live in fear of the critics we imagine.

As we mentioned in Chapter 1, this change in the nature of the stressors we face has turned the fight-or-flight response into a deadly enemy. In addition to generating anxiety and depression, prolonged stress is capable of suppressing the immune system, inhibiting growth, diminishing sexual appetite, and reducing the output of reproductive hormones. Our own metabolism has become our enemy.

Costs and benefits of modern life

Modern industrial society provides people with many good things, including longer life, improved health, greater comfort, luxury, and unparalleled opportunities for intellectual development. But at a cost. The cost is not born equally by everyone. Some people are better suited than others to our society, either because they were raised right or because they are genetically better adapted to modern conditions. Some people, no doubt, manage to feel good about themselves without much social support. (We don't actually know any such people, but do not doubt that they exist.) Those fortunate souls are unlikely to need the help of psychotherapists.

Of course, one can imagine a species that is different, a species whose individuals could all function easily in a society such as we have now. We are not such a species. It appears that humans function well only within certain limits. Outside its proper environment, the mind tends to go haywire. So people at all levels of modern society, rich and poor, suffer.

Hunting and gathering imposed restraints on behavior. Everyone had to "work" (hunt or gather) to survive. Everyone had to cooperate to survive. Everyone had to work and cooperate to gain a spouse. The competitive drives that we inherited from our mammalian and reptilian ancestors were diverted into serving the needs of creatures that had become interdependent. In particular, the deep-seated emotions that induce conformity held in check the vast egoistic potential of the newly enlarged brain.

In the modern world, competition and cooperation are no longer bound up together. On the international level, one great power enshrines the virtues of egotism, while the other insists on excesses of regimentation. Within our own nation, one party advocates the surpassing value of greed, while the other declares itself the sole possessor of compassion. On every level, from nation to individual, self-reliance and solidarity have been polarized. They have been separated from the conditions that made them effective survival strategies. Pieces of the hunting-gathering social mechanism, crafted by evolution, are flying around in our minds like shrapnel.

Under these conditions, it is very difficult for individuals to develop a successful working model of their environment. Confusion reigns on virtually every level. In the academic world, social scientists develop theories that bear almost no relationship to reality. In the world of work and business, people are constantly faced with forces that they cannot understand. As a result, few people have a sense of mastery over their lives. We believe that these conditions help to account for much of the soul-searching, the angst, the alienation, the anomie, the anxiety, the obsessiveness, the self-doubt, and the self-hatred one encounters in clinical practice.

Some people can survive by ignoring the complexities of modern life. They have the ability to simplify or restrict their attention. Other people have the type of intelligence that can create interpretations that work for them. Natural selection, after all, favors individuals who can develop alternative courses of action to suit changing environments. But the current environment is strange indeed and not everyone has the skills to cope.

Some Preliminary Conclusions

What is the practical significance of all this? We are tempted to start laying out some of our conclusions, but it is really too early to do so. They will emerge in the following chapters. For the moment, we will limit ourselves to a few brief and perhaps fairly obvious remarks.

First of all, we hope it is already clear to everyone that a biological perspective does not downgrade the importance of the environment in the genesis of psychological distress. We are anything but biological determinists.

Secondly, we see the *absence* of band-like social structures as a crucial factor in the lives of modern individuals. Psychotherapy can help people compensate for this absence. This puts the therapeutic relationship at the theoretical heart of psychotherapy. The therapeutic alliance can be understood as an attempt to create the support people once got from their bands. Once this support system is in place, the therapist can begin to actively strive to help the clients reduce their social isolation. One way to do this is to help clients improve the skills necessary to function in the social groups that *do* exist today—groups that might satisfy some of the needs that bands could have satisfied.

Consequently, we think that all therapists, even those doing individual psychotherapy, should think like systems theorists or like family/couple therapists. What are the array of supports, interests, and abilities surrounding the client? What is the history of those supports? Has there been a change to make living more difficult? What will mobilize supports? We certainly don't mean to imply that one shouldn't look to childhood or consider concepts of intrapsychic structure. But each individual should be seen in context.

Our position is that intensely individualistic solutions are less than satisfactory. This places us squarely in opposition to some strong traditions in the psychotherapeutic community. We oppose a primary emphasis on self-actualization and the "I" therapies. We also reject the notion that human motives are essentially selfish. We recognize that for some people, in some cultural contexts, an emphasis on strictly personal development is desirable, and even essential, but we believe that this tendency must be tempered by an awareness of the fact that humans are a social species.

Thirdly, we oppose the notion, common to many therapies, that the best way to help people is to let them flounder around until they find their own way out of their dilemmas. Most people are living in an environment they do not understand. The therapist will often have to offer them a way out. Not, of course, "The Way" — a dogmatic assertion of the therapist's reality — but, nevertheless, advice, guidance and coaching. Therapy must offer a roadmap of the new terrain.

In this spirit, we are proposing at least one new intervention. We have found that teaching clients about the changed environment can be a useful therapeutic technique. When appropriate, we convey to clients that their problems are due in part to the fact that they are living in a changed environment, an environment that is difficult for human beings. Problems result from a mismatch between normal genes (a good, intact self) and a changed environment. This kind of cognitive reframing doesn't always "take," but when it does, it can enhance self-acceptance, freeing people to put their energies into coping, instead of into the kind of relentless, futile self-denigration we so often see.

Note, in this context, that our theory explains why the quality of the therapeutic relationship has consistently been shown to be more important than the therapist's theoretical outlook. The relationship is important because relationships are important to human beings, and good relationships are hard to come by in the modern environment.

CHAPTER 3

Reciprocity and Psychotherapy

The holy passion of friendship is of so sweet and steady
and loyal and enduring a nature that it will last through
a whole lifetime. If not asked to lend money.
                                                        —Mark Twain

WHAT STANDS OUT MOST VIVIDLY in the lives of hunters and gatherers is the
importance of reciprocity. Sharing is ubiquitous. In one way or another,
people are always giving to each other and receiving from each other. Here is
how anthropologist Marjorie Shostak, then at Harvard and now at Emory
University in Atlanta, sums it up for the !Kung:

> Whatever possessions do exist are owned exclusively by individuals, who are free
> to dispose of them as they wish. Most items are eventually given away and become
> part of a network of goods that are frequently exchanged.

One of the most important aspects of sharing is the distribution of meat.
Anytime an animal is killed, the meat is shared out among the members of
the band. Distribution is based on two considerations, kinship and the
return of favors. People give to their relatives and to those from whom they
have received. There is sometimes disagreement about the amount each
person should get, but in general people seem to know what is coming to
them.

Distribution takes place according to elaborate rules. The rules differ
slightly from society to society, but only in detail. Here is an example from
the !Kung, as described by Richard Lee and Irven DeVore in *Kalahari Hunter-Gatherers*:

The owner of the animal is the owner of the first arrow to be effectively shot into the animal so that it penetrates enough for its poison to work. That person is responsible for the distribution. The owner may or may not be one of the hunters.

Robert Tonkinson, who studied the Mardudjara Aborigines of Australia, notes that the hunter generally receives one of the least choice cuts, for,

regardless of differences in skill and determination that exist among hunters, there is an unstated conviction that everything evens out in the long run.

In addition to sharing out the hunt, everyone is involved in the giving and receiving of gifts. All !Kung, says Shostak,

participate in the reciprocal giving of gifts, but each person gives to and receives from only a few partners. Gift-giving is a fairly formal affair, and people remember clearly who gave what to whom and when. These exchange relationships . . . may last a lifetime, and may even be passed on to one's children. . . .

As we said, the few possessions that do exist in hunter-gatherer life are owned by individuals, but most are eventually given away. As a result, valuable items tend to pass frequently from hand to hand. Just how effectively this system works was demonstrated by a little experiment done with the !Kung. The women of one particular band (band 1) were given necklaces made of cowrie shells. Each necklace had 20 shells. A year later, say Lee and DeVore (1976),

there was hardly a cowrie shell to be found in band 1. They had been given to relatives and friends, and they appeared not as whole necklaces, but in ones and twos in people's ornaments to the edges of the area.

A person who receives a gift is obliged to reciprocate. What this means is that anyone who receives a gift acquires a debt. The debt can be paid off by giving a gift or helping out at some later time. This system is open-ended in the sense that no one strives to pay off all obligations and be free of the system. People want to give and to get; they want to be involved in the system.

But sharing is not a matter of spontaneous generosity. It is the basis of the hunter-gatherer socioeconomic system. It creates a network of relationships and mutual obligations such that all participants can call upon each other in time of need. This network enables people to survive when hard times arrive; there is almost always someone, somewhere, who has an obligation to help out. Reciprocity, to hunter-gatherers, is a matter of survival, a matter of life and death. Here is how Asen Balikci describes the system among the Netsilik Eskimo:

> . . . there was very little driftwood available in the Netsilik area, and consequently very few wooden sledges were made. In addition, the scarcity of dog food obliged the Netsilik to keep very few dogs. . . . It was therefore essential for a hunter contemplating a distant winter journey to be able to borrow a sledge and some supplementary dogs if he didn't own enough. For such help the hunter turned to his close relatives. No payment was made for such temporary loans, but the sledge had to be returned in good order and with a new shoeing.

Reciprocal behavior such as we have been describing is rarely found among animals including primates. If our monkey-like vegetarian ancestors were like most other living primates, their capacity for reciprocal behavior was extremely limited. Somewhere along the line, we were transformed. The transformation seems to have accompanied the process of moving from the trees to the savanna grasslands, and from vegetarianism to meat-eating. In the process of providing us with the genes for hunting and gathering, mutation and natural selection also seem to have provided the genes that made reciprocal behavior possible.

Once some of our ancestors started to hunt and to exchange meat for other foods, cooperation, mutuality and reciprocity became important factors in survival. Having friends — or people who owed you favors — might keep you alive. Individuals who couldn't understand the rules or didn't know how to build a network of allies were less likely to survive, even if they had outstanding individual abilities. Thus, over time, the genes that promoted reciprocal altruism spread through the population that eventually evolved into the human species.

Once such a system is in existence, various additional traits enhance the ability to survive. A particularly important one is the ability and the will to keep track of what one owes and what one is owed. If one forgets what one is owed, one might not get a fair share for oneself and one's family. If, on the other hand, one forgets what one owes others, one risks the wrath of the "creditor." In either case, group life is disrupted. Consequently, people who can't keep their accounts straight tend to get selected out. They might be ostracized — a severe penalty where individual survival depends on membership in a group. Or they might be denied mates. In either case, their genes would not be transmitted to the next generation. Through some such process of selection, reciprocity and its associated mental capacities became as characteristic of human beings as our erect posture and highly developed brain.

It is interesting that chimpanzees and baboons don't share food at all, except on those relatively rare occasions when they hunt and kill. Even then, the sharing is limited; the animals who make the kill grudgingly allow others in the vicinity a few bites. Nevertheless, chimps and baboons do show some ability to engage in reciprocal behavior. We have already mentioned that olive baboons maintain long-term relationships—friendships. To a limited degree these friendships are based on reciprocity. Baboon friends show a tendency to help out individuals from whom they have received help in the past. Friends groom each other preferentially, and will provide mutual support when attacked by other members of the band. One good turn produces another. This is an especially interesting finding, because baboons are the only primates besides humans to descend to the savanna.

Chimp males form coalitions, which are described by Frans de Waal in a marvelously readable book, *Chimpanzee Politics: Power and Sex Among Apes*. De Waal discovered that the coalitions help their members maintain their ascendancy in the group. To some extent, these coalitions are based on reciprocity; a male member of a coalition will help out his partner in time of need. Our conclusion is that there must have been something in the brains of our ancestral species that prepared the way for the explosion of reciprocal behavior that characterizes human behavior.

The story of how biology moved to an understanding of the genetic basis of reciprocity—technically called reciprocal altruism—is interesting and important enough to merit a detour. Darwin's original formulation of evolution through natural selection placed *competition* at center stage. Darwin observed that if all species reproduced without being checked by outside forces, the population of the world would soon consume all available resources. It followed that all species, and indeed all individuals, were in competition with each other for scarce resources. The implication seemed to be that all organisms could be expected to look out only for themselves. The struggle for existence should be severe.

Suppose, some people argued, that by some chance, some noncompetitive individuals were born. They would not be able to survive, because they would be at a disadvantage; the others would overcome them. Therefore, noncompetitive individuals would leave fewer offspring than competitive ones. Thus, the evolutionary analysis of behavior led to the prediction that genes for "noncompetitiveness" would tend to be driven out of the gene pool. Misleading terms such as "nature red in tooth and claw" and "survival of the fittest" entered the language, and "fit" was taken by some people to mean strong and ruthless.

But this aspect of evolutionary theory didn't account for all the facts, as Darwin himself realized. Observation clearly indicated that in the real world, animals often behaved in a noncompetitive manner; helping and cooperation could be found in many species, even though biologists couldn't account for it. For many years, the conflict between theory and observation prevented evolutionary biology from becoming a useful tool for the analysis of social behavior.

In the 1960s, a series of researchers began to piece together a theory that could account for the existence of altruism and cooperation in the animal kingdom. The two leading figures in this process were the extraordinarily creative Robert Trivers, then at Harvard and now at the University of California, Santa Cruz, and Oxford biologist William D. Hamilton. In developing the notion of *kin selection*, Hamilton showed that if an individual's cooperative or altruistic behavior led to the survival of *relatives* carrying the same genes, cooperation and altruism could indeed be transmitted genetically from generation to generation. Since the relatives would (on the average) be carrying the same genes, they too would behave altruistically and would help *their* kin to survive, and so on, ad infinitum.

This work put theory in harmony with the facts. If one took into account the fact that altruistic acts probably benefited relatives who might, as a result, produce more offspring, one could understand how the social behavior of animals could come to be characterized by high degrees of cooperation.

This new orientation clarified the meaning of the term "fitness." No longer could "fit" be misinterpreted to mean "strong" or "competitive" or "ruthless," as the Social Darwinists had thought. The true meaning of "fit" became clear. The "fittest" are simply those who share the most genes with individuals of the next generation—whether those genes are transmitted through reproduction of self or through the reproduction of relatives. Thus, fitness can be achieved by competition, by cooperation, and even by self-sacrifice.

The old idea of fitness—the number of genes one transmits by reproduction—is now called Darwinian fitness, and the new idea of fitness—the number of genes one transmits by reproduction *plus* the effect one has on the copies of one's genes that are transmitted by one's relatives—was given the name "inclusive fitness."

The concept of inclusive fitness opened the way for a true science of social behavior. One of its first great achievements was to explain how sterility can be transmitted from generation to generation! The social insects—certain species of bees, ants and termites—are characterized by sterile castes, i.e., large numbers of individuals (workers) who don't reproduce. These castes are made up of sisters who are all daughters of a queen. By giving up their own reproductive opportunities, they improve the reproductive success of their mother (who also gives birth to individuals who are not sterile). In other words, the sterile sisters increase their inclusive fitness by aiding in the reproductive activity of a relative.

The replacement of "reproduction" or "Darwinian fitness" with "inclusive fitness" was a big step towards a meaningful biological interpretation of human behavior. There is now no reason to believe that humans are essentially selfish, as Freud, relying on the evolutionary concepts of his time, believed. The study of evolution indicates that empathy, helpfulness and cooperativeness are basic human traits. Of course, we are selfish too, when need be, for we have to take care of ourselves. Competition and cooperation are both innate. They can be shaped by the vicissitudes of life. Which will prevail in any given case will depend both on circumstance and on the nature of the individual.

Reciprocity and the Emotions

Emotions are at the heart of the predisposition towards reciprocity. Our most familiar emotions can be understood as having been developed to facilitate reciprocal relationships. Guilt and gratitude made us pay our debts. Sympathy and empathy induced us to give — and thereby helped each one of us to build up a fund of gratitude in others. Moral outrage led us to censure and punish those who did not live up to their responsibilities. Envy helped to make sure that sharing was customary and no one accumulated too much.

The intrepid Lorna Marshall, who, with her husband John Marshall and their two children, sallied out into the Kalahari to bring back the first scientific studies of the !Kung, gives us this vivid glimpse of the social function of emotion:

> Men and women speak of the persons to whom they have given or propose to give gifts. They express satisfaction or dissatisfaction with what they have received. If someone has delayed unexpectedly long in making a return gift, the people discuss this. One man was excused by his friends because his wife, they said, had got things into her hands and made him poor, so that he now had nothing suitable to give. Some people, on the other hand, were blamed for being ungenerous . . . or not very capable in managing their lives, and no one defended them for these defects or asked others to have patience with them.

The emotions which cemented the band are still alive in all normal human beings. These emotions have a direct impact on our thinking. Whether we want it to or not, the brain tends to keep track of what we owe others and what others owe us. Most of us cannot avoid such calculations even if we try. A sense of what is "fair" automatically incorporates itself into almost everyone's world view. Similarly, virtually everyone has a sense of what constitutes "betrayal" — which can be defined as a sense of not getting as much as we are owed. In fact, many investigators believe that the intense calculations involved in early human social organization were in part responsible for the evolution of increased intelligence.

In modern institutions we can see more remnants of reciprocity.[1] For example, duty and obligation can be understood as codified, rigidified, forms of reciprocity. Money, Harvard's Edward Wilson argues, can usefully be understood as the quantification of reciprocal altruism. If acquired honestly, the money a person has represents what is owed to that person by society. Writing, archaeologists have discovered, was first used to keep track of debts. "You scratch my back and I'll scratch yours" is the way our folk wisdom enshrines reciprocity. "Log rolling" is the political version.

Most religions echo this primeval wisdom. The New Testament states: "Do unto others as you would have them do unto you." In the Old Testament, the idea reads: "An eye for an eye and a tooth for a tooth."

The importance of reciprocity is indicated by the fact that we have a special word for individuals who are unable to engage in it: they are called psychopaths or sociopaths.[2]

Cheating

In nature, deception is important. Flowers try to look like insects, insects try to look like sticks, and natural selection decides who wins without prejudice against deceivers. Deception is important to humans too. As the exchange of food and favors became important for human survival, the ability

[1]We have never come across a description of a society in which the principle of reciprocity is unknown, except perhaps for the Ik (Turnbull, 1972), who were in the process of dying out. For illustrative purposes, we have provided a few sources in which the importance of reciprocity in posthunter-gatherer societies is particularly salient: Chagnon (1979), Lebra (1976), Lindholm (1982), Malinowski (1926), Meggitt (1977), Siskind (1975), and Stack (1975). The Meggitt work is particularly interesting for its treatment of revenge as a way of life; revenge is impossible for a creature that doesn't understand reciprocity.

[2]Readers familiar with developmental psychology will note that the position we have taken in this chapter is very different from that of Lawrence Kohlberg and his coworkers in the field of moral development. While we do not doubt that attitudes toward morality emerge in a series of stages, we do not find any support for the notion that an ever-greater degree of selflessness is a desirable outcome in human development.

to "cheat" in the altruism game also came into being. Cheaters are adept at simulating emotion for their own advantage. They produce sham guilt, sham gratitude, sham sympathy, and sham anger. This capacity probably built on our inherited tendency to bluff and threaten, a capacity which is universal in social animals. In any case, lying and cheating are particularly easy for creatures who can talk.

Other emotions also play a role in the reciprocity system. Just as natural selection produced cheaters, so it selected for the capacity to detect cheating. The feeling of suspicion is undoubtedly associated with anticipation of cheating. Because of the possibility of cheating, most human beings seem to be very concerned that their partners and associates are "really" feeling what they seem to be feeling (love, orgasm, commitment, etc.). Virtually every word we use is scrutinized for clues to its inner meaning. On the other hand, the feeling of trust would seem to be a fundamental accompaniment to harmonious reciprocity.

In a series of recent articles that are making a stir in the world of evolutionary biology, Stanford University psychologists Leda Cosmides and John Tooby have taken the case even further. They argue that to function in human society, the mind *must* be able to calculate so that *both parties* receive a benefit from a transaction or a relationship. This means that the mind must be able to balance its own interests against those of the other person(s) involved. Cosmides and Tooby have experimental evidence that there are specific mechanisms in the brain that are designed for this function and for this function alone. These mechanisms would serve to detect cheaters and also to prevent individuals from overestimating what is due to them. We will return to their ideas in a later chapter.

Reciprocity in Modern Society

Obviously, reciprocity is not given the highest value in modern industrial societies. The principles of exchange in large impersonal societies are different. The maxim "Business is business" sums it up for the capitalist world. The communist societies live by their own version of dog eat dog, whatever their ideology proclaims. Besides, doing for the State in the hope of being rewarded by the Party is far removed from personal reciprocity.

The rules of business and of the workplace in general are often in direct conflict with the rules of reciprocity. Where barter or money exists, an exchange is complete in itself. Neither side has an obligation to remain in the relationship. In fact, those who complete a mutually agreeable exchange are likely to say, with satisfaction and relief: "We're quits."

In hierarchical bureaucratic organizations, such as corporations and gov-

LETTER TO ANN LANDERS

Dear Ann Landers:
I have a different view on a recent column that was headed "Never lend money to relatives." My advice is, "Never borrow money from relatives."

When my wife and I were first married, we borrowed $500 from her parents. We paid against that loan every month, with interest, as agreed. Meanwhile, we went without a great many things so that we could honor our commitment.

The loan was paid back. The debt, however, never seemed to get paid. Every time we saw her parents, every conversation began with a reminder of "how we helped you out when you were up against it."

Believe me, Ann, I wish we had starved rather than borrow that piddly amount of money. Please tell your readers the other side of the story. You never get to know people until you are in their debt. My advice is to borrow from a bank or a credit union, or do without.
— J.L. in Texas

This incident shows how complicated the analysis of reciprocity gets in a money economy. Who is "right"? The parents are obviously putting too high a value on their help — too high for their own good, since they are alienating their son-in-law. But they are expressing, albeit in an obnoxious way, a profound biological feeling: you owe me because I helped you. The son-in-law, on the other hand, is operating according to the money economy; since he's paid back the loan, he feels he's paid off the debt.

In a money economy, people can "choose" which system to follow. Very often, they alternate, sometimes operating according to the reciprocity system and sometimes according to the money system — depending on what best serves their interests. This multiplies the chances that people will calculate reciprocity differently and therefore serves to undermine relationships.

ernments, the rules of behavior often contradict those of reciprocity. People are supposed to treat kin no differently from non-kin. Loyalty to one's friends and relatives is assigned such unsavory names as nepotism and patronage. These practices persist, but with stigma.

The emotions are no longer expected to play an important role in the economic system. Guilt, gratitude, envy and moral outrage have no respectable economic function. Indeed, morality has been replaced by legality, and the legal profession considers, or finds it convenient to consider, morality to be a separate realm.

In personal relationships, however, reciprocity is still expected. The new rules have not replaced the old ones, they have been added on. Many people have trouble coping with the resulting conflict. For example, in divorce, it is not unusual for couples to hasten to judicial resolution of their conflict, leaving more fundamental personal grievances dangling, unsatisfied. We have created a society whose formal rules are in conflict with those we are adapted to follow. The result is confusion and stress.

Another source of reciprocity-related problems derives from childhood experience in modern societies. As developmental psychologists Jean Piaget and Lawrence Kohlberg have argued, a sense of fairness emerges naturally, in a series of developmental stages, from the play of children. But in order to develop the balanced sense of right and obligations that characterizes a well-functioning adult human, a child must receive a proper upbringing, i.e., one that remains within the range of environments to which young humans are adapted. If children are deprived of affection, support, structure, and identity, they may well grow up unable to give and/or unable to take — unable to recognize what they receive as a gift, and unable to give gifts to others. The same thing may happen if a child is given too much and has to start out in life with a debt than can never be repaid.

The role of childhood in creating confusion about reciprocity is dramatically illustrated in the following case history. Roland was brought up in an unimaginably abusive home. Among other atrocities, he was locked up in an attic for a year and fed only through a slot. He was frequently beaten and made to stand at attention for hours at a time. The only person who treated him with any affection was an older brother, who was gay. This brother seduced him when he was nine. The brother later left home, leaving Roland to face the parents without any protection. Roland grew into an adult who was unable to pursue a career or form relationships. When he first came into therapy, he was desperately trying to reestablish contact with his mother, a woman who had stood by while he was being abused by his father. And he would frequently run errands and do extensive home maintenance for his brother, who had reappeared after suffering a crippling accident. Roland would then turn around and use much of his time in therapy to complain that he was being exploited.

His therapist pressed Roland to explain why he kept going back to relatives who had abused and betrayed him consistently. At first, Roland could not account for his actions. He simply repeated that he was confused. But finally he was able to express what he was feeling:

C: I go back to do work for him because I remember what he did for me and how he saved me from my father. But then, when I've done something for him, I start to feel angry about his walking out on me, and I feel like paying him back for that. So I go back and forth. Sometimes I'm paying him back, sometimes I'm paying him off . . . Now that I think about it, sometimes I feel like I have to help him to make up for what he didn't get from our father. I know that sounds crazy, because I didn't get anything either, but that's what I feel. Half the time I don't know what I feel. I'm confused. I guess I go back to feel the way it was, to feel like I was a kid again.

T: But it was terrible there.

C: Well, it was worth it. I see those families on TV [where all is lovey dovey], I don't think I could live that way.

The point of the passage is that Roland's whole life was marked by his inability to sort out what he had a right to expect in life, what he owed to others, and what others owed to him. His environment was simply too confusing to make sense of, and he therefore ended up with a distorted sense of reciprocity. Note that this formulation indicates the path that therapy had to take.

Modern psychology has developed without much awareness of reciprocity, but there is one major exception. In *Invisible Loyalties*, family therapists Ivan Boszormenyi-Nagy and Geraldine Spark (1984) wrote extensively about the debts family members think they owe to each other and to dead relatives. Boszormenyi-Nagy and Spark did not derive their argument from the study of the hunting-gathering adaptation, nor, as far as we are aware, did they make extensive use of the word reciprocity, but they placed the idea at the center of their analysis. Here is an excerpt:

> People may find it natural to live up to simple obligations in the current manifest give-and-take of their social interactions. However, the long-term responsibility for the "bookkeeping" of accrued obligations begins to burden the individual with demands for both an ordered memory and a capacity for postponed balancing of ledgers. It is an even greater demand to consider the entire family's accrued obligations. The larger the extended family, the wider the range of possible emotional benefits for the members, but also the larger the scope of the hierarchy of obligations. The roots of obligations may go back several generations and lie beyond the knowledge of those living (p. 102–3).

They then go on to describe some of the problems that arise from the existence of such obligations:

The rigidly unchangeable persistence of patterns of imbalance in the family's merit ledger can remain outside all members' awareness. Postponement of resolution or rebalancing can further be masked through involvement of one member in an outsider. An unbalanced overinvestment by the offspring of a spouse and children can result in unexpected explosion of retributive measures. It is well-known that murder occurs most frequently among people tied to each other through kinship or affection. Seemingly inexplicable eruptions of violence can find their explanation in the multigenerational merit ledger (p. 108).

The chaotic, meaningless accumulation of emotional debt that Boszor-menyi-Nagy and Spark describe derives from the fact that, in the modern world, the reciprocity system operates without reference to its original functions: survival, the creation of networks of potential helpers, the distribution of goods, and the maintenance of public order. Freed of this constraining context, the system often operates in a destructive, perverted way. It has become an anachronism, a kind of psychological appendix. People acquire debts they know not how. Many people never discover how to pay them off.

Reciprocity and Psychotherapy

We believe that many of the people who come in for psychotherapy can best be understood as having pathologies of reciprocity. They aren't correctly weighting their emotional rights and duties—their obligations to others, and the obligations of others to them. People who suffer from a pathology of reciprocity find it difficult to get along with others. Because they are unable to derive emotional satisfaction from social relationships, their self-esteem is low, and they are prone to confusion, anxiety and depression.

Pathologies of reciprocity can be divided into two broad categories: guilt and entitlement. Guilty people feel that they have given too little or received too much. Entitled people feel that they have given too much or received too little.

Giving and receiving must be understood in a very large sense. A man who has not achieved what he thinks his father wanted him to achieve may feel guilty for not having *given* enough to his father. A woman who, as a child, did not behave properly in school, may feel that she has not *given* her mother what her mother deserves. Children who were spoiled or even especially cherished by their parents may feel that they have received more than they can ever pay back. Children who were deprived may grow up feeling that the world owes them a living.

The desire to be perfect can be understood as an expression of reciprocity calculations. Some people think they have to be perfect in order to deserve to be alive. Similarly, the feeling of being a total failure can also express reciprocity. Some people think they have failed because they haven't met someone's perfectly arbitrary expectations.

In the hunter-gatherer environment, everyone had to keep track, *in their heads*, of their debits and credits. This reckoning still goes on. It surfaces when clients begin to talk freely to the therapist. One hears two kinds of material: a list of grievances and injuries, and another list of failures to meet expectations and obligations. "There are all those people out there who didn't do what they were supposed to do," say some people. "There were all those things that I was supposed to do and didn't," say others. And most people have both kinds of lists. One could almost say that the internal dialogue is the ledger book of reciprocity.

Many have created in their minds phantasmagorical debts that burden them with guilt — debts to dead parents, to ancestors, to "humanity," to God, and even to no one in particular. Others, and often the same ones, seem unable to recognize that they might owe something to people who have befriended them and given to them unstintingly. Still others, and often the same ones, feel they are entitled to things that aren't coming to them, but don't realize what they are in fact entitled to, or what they have in fact been deprived of.

These ruminations produce a welter of emotions. Some people are angry about what they are not getting, some people are depressed. Some are on the verge of violence, some on the brink of suicide. Some are determined to get what is coming to them, and some are sitting on the sidelines, content to complain. Some are full of angst because they haven't done what they should (paid what they owe). Furthermore, many people oscillate between these emotions, producing difficult, unstable, unpredictable behavior.

The job of the therapist is to enable people to calculate reciprocity in such a way as will enable them to engage in satisfying social relationships. Therapists must not of course define the client's rights and obligations. Rather, they make the operation of the system clear, reveal the roots of the client's pathology, and thus free the client up to get emotional nourishment from other people.

In the rest of this chapter, we will provide excerpts from case histories to illustrate the connection between reciprocity and various commonly-encountered clinical phenomena. We will start with guilt and entitlement.

Guilt

After several months of therapy, Tom, a college professor, discovered that he had a "judge" in his head. Like so many other people in the same situation, he was living his life as if he were on trial. What was interesting about his case was that he spontaneously related his inner dialogue to reciprocity:

> It's as if I owe things to other people. I owe them favors, or to do what they ask me. That I can understand. But I also seem to owe them to behave in a certain way, to live up to their image of me, maybe, so that they can feel good. I seem to be responsible for how other people feel, my parents especially, but even my friends. Or strangers, people who serve me in restaurants. I've been elected to make things right.

Tom's whole life had been fashioned by this distortion in his personal accounting system. He had lived for years with a wife who didn't want to have sex with him; it hadn't occurred to him that he had a right to something else. He had had a few affairs, but felt terribly guilty about them. He had been unable to complete the book he was working on, even though he had an enthusiastic publisher who thought the book would give him a national reputation. In the sessions, he was markedly uncomfortable whenever he had to talk about himself. He preferred to talk about the problems he was creating for other people.

Given his level of insight, the therapist moved quickly to engage him in some self-assertion exercises: deliberate attempts to ask for, or demand, what he wanted. He suffered greatly carrying them out. At first he thought he would die of guilt. But soon he realized that nothing catastrophic was going to happen if he expressed his desires. He gained some distance on the feeling of guilt and carried out the assignments more easily. Following that, his sense of self began to change as well; he began to see himself as a person with rights as well as obligations.

Entitlement

Although Roger was not technically "paranoid," he spent all his time in therapy trying to prove to me that the world was persecuting him, or better, discriminating against him. He was totally unaware that he brought all his troubles on himself, through his cutting, insulting "humor," and his total inability to prevent himself from arguing about everything that was said to him.

One example will give the measure of his unrealistic expectations of the world:

I invented this [widget], it really was great, and I sent it off to a company that asks for inventions, and they didn't even answer me. They didn't even write to thank me for sending it in. I went to all this trouble, worked the whole thing out, packaged it, I sent them a nice note, and they just ignored me. Now, am I bringing that on myself? Are you going to tell me that it's my fault? They put other people's stuff on the air. People just don't give me a break, I don't know what it is.

Roger expected reciprocity from the world, but he overvalued his own contribution. He expected to receive far more than the real value of his contribution. His inflated sense of self thus prevented him from entering into satisfactory relationships with anyone. Therapy focused on helping Roger to understand the rules of the reciprocity system, as well as on getting him to confront his grandiosity.

It might seem paradoxical to talk of entitlement in Samantha's case. She expected little from other people. But she gave almost nothing, and therefore the little she expected was unreasonable.

Samantha was about 40 when she first came in to therapy. She was of average intelligence, but had never held anything but low-paying jobs, and had never had a husband or a long-term relationship. Her extreme sensitivity and emotional outbursts destroyed all her work and personal relationships. After she lost what must have been the tenth job since beginning therapy, she came in crying and complaining about the boss. The therapist confronted her rather sharply, and told her that as long as she reacted emotionally to instruction and criticism, she would never be able to get the retraining that we were hoping for. Here is the dialogue that followed:

T: You're always concerned with how people see you and treat you, and with what you need. Have you ever thought of what other people need from you?
C: (looking stunned) My boss needs something from me?

Her limited sense of self and low-self esteem made it impossible for her to recognize other people's needs or to perceive her obligations in social situations. She was entitled and deprived at one and the same time.

Reciprocity and the borderline spectrum

Most observers would agree that one of the most common characteristics of people seen in psychotherapy is a pervasive dissatisfaction with self, often accompanied by compensatory fantasies of perfection and/or unlimited power. The tendency to oscillate between a grandiose and a negative self-representation is found in its most extreme form in people characterized by what psychoanalyst Otto Kernberg calls borderline personality organization. Borderline, narcissistic and histrionic personalities tend to oscillate between a highly idealized and a totally negative self-representation. They sometimes see themselves as perfect, sometimes as worthless, and their feelings about others tend to oscillate in the same manner. There is no in-between state.

We have found that this tendency toward self-denigration and self-aggrandizement is generally associated with distortions in the calculation of reciprocity. In borderline personality organization, the concept of reciprocity apparently changes along with the self-representation. When such people are seeing themselves as perfect, they don't believe they owe anything to anyone. This may be because they are simultaneously seeing others as "bad." When they are seeing themselves as worthless or evil, on the other hand, they don't think they deserve anything. Hence, they can be gushingly grateful at one moment and coldly demanding at the next.

Furthermore, they often make commitments in one state that they forget when they've switched into another state. As a result, they regularly let their friends down, often without knowing it. They go through life accumulating resentment rather than favors. Naturally, they are unable to sustain satisfactory relationships over time. The failure to sustain relationships feeds back on their self-image, confirming their negative opinion of self and making escape into a fantasy of perfection all the more attractive.

The following case description represents an analysis of the borderline problem from the point of view of reciprocity.

Allison found it almost impossible to accept gifts or friendly gestures. First of all, the obligation to return the gift bore heavily on her. She saw it as a threat to her freedom and ultimately to her self. What if she didn't want to return the gift? Would she have to do it anyway? And if she had to commit this act, what meaning did her life have? She would often get angry thinking about this, and would, for a week or a even a month, get completely absorbed in an inner dialogue concerning the value of continuing her life. She would emerge having totally forgotten the gift that set her off.

The content of the inner dialogue came out with difficulty in our sessions. Since she obviously could not be worthy of the gift, she felt that she had fooled the gift-giver. This made her feel terribly guilty. The guilt produced anger, which at first she turned on herself. The "deception" threatened her integrity, making her feel dishonest and cheap. Ultimately, she turned the anger onto the gift-giver, as the person who was responsible for making her feel bad.

Some part of her could recognize that this anger was unjustified, so she would get angry at herself for being angry at the gift-giver, and would try to compensate. This flung her into the opposite behavior. She would exaggerate her obligation, and eventually start to feel that she had to comply with every one of the giver's wishes. Essentially, she would see herself as a slave, and the giver as the master. Naturally, she couldn't sustain this position for long, and would again find herself in a rage—at the giver, for being a tyrant, and at herself, for being so spineless. By this time, she would find it impossible to have any relationship at all with the giver.

Allison also found it almost impossible to give, because for her, giving represented a total commitment, a merging. Part of her desired it, but part of her feared it, because it represented the obliteration of her personality. She feared that her gift would be misunderstood by the recipient, who would then expect this total commitment, which she would be bound to refuse. This refusal, she felt, would create disappointment and pain, and so she generally did not make the gesture in the first place.

She would make impulsive, and very generous, gifts—of objects and of herself—when she was feeling good about herself, but these gestures would invariably be followed by flight. Thus, she inflicted in reality the pain that she tried so desperately to avoid.

In the sessions, her therapist used the hunter-gatherer reciprocity system as a means to discuss Allison's effect on other people without appearing to criticize her behavior in any way. The therapist started by talking about the difficulties of establishing stable relationships in a modern, industrial society. Then he pointed out how much easier it was under other conditions, without specifically stressing the special position of hunter-gatherers in the study of human evolution. The altered social conditions in which we live provided a framework for discussing individual behavior in a nonthreatening manner. This subject could be discussed with nothing at stake. The following passage may help to provide a picture of this use of the material. (Intermediate steps, gradual approaches, false starts, and detours have been eliminated for the sake of brevity).

T: Picture a good friend of yours who is a member of a band. Someone offers her a gift. What does she feel?
C: Panic.
T: OK. She feels panic. What does she have to do?
C: Control it.

RECIPROCITY AND COMMUNICATION

Implied messages about reciprocity can be found in much of what people say to each other. Take for example the following exchange, which occurred between a man and his wife in a couples session:

Wife: Would you like to have roast beef for dinner tonight?
Husband: Fine.

The issue here is the meaning of the word "fine." When questioned, the husband said he was trying to be easy to please. He couldn't understand why his wife got angry.

The wife's question meant: "Can I please you by making a special dish?" which translates as "Can I do something for you?" The husband's answer meant: "It's OK by me if you want to," which translates as "I will do it for you, as a favor." The wife was angry because she didn't see his willingness to eat roast beef as a favor to her.

If the meaning of the messages is not clarified, both parties to such an exchange will end it thinking that they have done something for the other person, and will therefore (unconsciously) expect something to be done for them in the future. The discrepant calculation of reciprocity, even in such minor form, can eventually build up to the point where it destroys a marriage.

T: Let yourself imagine her controlling it.
C: (Pause) I've done it.
T: Good. What does she get out of it?
C: She gets to be part of the group.
T: What's your sense of what the other people are feeling?
C: Together. They're dancing now.
T: Imagine joining the group. Dance along with them.
C: (Pause) I can't get into the dance. But it feels good just being with them. . . .

At a subsequent session, we returned to this scene:

T: What would happen if she kept on taking gifts and never returned any?

C: They would get awfully tired of her, I guess. They'd stop giving to her and probably wouldn't want her around anymore. I don't know. Maybe they'd even drive her away. . . .

Allison, like many clients, found the hunter-gatherer reciprocity system attractive in theory, and it gradually became something of a model for her. The therapist used it to talk indirectly about her inability to engage in reciprocal relationships. Because she could perceive the orderliness in it, she could use it to revise her way of thinking about her own relationships, without self-criticism. For weren't therapist and client talking about a societal issue, rather than a personal failure? When she could talk about her effect on other people without an explosion of anger or a retreat into sullen silence, the need for indirectness diminished, and the explicit use of the anthropological material declined.

Reciprocity and depression

Depression apparently alters the calculation of reciprocity. People who are subject to bouts of depression seem to experience changes in their sense of obligation and entitlement. When depressed, they think that they deserve nothing; when they are feeling better, they have a more balanced sense of rights and obligations. Here is an example:

Winnie had made a fairly decent life for herself. She had a husband, several children and a modest career. But she was subject to frequent bouts of depression, which were becoming more and more irksome. For the last few years, she had been depressed more often than not.

She had good reason to be depressed. Shortly after her birth, she had been abandoned by her mother. The mother reclaimed her without warning when she was seven, thus causing Winnie to lose the only family she had ever known. Worse, the mother turned out to be subject to extreme mood swings. When she was up, she was very very nice, but when she was down, she was horrid. Winnie was indelibly marked by this erratic reward schedule. She had spent her adult years trying to get love and support from her mother. Failing this, she had begun trying to get her mother to discuss her mood swings rationally.

By the time she started therapy, Winnie had gained some awareness of this dynamic. Challenged to explain why she continued to associate with her mother, she stated:

When I'm depressed, I feel that blood is thicker than water. She's in trouble, I have to be there for her. When I'm feeling good, I think: "I don't have to take this anymore."

To put it in terms of the reciprocity system: When depressed, Winnie thought she owed her unhappy mother some support. When not depressed, Winnie felt she didn't owe her mother so much, and deserved more for herself. We think that this phenomenon will be found in most if not all people who suffer from recurring bouts of depression.

Some Forms and Disguises of Reciprocity

Reciprocity comes in many forms and wears many disguises. The following clinical examples will illustrate some of them. We hope that readers will recognize some of these same patterns in their clients. (Note that extensive extracts from sessions involving reciprocity-related issues appear in Chapter 13.)

Revenge

Orlando, a craftsman from a strong ethnic background, had spent his life trying to live according to the rules he had learned from his father. He believed that if he worked hard, did the best job possible, didn't make waves, and didn't ask for anything, his employers would respect him and reward him with raises. As a result, he was chronically underpaid. However, he refused to give up this strategy. He believed it was right, period. He felt that employers who didn't give him his due would eventually lose out, and he drifted from job to job looking for an employer who would recognize his qualities.

One could of course analyze this behavior in terms of a "search for the father" and there is some truth in this approach. However, it misses the essential point. Orlando's values were good. His expectation of reciprocity would have made him an ideal member of a band. But these values were simply not adapted to modern society.

Orlando did not understand why he was not successful, but he refused to complain. He presented himself as a calm, reasonable man who was going to bear his burden stoically. However, as therapy progressed, he began to talk more and more about the people who had not "done right" by him. The therapist taught him a relaxation technique and gave him a simple instruction: "Let go, say whatever comes into your mind." His response was a surprise. He began to describe violent fantasies of revenge. Furthermore, it was clear that he could barely distinguish between fantasy and intention. He later reported that the fantasies were always near the surface—he had to expend a great deal of effort to keep them under control.

Therapy aimed to validate his values while allowing him to modify his

---

RECIPROCITY AND TRANSFERENCE

Despite substantial improvement in his career and personal life, Carny, a 33-year-old man of working-class origins, had remained suspicious of the therapist's intentions through four years of therapy. Among other things, he lost no opportunity to joke about the high fees he was being charged, even though he had always paid substantially less than the going rate.

He came in one day complaining bitterly about a brother who had ripped him off. Since Carny had become successful, he had been trying to help other members of his family, and they had invariably responded by playing him for a sucker. Carny was the identified patient in his family, and was generally treated like a moron. However, he kept heaping favors on his kin, in hope of winning their approval and acceptance. We had discussed this compulsion many times. This time, he seemed ready to deal: "Why is it that I am so family-oriented?" he asked.

The therapist used the opportunity to point out that kinship and reciprocity were two fundamental bases of human social life, then added:

T: You are totally involved with family. You pay no attention to reciprocity in other relationships. You spend your life with people who rip you off. You don't demand that people treat you in kind. You give too much to your kin, and then get angry when they don't give you as much in return.

(*continued*)

behavior so as to function more successfully in his environment. When he understood his predicament, the violent fantasies subsided, and he was able to make more adaptive career choices.

Blackmail

Patty had been in therapies of various kinds for years without ever making any progress. She was an extremely difficult person to tolerate. She would come into the session, sprawl in her chair, yawn obnoxiously, and stare off into space until asked a question. Then she would generally reply: "What do you want to know?" or "What do you want me to say about it?" When pressed, she would try to make the therapist feel guilty about harassing her.

RECIPROCITY AND TRANSFERENCE (*continued*)

C: (After a silence) You're saying that I don't notice when other people give me things, and I don't care when they don't give me anything . . .

T: Well, did it ever occur to you that you might be getting your money's worth from me? My sense is that you treat me like a business competitor. You try to get as much and give as little as you can.

C: Are you saying that I should come in and offer you more money every once and awhile?

T: That sounds ridiculous to you, doesn't it?

C: Yes.

T: Would you be surprised that other people do?

C: (Taken aback) Why do they do that?

T: Perhaps because they started making more, and think it's only fair.

C: (With a sneer) Could there be another reason?

T: What do you think?

C: You don't think it's to make you like them?

T: Well, I guess that's the way *you* would see it.

C: (After a long silence) The idea that you're saying that I have been paying too little could really make me paranoid, but I'm going to think about it.

The session led to a reduction in Carny's suspiciousness and to a much greater sense of common endeavor.

   Note: This material was not used to raise the client's fee. We realize that the above passage represents a risky intervention. Making a client aware that he had been receiving value for services rendered could generate guilt. But in this case, bringing the client to an awareness of his relationship with the therapist and with all non-kin seemed more important.

About a year into therapy, while answering a question about her job, she suddenly stated that she was a nice person. Shocked, the therapist asked her what she meant by "nice." She replied that she did things for others and didn't ask them to do anything for her.

T: Is that being nice, or is it being a doormat?

C: I don't understand.

T: Well, it seems to me you're letting people push you around.

C: I don't see that.
T: Well, look at it this way. If you continue to do things for others when they don't do anything for you, you'll make them feel guilty. Is that nice?
C: (after a silence) But maybe I can make them do something for me that way.
T: Perhaps you can. It may work. But is it "nice?" Aren't you trying to force people to do something for you that they don't want to do?

The conversation went on like that for a long time. Later on, the therapist tried to point out to her that hiding what she wanted was also not "nice," because it made it impossible for other people to give her pleasure and thereby discharge their obligations (not to say make themselves feel good). She was unable to grasp this point at the time.

This is an interesting, and fairly common, pathology of reciprocity. Patty understood part of the rule, namely that the person accepting a favor incurs an obligation. But she couldn't see another part of the rule, namely, that one must take as well as give. Consequently, she couldn't understand her role in the system, nor why people treated her as they did.

Self-destructive behavior

It may seem odd, but some self-destructive behavior also seems to be the result of a pathology of reciprocity. Most therapists have encountered individuals who seem to be hurting themselves in order to get back at someone. The most common expression of this is: "He'll be sorry." Suicide often seems to be the expression of a desire to hurt someone else — to get revenge for some injury, real or imagined.

The underlying perception of the person who damages self to get back at someone is correct — the action *will* generally be painful to the person it is designed to hurt. Why this should be so is not self-evident, but one can hazard an explanation. When someone we are close to injures him/herself, a natural reaction is to ask ourselves what we did wrong, i.e., in what way did we fail to live up to our obligations. Even if we cannot find anything really wrong in our actions, we find it hard to escape guilt. This is probably because the reciprocity system, unlike the money or barter system, is vague and open-ended. There is no final, unambiguous accounting of debts and obligations.

In a larger sense, the ability of a human to hurt another through a self-destructive action is a function of the fact that humans are a social species. Empathy was essential to survival in a band, and is probably essential for normal living in any human society. Most of us cannot help feeling the pain of others. This too is a function of the reciprocity system; empathy, like guilt, leads us to live up to our obligations.

The case of Sheila provides a good example of the connection between self-destructive behavior and reciprocity. Sheila had originally come into therapy because she wanted to become thin. Years of prior (insight-oriented) therapy had not helped. Despite all the time she had spent probing her past, she affirmed, and seemed convinced, that she had had an ideal childhood. She took violent exception to any attempt to find causal explanations in her parents' behavior.

Exploration revealed that Sheila had been fat as a child and was not as academically gifted as most other people in her family. Furthermore, she had been raised by a father and stepmother. From her low self-esteem, one could surmise that they probably hadn't liked her very much, but no evidence was forthcoming.

Starting in adolescence, Sheila undertook a series of successful diets, but invariably put the weight back on. She was bewildered. She claimed never to feel hunger, and insisted she wanted to be thin more than anything in the world.

In psychotherapy, we discovered, not surprisingly, that she was using the weight as a shield and an excuse. She found compliments unpleasant, because she didn't believe a fat person deserved any praise. She eventually realized that she was blaming all her problems on her fat. "If I was to get thin, I wouldn't have any excuse anymore." However, none of these realizations helped her to control her eating.

More or less out of frustration, her therapist asked who she was hurting by keeping herself so fat. She insisted that she was only hurting herself. But one day, after a relaxation exercise, while she was in what seemed like a hypnotic trance, the following exchange ensued:

T: Are you trying to prove to me that I can't help you?
C: No.
T: So what is keeping you fat?
C: (In an altered tone) If I get thin, how will they know that they did bad things to me?

From this session on, Sheila began to discuss her childhood in more reasonable terms. She stopped bridling when her father's wife was referred to as her stepmother, and she began to admit the possibility that there might be a connection between her upbringing and her weight problem. However, she has not, as of this writing, overcome her eating disorder.

This example does not of course "prove" anything, but we feel it is illustrative. Virtually everyone has known someone who is trying to get revenge on someone else through self-destructive acts. When analyzed in terms of the reciprocity system, this otherwise bizarre quirk of human behavior turns out to be readily comprehensible.

One can see the connection between reciprocity and self-destructive behavior very clearly in some forms of sexual behavior. In sex, taking is very close to giving. One desires the pleasure of one's partner. Thus it is possible to hurt someone by being frigid, indifferent, premature, or impotent, all behaviors which are primarily destructive to the self.

Antisocial behavior

Zach was a convicted rapist, with a long history of violence against both men and women. He had no solid relationships in his life, with either men or women. He had been rejected for psychotherapy by a series of clinics, whose directors thought he was a poor risk. Most people who knew his case thought that he was hopelessly lacking in compassion, that he was incapable of feeling empathy for his victims, and that he had no sense of right and wrong.

He was in therapy for over a year before there was any reason to believe that this judgment was incorrect. But one day, he reported committing a small crime and then making amends for it. During the philosophical discussion of morality that followed, he revealed that he did have a sense of right and wrong. The problem was, it was distorted beyond recognition.

Zach felt that what he was doing when committing a crime was "right." His rationale was as follows: He had had a deprived childhood, and had been the subject of terrible abuse. Therefore, whatever he could get back, he deserved. Since even his parents had abused him, everyone else was likely to do so as well. Therefore, he had to strike out at others before they attacked him. Besides, "they" were part of society, and society owed him.

What people in later life did for him never made up for what he had lost, and therefore, he never felt that he owed anyone anything, no matter what they did for him.

Before this point in therapy, Zach's "calculation" of reciprocal obligations was primarily unconscious. As he verbalized it, he had the impression that he had always known it, but in truth, he had never been able to express it to anyone before, and he hadn't known that this way of thinking was in any way unusual; he assumed everyone calculated in the same way.

We cannot be sure that Zach's method of calculating was purely the product of his environment. Not every abused child becomes a violent criminal. Some become victims. Perhaps the circuits that calculate reciprocity were, in Zach's case, biased from conception in favor of rights as against obligations, in which case the environment he grew up in would have served as an aggravating factor, one that tipped the balance towards criminal behavior. It seems probable to us that, as is so often the case, both genetic and environmental factors played a role here.

Below will be found an excerpt from a session with Zach. It helps to illustrate one way the concept of reciprocity can be used in therapy. We should state that the therapist hesitated a long time before introducing the topic of reciprocity, because he was afraid—afraid to discover that Zach simply could not understand, and therefore engage in, reciprocal behavior. This fear proved to be ill-founded.

Zach opened one session by defining himself as "unscrupulous." This seemed like a good opening and served as the springboard for the following dialogue:

T: You know, that makes me want to talk to you about reciprocity.
C: That's a word that's new to me.
T: Well, it's a little hard to explain. It has to do with relationships. Suppose you do a favor for someone. If you need a favor later, you will probably come to that guy, and if he doesn't help you out, you'll be mad.
C: Yeah, I know exactly what you're talking about. My wife didn't want me to stay in the house last night, so I asked my friend if I could stay over with her, and I had a sense that I owed her, so I brought over an album today, and I'll keep doing stuff like that until I feel that it's clear.

The therapist was of course surprised and delighted. Here was the client, running the complete set of calculations, just like any normal person. The prognosis took a strong turn for the better.

Meanwhile, it seemed highly probable that his calculation of reciprocity was somewhat different from that of most people. That hypothesis guided the rest of the session.

T: OK, you've got it. Now here is what I think. (Here, the therapist laid out the notion that the calculation of reciprocity is a biological trait of the human being.) You are like everyone else in this respect, which has to be reassuring.
C: (With stunning insight) But I think I calculate differently than most people.
T: That's exactly what I think. There is a conventional way of calculating what you are owed and what you owe, and your way might be different. Probably because of the way you were raised.

C: I think I calculate differently because I didn't get what other people got. (Here the client laid out the abuse he had received in childhood.) So I don't see what the conventional way of calculating has in it for me.

T: Well, the conventional way is what makes relationships possible.

C: I'm glad you say the conventional way. It has nothing to do with right and wrong, then, or with really owing.

T: That's really another question. I'm talking about getting along with people. If people calculate too differently, they can't stay in relationships with each other. They get angry. My guess is that most rifts between people occur because the two parties are calculating reciprocity different-ly. Now the thing is, everybody does it somewhat differently, and most people think that they are owed more than they owe. Which means that there is always a potential for rifts. You have to learn how to tolerate this. Now my guess is that you can't stand it.

C: You're right. If I see that someone thinks I owe them, I start to feel guilty, and that drives me wild. I can't stand it. I'm backed into a corner. There's been too much guilt in my life. When I was a kid, my father would have fights with my mother, and she would drive off, and he would say to me: "You see, your mother is going to kill herself, and it's your fault."

T: Your fault?

C: Yes. He would have been beating on me and she would say some-thing to try to get him to stop, and he would turn on her, so it would be my fault.

T: No wonder you can't tolerate guilt. . . . well, there you have it. You feel guilt, you get angry, you get into a fight, you destroy a relationship and you get into trouble. . . . I think you need to be able to tolerate feeling the guilt. Because you're always going to be surrounded by people who think you owe them, and if you get mad, you're going to get into trouble.

C: I think you're right. Guilt is basic. I've got to be able to let myself feel it.

T: And that doesn't mean that you have to agree with what the other guy calculates. You have to let other people calculate the way they calcu-late. You'll make your own calculation, you'll have your own sense of it, you won't be frightened when you feel the guilt, and you'll be able to balance what you owe against what you are owed much more accurately, or better, much more conventionally . . .

We feel that the emphasis on "conventional" calculation, rather than right and wrong, was an important part of this conversation. "Right and wrong" would have put the client on the defensive, and would have confused the issue. Was he "wrong" to feel that he had something coming, given the abuse he suffered as a child? By making right and wrong irrelevant, we were able to change his calculation without making him feel he had been defeated.

Note that this relatively nonjudgmental approach reflects the biological approach to morality. Morality is seen as a biological trait, manifested in an innate tendency towards reciprocal altruism, given favorable environmental conditions. It is something that one feels. What we *feel* is right may or may not *be* right, but *that* we feel that some things are right and some things are wrong is an unquestionable fact.

We do not know if Zach was a sociopath. Is he not, because he can understand reciprocity, while true sociopaths can't? Or are the people we call sociopaths simply calculating a bit differently from us, because of adverse circumstances? Further research on this question would be desirable.

Cheating and the therapist

The case of Zach brings up a more general theoretical problem. People tend to cheat in reciprocal relationships if they feel they can get away with it. How should therapists deal with this? We feel that clinicians need to understand that it is natural and normal for people to try to promote their own selfish interests, just as it is natural and normal for them to need the support and esteem of others. Clinicians should not impose moralistic standards derived from other belief systems.

When clients tell us about cheating, we believe the correct intervention is still to indicate that the behavior is natural. Then, we point out the dangers and drawbacks. We try to get the client to evaluate what there is to lose.

The consequences of cheating are of two kinds, which need to be distinguished clearly. If the client is found out, there will be loss of face and social isolation. Found out or not, there will be guilt, shame, and low self-esteem (provided the client is not sociopathic). There is generally a trade-off between acting selfishly and feeling good about self, and this trade-off is what the clinician needs to keep in mind.

Enough for now. Extensive reciprocity-related therapeutic dialogues will be found in Part Two. Those extracts from case histories further illustrate some of the ways the concept of reciprocity can be used in psychotherapy. In the next two chapters, we will be looking at childhood and development, with particular emphasis on how the environment of childhood has changed since the decline of hunting and gathering.

RECIPROCITY AND INADEQUACY

Wally came in wanting to talk about a discussion he had had with his girlfriend. She had been giving him many compliments and lavishing attention on him. He liked it at first, but then it began grating on him. He gradually realized that when treated well he begins to expect that unpleasant demands will be made on him.

We explored the issue. He first thought was that he was uncomfortable because he didn't like his lover enough. He then realized that the explanation was inadequate. Encouraged to look for the roots of his discomfort, Wally soon discovered that the demand was disagreeable because it triggered an unpleasant thought: "I won't be able to reciprocate." He traced this thought to his childhood experience of being unable to protect his mother from his abusive father. "I was inadequate then, when it really counted. I don't see how I can be adequate now."

Later, he continued along these lines: "I'm beginning to feel that there is something in me that is working against me, that is tricking me, that is working against my best interests. I feel that I am betraying myself and also that I might betray other people, by not being able to repay them in kind."

Most of the time, Wally felt that he had nothing to offer to anyone, and therefore could not stand it when someone offered something to him. It should be noted in passing, however, that some of the time, Wally expressed grandiose ideas about who he was and what he should achieve, and in those states, he didn't think that anyone was good enough for him. Only when he realized that he oscillated between these two positions was he able to begin engaging successfully in reciprocal relationships.

CHAPTER 4

The Natural Environment of Childhood

No one can make you feel inferior
without your consent.
— Eleanor Roosevelt

OUR UNDERSTANDING OF CHILD-REARING in the natural environment is based on what we know about child-rearing in 20th century hunting and gathering bands. We rely on the observations of anthropologists who are very different persons, and who approach their work with very different sensibilities. Colin Turnbull, the celebrated Englishman who lived with the Mbuti (Pygmies) for several years, portrayed them with lyrical charm. Jean Briggs, who lived for a year as the adopted daughter of an Inuit (Eskimo) family, described her experiences eloquently, but with more restraint. Former Harvard anthropologist Melvin Konner described infancy among the !Kung (Bushmen) of the Kalahari in measured scientific prose (1976). Marjorie Shostak, who witnessed the !Kung in their last years as true foragers, found more conflict than most other witnesses. Yet all observers[1] agree on the main facts. In virtually all hunting and gathering bands:

[1]Our account of child rearing among foraging peoples is based mainly on a review of the following works: Balikci, 1970; Berndt & Berndt, 1964; Bernhard, 1988; Boas, 1888; Briggs, 1970; Dahlberg, 1981; DeVore & Konner, 1974; Draper, 1976; Elkin, 1938/1964; Freuchen, 1961; Gould, 1969; Greenway, 1972; Hart and Pilling, 1979; Howell, 1979; Jenness, 1928; Konner, 1982; Lee, 1979; Lee & DeVore, 1968; Marshall, 1976; Meggitt, 1962; Mowat, 1951/1977; Roheim, 1974; Shostak, 1981; Steffansson, 1951; Thomas, 1959; Tonkinson, 1978; Turnbull, 1962, 1983; Waipuldanya, 1962/1970; Williams and Hunn, 1981. The composite that we have created stresses the features that these widely separated cultures have in common. The quotes are designed to give examples of these common features, not to "prove" the points we are making.

1. After the first year of life, children are raised by many adults, not just the biological parents, and even during the first year there are always other adults around to help out and provide extra attention.

2. Parenting is public and can't be hidden from the group.

3. There is no formal education (schooling).

4. Children learn by imitation.

5. Play and learning are inseparable.

6. Children are allowed to develop at their own pace.

7. Children play in mixed age groups, so much necessary information is transmitted from the older children to the younger ones.

8. All aspects of adult life, including work and sex, are clearly visible to children of all ages.

9. Adults are extremely indulgent towards young children.

10. There is almost no nagging.

11. Gender roles are well-defined and absolutely clear.

12. Sexuality is encouraged or at least not condemned as it is in our society.

13. Finally, the dangerousness of the outside world — the physical environment — is clear and palpable (through the senses) even to infants.

In some societies, in particular those of Australia, older children are subject to very harsh discipline, including tests of endurance and courage that require enormous self-control. These measures, which include ritual wounds such as subincision of the penis, might seem to contradict the notion that hunter-gatherers are indulgent to children. Not so. The disciplinary measures are not punishments but rituals clearly designed to signal the end of childhood. They are not applied by parents, but by other adults in the band. Finally, they are acceptable because it is clear, even to the children, that all individuals must be able to face severe hardships in a remarkably difficult environment.

The key idea of this chapter is that the natural environment *constrains* child-rearing. The word "constrain" needs some explaining. It refers to the way in which the setting, on the average, puts some limits on what can happen. If we say a salad bowl constrains a salad, we are saying that while lots of exciting things can happen inside the salad, like sliced tomatoes meeting anchovies, some things can happen only very rarely, like anchovies sliding onto the floor.

The social environment of a band constrains variation in the behavior of individuals. Suppose, for example, that an individual in a band was inclined (predisposed) to beating his child. The chances are he wouldn't be able to. Hitting children is not socially acceptable, and since there are no walls, no one can hit children in private. Even if there were a "deviant parent" in a band, the degree of harm such an individual could do would be strictly limited.

Because of the public nature of parenting, children are generally brought up in the same way from generation to generation. Idiosyncratic child-rearing is kept to a minimum, and thus does not get passed along the way it does in our society. Without thought or effort, parents and other adults behave in ways that will help the child grow up into a socially acceptable, productive adult. The entire system works as an integrated unit, with children automatically learning what is necessary for proper development.

The children of hunter-gatherers certainly do not learn as *much* as children learn in our society, but they learn what they need to know.

Childhood in Hunter-Gatherer Societies

To provide a vivid picture of childhood in hunter-gatherer societies, we will quote extensively from ethnographic accounts. Most quotations are about two peoples, the !Kung and the Mbuti. We have used the !Kung and the Mbuti simply because these are the two groups about which we have the most detailed information. A warning: the Mbuti and the !Kung are among the most peaceful and cooperative of peoples. We understand that not every hunter-gatherer group could be expected to have so idyllic a life and be as attractive to the contemporary reader.

Birth

In hunter-gatherer bands, children who survive are wanted. Unwanted children are gotten rid of, one way or another. Infanticide is not common, but no mother is forced to keep a child that she doesn't want or can't take care of. Children are wanted not only by the parents, but by the entire band. All the adults consider themselves in some degree to be the parents of every child, which is quite natural, since most people in the band are closely related. There is competition to see and hold newborn infants, and there are always experienced parents around to transmit the traditions of the ancestors to first-time mothers. The role of mother commands the respect of everyone in the group. Giving birth gives a woman the final badge of courage and adulthood.

Throughout the first few years of life, children are in almost constant contact with their mothers. They are carried close to their mother's body when she moves around, they accompany her to work, they sleep against her body, and they feed on demand. The !Kung infants have continual access to their mother's breast, day and night, and nurse several times an hour, usually for at least three years. Children sleep beside their mothers at night, and during the day are carried in a sling, skin-to-skin on their mother's hip, wherever she goes, at work or at play. If they are physically separated, it is usually for short periods when the father, siblings, cousins, grandparents, aunts, uncles or friends of the family are playing with the baby while the mother sits nearby.

Fathers are generally indulgent, affectionate, and devoted, forming very intense mutual attachments with their children. Fathers are not viewed as figures of awesome authority, and their relationships with their children, says Shostak (1981), are "intimate, nurturant and physically close."

Colin Turnbull (1983), who admittedly inclined to the idyllic, tells us that a Mbuti child:

> . . . was conceived in love and joy, and that is how it is born, equally wanted and welcome whether it is a girl child or a boy child. . . . The infant emerges easily, helped only by the mother's hands or those of a friend, and is immediately placed to the mother's breast as she lies down. The umbilical cord is cut in anything from a few minutes to as much as an hour or more later. At that time or soon after, the father and close friends may be invited to see the child, who by then is happily suckling. Women say this is a decision made by the mother and the child. When I have been present in the camp at the time of a birth, the newborn infant has sometimes given two or three tiny bleats . . . but then it has better things to do than cry, such as explore its mother's body, feel her warmth, try the new and satisfying experience of drinking its mother's milk, all the while being reassured by the familiar sounds of her voice, singing the newborn's own special lullaby [which the mother had been singing before birth]. . . .

Not long after birth, the child begins to be exposed to the other members of the band. It will be handed around and stroked by virtually all the adults, who then become available as backup parents. Turnbull (1983) describes this process among the Mbuti:

> The child, who has been in constant contact only with the mother, is presented to the camp. The mother emerges from her *endu* (leaf hut), and hands the child, wrapped in sweet-smelling bark cloth, to a few of her assembled family and close friends, not just to look at, but to hold close to their bodies. The infant learns that there is a plurality of warm bodies, similar in warmth (which is comforting) but dissimilar in smells and rhythmic movements and sounds. If it is disconcerted enough to cry in protest, its mother immediately takes it back and puts it to her breast. Thus an initial model of predictability and security is reinforced. . . .

Exploration and separation

Separation from the mother is a gradual process among hunter-gatherers. Early exploration takes place within the camp, in a protected environment where all the adults are potential friends and no area within reach of the infant is dangerous, with the possible exception of the hearth fires. Turnbull's (1983) account is the most extensive one we have, so we will continue to quote from it extensively:

> Infancy is by no means a time of total protection but rather one of controlled experimentation and perpetual learning. It is the time for exploring territory. Now that it has left the very clearly defined territory of the womb, the newborn utilizes every sense available to it to explore the new territory that is its mother's body. There is not an inch of that new world that the infant has not explored within the first few weeks of life. And while exploring the relatively familiar confines of his mother's body in total security, it is constantly being introduced to other sensations that will also be associated with total security in the future. . . .

Once the child can crawl, it has access to a new space, the parents' living environment — hut, shelter, igloo, etc. This space is relatively safe, but has some dangers that the child can perceive. The parents will probably allow the child to discover these dangers on its own. Says Turnbull:

> The floor of the *endu* (hut) will be explored just as thoroughly as was the mother's body. A thorn brought in when the father returned from the hunt, a biting ant, or the sharp edge of a leaf or sliver of bamboo may cause the child trouble; but rather than prevent it from discovering these things, the mother will either leave it to discover them alone or help it discover their harmful potential and the fact that harm can be avoided or readily alleviated. . . .

As a child gets older, it will enter the larger world of the camp. As it explores, it will learn vital lessons about territory and kinship. The closer it stays to its own shelter, the more likely it is that its own parents will comfort it if it runs into trouble. If it wanders away, it is more likely to be picked up by one of the other adults. This expands the child's concept of safe territory, contributes to its sense of security, and encourages it to explore. If it starts to stray from the encampment, however, it will find itself being brought back, perhaps with surprising roughness. In this way, it learns the boundaries of the band's territory, and the distinction between safe and dangerous.

Weaning is of course a key step in the separation process. It generally does not occur until the child is between three and four, Shostak tells us, which is when mothers usually become pregnant again. Thus the tension associated with weaning is compounded by the jealousy occasioned by the arrival of a new sibling. As a result, weaning is perhaps the most conflict-ridden period in the life of a child. Children are loath to give up the breast, and continue to attempt to nurse long after the mother wants them to stop. Nisa, Shostak's chief informant, had very negative memories of this period in her life:

> When mother was pregnant with Kumsa [a brother], I was also crying. I wanted to nurse! Once, when we were living in the bush and away from other people, I was especially full of tears. I cried all the time. That was when my father said he was going to beat me to death [an expression commonly used as an empty threat, says Shostak]. I was too full of tears and too full of crying. He had a big branch in his hand when he grabbed me, but he didn't hit me; he was only trying to frighten me.

Nisa may have been exaggerating. Observations by anthropologists do not indicate that children are beaten by their parents, or even routinely threatened.

Among many peoples, weaning from the breast is followed by weaning from the sling. This also is a time of strife. Says Shostak:

> !Kung children love to be carried. They love the contact with their mothers and they love not having to walk under the pressure of keeping up. As their mothers begin to suggest and then to insist that they walk along beside them, temper tantrums once again erupt. Children refuse to walk, demand to be carried, and will not agree to be left behind in the village while their mothers gather for the day.

Parent-offspring conflict: A theoretical aside

The ubiquity of conflict at weaning lends support to the theory of parent-offspring conflict, another concept developed by Robert Trivers (1974). Trivers argued that the behavior of both parents and offspring must be understood as individual attempts to maximize inclusive fitness. Viewed from this perspective, the interests of parents and offspring overlap to a large extent, but they are not identical. For example, in a crisis, a parent could conceivably increase inclusive fitness by abandoning a child, to the detriment of the child's fitness.

Weaning is an instance of parent-offspring conflict. Generally, the offspring will attempt to gain more parental investment (milk, attention, care, etc.) than parents are willing to give, especially when parents have more than one offspring. Robert Hinde (1984), the great Cambridge University animal behaviorist, discovered that the mothers of infant rhesus monkeys do indeed push their offspring away during the weaning period, and this phenomenon has been confirmed in various other species. Interestingly enough, the evidence indicates that this type of maternal behavior fosters the offspring's exploratory behavior and independence.

The importance of this concept is as follows: *some* degree of conflict between parent and offspring is natural. One should not regard a totally conflict-free environment as an ideal. Conflict is not always harmful. Surely it should not necessarily be interpreted as a sign of individual psychopathology or of a malfunctioning family unit.

Freud's "castration anxiety" and "Oedipus complex" can best be understood as dramatizations of parent-offspring conflict, writ huge by a fertile imagination working in a culture that had turned the father into a distant, all-powerful ogre. The weakness of Freud's theory was apparent from the beginning. Freud himself recognized that girls have conflicts with their parents as well as boys, and this should have warned him that his interpretation was off the mark. Instead he invented the "Electra complex" to account for the conflict he found in girls and to restore the symmetry his theory otherwise lacked.

The play group

The !Kung are aware that weaning is stressful for children and they try to compensate. A father may spend more time with the child or the child may be sent off to a relative in a nearby group. But what really facilitates the transition is the existence of the play group. Once they are weaned, and until they are adults, children spend much of their time playing together as a group or simply hanging out. They are not expected to do any work or to help with any adult task.

Note that the play group is definitely not a peer group. The play group contains all the children who haven't reached puberty yet. Naturally, the older children are the leaders and, in effect, take much of the burden of child care off the shoulders of the adults. Much of what we would call "parenting" is performed by the older children.

As soon as children discover that play in the group is more appealing than the struggle to get a greater share of their mother's attention, the weaning crisis wanes.

Learning to get along

The play group has a crucial role in transmitting the central values of the band. The games the children play teach them the importance of cooperation and sharing right along with the skills of hunting and gathering. The games are not supervised or directed by the adults but they don't have to be. What the children learn reflects the values of the adults of the band because the children can see the adults function and can understand the importance of the rules of adult behavior. They can see that knowing how to get along with others is just as important as knowing how to throw a spear, build a shelter, or find a water-holding root in a trackless desert. Consequently, the values of the group get transmitted from generation to generation, right along with the physical skills that promote survival.

The appropriateness of the values are obvious. Injury, ostracism and even death stalk those who cannot follow the rules. In an environment that does not easily forgive mistakes, deviant behavior is not likely to persist over long periods of time. Hence, there is little possibility that the children's group will fail to transmit what is important for the children to know.

The role of observation

The education of hunter-gatherer children begins at birth and its methods change very little over the years. As Gary Bernhard demonstrated in *Primates in the Classroom*, a powerful analysis of learning among monkeys, apes and humans, hunter-gatherer children are "taught" almost nothing; they learn by watching their elders.

The subsistence activities of both men and women — their "jobs" — are not hidden from view. Children can observe the entire range of adult activities from their earliest years. Since they aren't insulated from reality, the children grow up to act like responsible adults without taking lessons or going to school. They know their roles by heart before they are called upon to play them for real. They have had a chance to practice before doing anything that counts.

Child-rearing takes place while the women are going about the business of adult life. The children are simply there as the mothers build shelters, gather, prepare food and perform other essential tasks. Children have a choice. They can watch as the women work or play by themselves. In either case, they will be doing what they want. Children also have plenty of opportunity to observe the men at work. Children aren't taken along on the hunt, but few men hunt more than three times a week. The rest of the time they are in camp where they work and relax in the midst of the children. All the children can see what fathers and mothers do.

Since children aren't "taught," parenting is not a high-pressure activity. Adults don't spend their time harassing children who don't want to "study." Children learn what they need to learn because they find adult activities interesting enough to copy. Furthermore, since children aren't in general expected to contribute to the maintenance of the group until they grow up, there is no need to coerce them into doing "useful work." Children watch the adults when they want to, and play by themselves when it suits them. The adults don't have to hassle them all the time "for their own good."

Parents are seldom if ever driven to frustration and rage by the demands of children for attention simply because no adult is ever expected to remain alone with small children for any length of time. A mother doesn't raise her child by herself; she is surrounded at all times by other adults. Her children have other children to play with and other adults to relate to. She does not have to bear the burden of spending entire days trying, with no support and no relief, to meet all the needs of a small child.

Discipline, indulgence, and the physical environment

Under these circumstances, adults rarely have to act as disciplinarians. Children are punished primarily when they do something to endanger themselves or their companions. If they irritate the adults with complaints, they might be yelled at and threatened, but actual incidents of beatings are extremely rare. All observers agree that by Western standards hunter-gatherers are extremely indulgent of young children. As we mentioned before, even the Australian Aborigines, with their extremely severe initiation rites, rarely if ever punish young children.

But this treatment doesn't seem to "spoil" anyone. Despite the relative freedom of the early years, children grow up willing and able to take care of themselves and willing to fulfill their responsibilities. Why?

One doesn't have to look far for the reason. Danger provides all the "discipline" that children need. The dangers that menace the band are obvious to all. The group lives amid wild animals, in temporary shelters, in the constant presence of disease, injury and death. Children can't help seeing what they are going to face when they grow up. Consequently, they reach adulthood with a strong sense of responsibility. They understand what adults do. The social environment can be as supportive as it is because the physical environment is as demanding as *it* is.

The major constraints on a child's life derive from the nature of adult work and the relationship of the band to its environment, not from characteristics of a parent's personality. The camp of a !Kung band, for example, is simply a cleared space surrounded by huts that are backed right up against the wilderness. Patricia Draper, another in the long line of outstanding Harvard-trained observers who have spent time in the Kalahari, vividly describes the scene: Behind each hut "stretches the Kalahari bush, which, from a child's vantage point, is vast, undifferentiated and unsocialized."

Children soon grow to understand the dangers that lie beyond the confines of the clearing; it doesn't take much to make them realize that they will someday have to rely on themselves.

Taken together, these characteristics of parenting in hunter-gatherer societies ensure that children aren't constantly being forced to do things that they can't do or don't want to do. As a result, they aren't systematically exposed to failure. And because they are successful at what they do, they do not routinely experience self-doubt and anguished self-examination. They learn that what they want is legitimate. This "validation of desire" serves them well in later life.

These same characteristics of the learning environment ensure that adults do not become huge, menacing figures endowed with superhuman qualities. We know that in our society children often absorb into their unconscious the image of an omnipotent father figure or an all-encompassing mother—images that sometimes remain with them all their lives. The characteristics of the hunting-gathering adaptation would seem to make this less likely.

Sexuality and identity

Freud shocked the Western world with his so-called discovery of childhood sexuality. The hunter-gatherers would not have been surprised. They are aware of it and seem to have no problems with it. Some of them actively encourage the expression of sexuality in children. We know of no case where sexuality is suppressed. However, one should note that, with the exception of Turnbull and Shostak, most ethnographers are remarkably silent on the subject of hunter-gatherer sex.

Among the Mbuti, says Turnbull (1983), children who are still in the stage of playing together in a *bopi* (a special playground set aside for them in the camp), begin to learn about sexuality by watching girls and boys on the threshold of maturity. Almost immediately, they begin to "explore each others' bodies without discrimination and will even imitate the act of copulation in the form of dance." No one thinks amiss of this and of course no one tries to stop it. Turnbull, in trying to describe the attitude of adults towards the emerging sexuality of the young, says that they actually consider it a "purifying element." They see it as being related to "giving rather than taking life."

The older children are astonishingly relaxed about their bodies and their emerging sexuality. Young boys sleep in each other's arms. Sometimes it happens that one of them ejaculates. No one even comments. Nevertheless, Turnbull claims that he never came across a single case of homosexual intercourse. (He didn't report on the girls, because he slept in a different area and didn't have any firsthand knowledge.)

Among the !Kung, the adults don't appear to actively encourage sex play but they don't try very hard to stop it. Here are some of Nisa's memories of her childhood:

> At night, when a child lies beside her mother, in front, and her father lies down behind and her mother and father make love, the child watches. Her parents don't worry about her, a small child, and her father just has sex with her mother. Because, even if a child sees, even if she hears her parents doing their work at night, she is unaware of what it is her parents are doing . . . [as she gets older, she begins to understand that her] mother and father are making love. At first she thinks, "So, that's another thing people do with their genitals." Then if the child is a little boy, he'll take the little girl, or perhaps his sister, and do the same thing to her; he'll teach himself . . . And once he's learned it, he'll try to play that way with everyone. . . .
>
> That's what an older child does. He waits until he is with a little girl and lies down with her. He takes some saliva, rubs it on her genitals, gets on top and pokes around with his semi-erection, as though he were actually having intercourse, but he is not. Because even though young boys can get hard, they don't really enter little girls. . . . At first, girls refuse that kind of play—they say all that poking around hurts. But when they are a little older, they agree to it and eventually, even like it.

One must of course note that in all hunter-gatherer societies about which we have information, children sleep near their parents and hear, if not see, sexual activity from the time they are born, with no apparent ill-effect.

Initiation rites

The passage to adulthood is invariably marked by ceremonies in which boys become men. The rituals typically involve trials of stoicism and courage, transmission of the secrets of the elders, and proof of skill in hunting. These events formally signify to boys that they are adults, that they have achieved a special status in the group, and that they have met the standards by which men are judged.

Many hunter-gatherer groups also celebrate the great milestones in the life of a female. Among the Mbuti, the *elima*, a celebration of a girl's attainment of puberty, is perhaps the most important rite in the life of the group. Menstruation "is an event that is met with extreme joy, for it means that the girl now has the potential of becoming a woman, which for them means becoming a mother" (Turnbull, 1983). During the *elima*, the boys try to force their way into the structure that houses the girls. The boys have to be beaten by the girls before they can enter the *elima* house, and even then they still have to fight their way through a barricade of well-armed and determined adult women. But eventually the boys do get in and the ceremony develops into a festival of courtship. Events such as these function strongly to reinforce identity and self-esteem. They teach people to be proud of being themselves.

Not all hunter-gatherer societies have initiation rites for girls, probably because the advent of adulthood among females is so clearly heralded by nature. Menstruation is a clear sign of the end of girlhood, marriage generally takes place soon afterwards, and giving birth is a self-evident demonstration of adulthood.

In adult life, sexuality is often a source of stress and conflict for hunter-gatherers, just as it is in other societies, but the sexuality of children is not subject to suppression. This implicit philosophical and moral stance has an essential psychological function. Children learn that they are good people. They learn that what is going on inside them is valuable and important. They experience their physical development as a series of successes. They know who and what they are, and what they will be called upon to do.

Children who are brought up to rejoice in their natural functions don't have to learn to accept themselves; there doesn't seem to be any way they could imagine what it might be like to reject themselves. For boys, this degree of self-possession means, among other things, that almost all of them will be sufficiently self-confident to attract and hold at least one woman; for girls, it means, among other things, that they will not grow up thinking that finding a man is the only important task in their lives. Everyone (who survives) becomes a mature adult, able to meet the heavy responsibilities of a life in which everybody is everybody else's safety net.

So, genes and environment again. We believe that children are born with a need for child-rearing practices that do not deviate too much from those described in this chapter. Human genes specify the types of social environments that will produce healthy adults, just as they specify the types of diets that will produce healthy adults. Not any environment will do, if children are to grow up with a strong sense of self and an integrated identity. In the next chapter, we will look at child-rearing in the modern environment and its role in generating psychological distress.

CHAPTER 5

Childhood and Psychopathology

CLEARLY, THERE ARE MANY DIFFERENCES between parenting in hunter-gatherer societies and parenting in industrial societies. In this chapter we focus on differences that we think have adverse effects on children, especially for the development of their self-esteem, autonomy, identity, capacity for intimacy and sense of reciprocity. A key—perhaps *the* key—difference is that children are now reared in nuclear (and even single-parent) families rather than in communal bands. There are two consequences. One, the number of caretakers is reduced. Two, child-rearing now takes place largely in private; only the parents know what is going on. Because of privacy, mistreatment of children can occur that would never be tolerated in the open life of a hunting and gathering band. And because few adults are around to share the caretaking, minor shortcomings of the parents take on exaggerated importance. In other words, there is an increase in both real and imagined abuse.

The Home

In industrial societies, children are raised in walled enclosures—behind closed doors. What goes on between parent and child is shielded from the critical eyes of the community. In the privacy of the home, systematic deviation from community norms is possible and commonplace. The same privacy also makes hypocrisy possible, and thus contributes to the excessive development of shame and guilt.

The lack of firm traditional norms for raising children further complicates the situation. In America, where beliefs and traditions change rapidly, where no universally accepted traditions are available to guide parenting, child-rearing has become a matter of improvisation. Parents invent what they do, patching together pieces of what they learned at home, what they observe in the homes of friends they admire, and what they glean from celebrated baby doctors. They combine elements of diverse traditions, hoping that they can correct what they thought were shortcomings in their own rearing.

The combination of privacy and improvisation is dangerous. At worst, it can facilitate drastic deviance, such as incest and physical abuse. It leads to less dramatic problems, such as scapegoating, overprotection, and failure to provide clarity about roles and expectations. Alcoholic families, typically isolated and secretive, are particularly infamous for both gross abuse and subtler problems.

We are not going to stress the evil effects of obvious abuse. Others have done so very effectively, and the evolutionary perspective has nothing to add. We will stress the problems created by what, in the West, is considered normal behavior by well-intentioned parents.

Western child-rearing emphasizes separation and independence. Children are encouraged to sleep in their own beds, and then, if possible, in their own rooms. From a very early age, they are taught to think for themselves, to question authority, and to do "their own thing." One can understand why. Western children must eventually go off to school with strangers, go away to college, move to new locations for jobs, etc. But the emphasis on independence tends to downplay the importance of community and affiliation. Western education does not emphasize these values, and thus tends to create adults who are emotionally isolated.

In nuclear families, children are dependent on their parents for everything: security, validation, love, companionship, and guidance. When there is conflict with the parents, the children frequently have nowhere to go for comfort and support. They must rely almost exclusively on the emotional output of their parents. Under these conditions, parental shortcomings, even trivial ones, become much too important to the children. Every episode of parental disapproval — and they inevitably occur — can deal a painful blow to a child's self-esteem. Naturally, children who are temperamentally sensitive suffer the most.

Consider, for example, Randy's feelings about his parents. In his late twenties he still has a pervasive need to justify himself to himself, he knows not why. In therapy, he describes his past:

> My parents loved me and tried to help me. But they always wanted me to succeed according to *their* standards. I always figured they would never accept what I wanted to do with my life.

Did these parents really do anything wrong? Clearly, they were devoted to their child's welfare; if they failed to convey to their child a sense of his own worth, it was not from want of trying. The mere fact of having "their own standards" was, for this particular boy, enough to create a problem.

Modern parents have to walk an exceptionally fine line between approving their children's initiatives and indulging their whims. They have to avoid creating low self-esteem without giving rise to spoiled brats. They have to teach proper behavior in an artificial world, without teaching children that what they do naturally is bad. It is a difficult task for two parents who love each other and have satisfying, exciting lives. It is extremely difficult for anyone else.

Just as the shortcomings of parents can become disproportionately significant, so can those of the children. Difficult children have immense power to disrupt their parents' lives. In a band, where parenting is diffused, and where childcare is not the exclusive focus of any one person's day, a difficult child cannot have nearly as much effect on the psychological well-being of any one adult. In our society, difficult children can drive their parents to distraction. A vicious circle can result: parents who are fatigued and upset handle children badly, the children get more upset, which drives the parents to distraction.

Mistreatment of children is not the only problem. At the other end of the spectrum, one finds parents who try to give their children "everything." These children are likely to expect too much of the world. They may well be unable to appreciate what has been done for them. They may therefore have difficulty developing an appropriate sense of responsibility. They may have trouble engaging in reciprocal relationships.

Both deprivation and overindulgence are pathways to flawed reciprocity. Children who don't receive enough don't want to give; children who get too much don't learn that they have to give something back.

Mothering

Until very recently, it was an ideal for mothers in most Western societies to spend their days at home, taking care of the children. This often meant that the mothers were left without the company of other adults. Many of the women in this situation ended up bored, irritable and depressed. The situation was particularly intolerable for well-educated women with a strong need for more sophisticated company than children can provide. The result was a longing for other pursuits and anger at being thought of as "merely a mother." Of course, many women in this position managed — and still manage — to do a creditable job despite their longings, but we feel that the children pay a price. *Born Unwanted*, a recent study by Henry David of the Transnational Research Institute in Bethesda, reveals just how important being wanted actually is.

At present, of course, more and more women are working. But unlike the work of gathering (and even farming), modern work takes women away from their children. Contemporary women often have to choose between career and home. In Chapter 8 we will discuss the effects of this dilemma on the women themselves. Here, it is enough to say that an absent mother is not what a child needs.

Fathering

In industrial society, fathers are generally absent from the home during most of the day. Industrial work and most professional work generally take place in special settings: factory, office or lab. Because the workplace is out of the home, children can observe only a limited range of adult activities. They cannot learn what they need to know about adult life by imitation. And because the daily work of the father is not observed by his children, his contribution to their welfare can go unappreciated. Even though he may be working desperately hard, they may understand nothing of his struggle. They may only experience a tired, distant giant who ignores them or is expected to discipline them. Children raised under these circumstances may grow up without an adequate sense of what they have been given, and thus will have difficulty assessing reciprocal obligations.

Day-care

As of this moment, more and more children are being raised in day-care centers. This does involve more adults in caring for children, and so might at first glance seem like a step in the right direction. Indeed, day-care is very probably preferable to some home environments, and some studies indicate that children who attend day-care develop certain cognitive skills more rapidly than children who don't. But these studies compare day-care to present-day home-care. We are contrasting day-care with life in a band.

Stories Then and Now

Looking forward to motherhood, Pygmy women sing and tell stories to their children before they are even born—stories that are later to become part of the child's lore about his or her personal history. No doubt, many women today have equally positive feelings about their unborn children. But many women don't; they experience pregnancy as an imposition and a constraint. This passage from a novel by Oriana Fallaci, *Letter to a Child Never Born*, is not typical, but it is symptomatic:

> What a lot of demands you make, Child. First you lay claim to my body and deprive it of its most elementary right: to move around. Then you even pretend to control my heart and mind, atrophying them, blocking them, robbing them of their capacity to feel, think, live. That's too much. Child, we'd better come to terms . . . I'll give you my body, but my mind, no. My reactions, no. Those I keep for myself. And along with them I claim the reward of my own little pleasures. In fact, I'm now drinking a good slug of whisky and smoking a pack of cigarettes . . . Because I'm fed up with you.

This embarrassingly frank expression of emotion points to a sad fact about modern society. Children, possibly because they are now a cause of endless expenditure rather than a promise of future income, are often experienced as a burden rather than a promise. Here is a story told to us by a client, who was a twin.

> Mother often used to say that if she had known then what she knew now, she would never have had children. We heard that story so often that we developed a standard response: "So tell us, Mom, which one of us would you have gotten rid of?"

The day-care system could theoretically be modified to make something that roughly approximates child-rearing in a band, but to do so would require major changes in architecture and society. One way to do it would be to have mothers form small groups which would, collectively, take care of the children, on a rotating basis. Each group would be the core of a community. Each would have a space set aside, either in a residence or a place of employment. The space would contain equipment (computers, art supplies, etc.) which would allow each mother who so desires to engage in a productive adult activity. Time off for jobs would be arranged so that some of the mothers would always be there for the children. Other people—fathers, grandparents, friends, etc.—would participate in the life of the community as desired, but no paid child-care workers would be allowed. America is not ready to make this kind of investment in its children.

As it stands, the system is flawed. The recent scandals involving child abuse by day-care workers are discouraging, but not really surprising. Day-care workers are strangers. They cannot be expected to function as responsibly as members of a hunting and gathering band, each of whom can expect to have lifelong involvement with every child born to the band. The low pay and lack of prestige of child-care work doesn't help either.

Complexity

Our world is hard for children to understand. They are unable to take in or understand the complicated social, economic and psychological pressures that are acting on adults. They can't understand why their parents are frequently upset, angry, frustrated or depressed. They blame themselves, but without knowing exactly why. As a result, they are often stuck with a vague sense that they have done something wrong. They may grow up thinking that they are too stupid to understand the world.

In the hunting and gathering bands in which humans evolved, the family was the means of survival, the core of the small groups in which one lived and upon which one relied throughout life. Today the family, though essential for security and the optimal development of human talents, is apt to be a problem, often something that has to be escaped from. People must leave to live their own lives, the lives they want to create for themselves. But attachment, which is as fundamental to humans as breathing, has a loyalty aspect. To leave seems like disloyalty and creates inner conflict. To detach costs dear.

The School

Because children are unable to learn enough at home, they are sent off to schools. At school they are obliged to engage in activities chosen by adults; they have limited opportunity for spontaneous activities they choose themselves. Since their performance in school will affect their futures in ways they can't understand, they must submit to discipline that doesn't make much sense. They are often bored, discouraged and resentful, because schoolwork seems, and often is, unrelated to real life.

At school, children are under intense pressure to perform. In class and on the playing fields, in communist as well as capitalist societies, their perfor-

PERMISSIVE EDUCATION

Some experimental schools, particularly those based on the principles of "permissive education," might seem at first glance to resemble the natural form of learning found in hunter-gatherer societies, but this is an illusion. Children in places like Summerhill are not exposed to a model of adult life that they can imitate at their own pace. Rather, they are obliged to invent their own social structures from scratch. And they have no idea what kind of challenges these inventions will have to meet. This is an invitation to chaos.

It is very difficult to use evolutionary biology as a basis for devising policies and social reforms. Society cannot go back. Nevertheless, a knowledge of evolution can assist people in avoiding mistakes that they might otherwise make. Gary Bernhard's *Primates in the Classroom: An Evolutionary Perspective on Children's Learning*, is a case in point. His analysis of what might be done to improve the schools should be on every educator's reading list.

mance is measured comparatively. The winners of the competitions develop great skills. Unfortunately, winners may regard their social relationships as of secondary importance. The losers—and there are far more of them— often come away from the experience with a nagging sense of inferiority that lasts throughout life.

Because performance in school is so important to a child's future, responsible parents must do whatever they can to help their children succeed. Children cannot be allowed to proceed at their own pace. They have to be induced or compelled to perform. As a result, well-meaning nagging has become the great art form of American parenting.

Some children do just fine, of course. They win prizes and games, esteem their teachers and peers, feel secure in their identities. Presumably, they were equipped by both nature and nurture to deal with the changed environment. Psychotherapists will more often encounter those who were not so equipped.

Fear, Danger, and Cognition

There are clear differences between the types of fear-provoking situations that Western children encounter and those experienced by hunter-gatherer children. These differences may have an impact on the way children experience and eventually understand the world.

Children are innately afraid of certain things, such as loud noises, the dark, and, after about nine months, strangers. In the natural environment, such signals indicated danger. Since the mind of the child is innately prepared to be afraid of these signals, the fears of hunter-gatherer children helped them to make sense of the world. When innately frightening things happened, the adults were afraid too. Children and adults experienced together what was frightening for both—obvious dangers such as lions, snakes, and being left alone exposed to hunger or dangerous creatures. Fears had identifiable causes. Everyone grasped the problem and all were drawn together by the experience.

The dangers of the modern world are much more difficult to grasp. In a city, or even a small town, many of the things that menace children are silent and apparently innocuous. For example, electrical outlets are not obviously dangerous. They do not give off any warnings, they sit quietly, they seem useful. But children must be taught to stay away. Children must learn, and learn early—when they are just beginning to crawl and poke around in interesting places—about the lethal nature of the innocent-looking sockets. They must learn from verbal warnings and anxious reactions that they cannot really understand.

An extreme example of a not-obvious danger is the fear of a nuclear holocaust. A future nuclear war is an abstraction that even adults have a hard time grasping. It is a theoretical danger, one that is not palpable to the senses; nothing shows for a child to see or feel. Only through careful explanations can children even begin to understand the nature of the threat. This kind of fear does not map onto the child's emotional system. It does not serve to make sense of the world; rather, it serves to make the world appear incomprehensible. We believe that it may contribute to the prevalence of free-floating anxiety in adulthood.

Danger: Inside or outside?

For children, the comforting experiences of attachment serve as the foundation for a sense of what is safe. Distressing experiences away from their mothers send them scrambling back for comfort, highlighting the contrast between safe and dangerous. Feeling threatened and feeling comforted become fundamental ways of experiencing the world. In this way, attachment is linked to a basic cognitive function: understanding things as either safe or dangerous. In the natural course of events, the family (band) is safe and the external environment is dangerous.

Obviously, if real abuse, sexual or physical, is being perpetrated on the child, the danger in the house will be far greater than that outside. But even in the so-called normal family, the same reversed relationship between danger inside and danger outside may hold. If the tension in the house is greater than the threats the child senses outside the home, the child may experience the family as dangerous. This turns fundamentals upside down: the family, which should be safe, is dangerous; the outside world, which should be approached warily, is safer than home. Children in this predicament may experience nothing as safe. We think this might contribute to a fear of intimacy — fear of those with whom one should feel safe.

(As social psychologists such as Stanley Schacter have shown, a similar dynamic operates with with respect to an external enemy. When there is one, aggression is directed outside, with a corresponding increase in internal cohesion and solidarity. We think it follows that if there is no external enemy, people inside the family can come to be seen as sources of danger, with a consequent increase in intra-familial strife.)

The importance of a challenging external environment is often overlooked. Indeed, the thrust of civilization has been to tame the environment, and many writers seem to think that when the whole planet is domesticated, all will be well. This utopian viewpoint does not take into account the psychological function of danger. Some individuals have a particular need for a challenging external environment, and in all cases, external danger helps to cement family (and social) solidarity. The we/they effect may have drawbacks in the nuclear age, but it cannot be wished away.

Could it be that the fascination youngsters have for horror movies actually serves a function? If such movies are surrogates for the palpable dangers that no longer exist, perhaps they serve, in some bizarre way, to make home and family seem more attractive. It is difficult even to speculate about what happens when such shows appear on TV screens inside the house .

Of course, there are children who live in dangerous neighborhoods, and who can, when old enough, perceive only too well the nature of the danger that threatens them. Does this negate the argument we have put forward? We don't think so. Living in a high crime area is an additional burden on a child, but it is not the equivalent of living in a band that is surrounded by a dangerous external environment. For one thing, a school is supposed to be safe. It is a place where parents *send* their children. For another, one cannot assume that the home in which such children live is particularly safe or supportive. Thus children who live in high crime areas are not living in an approximation of the natural environment. They are living in a man-made jungle for which they are not equipped by nature.

To summarize: The pressure exerted by the environment once constrained human behavior and kept it functional. The environment forced everyone to be self-reliant *and* to be interdependent. It kept the band and the family together, and it kept the behavior of parents in line with the needs of children — particularly the need for structure. In the absence of this external pressure, behavior can get out of hand, taking unpredictable and idiosyncratic forms. Great creativity can result; some children develop their talents to the maximum. But great damage also can result, leading to the kinds of psychological distress that we see in clinical practice.

The pressures and dangers in our society do not produce constructive constraints, like those in hunting-gathering bands. For example, the challenges of hierarchical societies tend to beat down the self-esteem of many if not most of the adults who compete for places of privilege within them. The emotional and psychological pressures of modern life do not kill outright, like drought, wild elephants or poisonous plants, but they cause unremitting tension and recurring helpless rage. Not surprisingly, parents, helpless to retaliate against the forces that torment them, sometimes take it out on their own children.

Some Recent Developments

Some trends in this generation are moving us ever farther from the natural environment. Children are no longer seen as a source of support in old age; social security and insurance, now essential social institutions, have displaced them as sources of financial security.[1] This accentuates the trend toward seeing children as impediments to personal gratification. Secondly, the number of single-parent families is increasing, further reducing the number of primary caretakers in the average home. Finally, the increasing availability of money encourages parents to substitute objects for attention, renders children more materialistic, and puts drugs within the reach of almost any child with a decent allowance. None of these developments can be expected to improve our child-rearing environment.

Technology is another factor that is altering the environment of childhood in ways that can't be grasped in advance. Take for example the listening devices that some parents have installed to monitor the activities of their children. These devices were developed because many children now have

---

[1]This has also created problems for the elderly. As Richard Alexander says, in *The Biology of Moral Systems:* "The whole problem of care for the aged has arisen, not so much because we live longer, but because familial bonds have been fractured."

their own private rooms—in itself a significant change in the environment of childhood. Perhaps the added safety is desirable. But the existence of this technology means that parents can know what is going on without being present—without the child's knowing that s/he is being monitored. Can we be sure that this will have no effect on children?

We know of at least one case where this technology is being used in what is, to say the least, an unsettling way. In casual conversation one day, a well-educated, upper-middle-class mother demonstrated, spontaneously and without any hesitation, the new use she had found for the monitoring apparatus. After turning the intercom on to hear what her four-year-old was doing, she switched it to its speaker mode and admonished him "over the air." Here is part of the conversation:

Mother: (from upstairs) Arnie, stop doing that!
Arnie: (in a startled, frightened voice) What do you mean? Where are you? How do you know what I'm doing?
Mother: This is your Magic Mom. I know everything you do all the time, even when I'm not with you. Now stop playing with. . .

We'll leave it to the reader to imagine what Arnie might be asked to stop playing with.

Psychological Consequences

To completely analyze the consequences of these changes in the environment of childhood would require a separate book. In the following section, we will discuss a few areas where damaging consequences are most likely.

Problems of autonomy and intimacy

Autonomy and intimacy, like independence and affiliation, are sometimes seen as opposites, but we believe it makes more sense to see them as complementary facets of interpersonal competence. This competence grows out of the support, approval, and encouragement children receive from their parents and extended family. From a solid emotional base, children derive a sense of self-worth that enables them to stand on their own feet, reveal themselves to others, and provide support and encouragement to those who need it.

Hence, autonomy and the ability to sustain intimacy spring from good experiences in attachment[2] and individuation. The bonds that link children to their parents are transmuted into self-reliance and affiliation. In later life, these strengths help adults to make allies who will help them contend with the challenges of the environment.

We have already described how attachment in hunter-gatherer societies is different from ours. Because parenting is diffused, children are less dependent on their parents, and therefore less likely to be scarred by parental deficiencies. Children have many more opportunities to learn how to relate to adults and to other children of different ages. They are therefore less likely to be deprived of the emotional nutrients needed to develop self-reliance and the capacity for both reciprocity and intimacy. There is little if anything analogous to child abuse, excess pressure to perform, nagging, and general dissatisfaction of women with the role of mothering.

In this connection, it is noteworthy that children who are abused, neglected or deprived often become *more* attached to their parents than children who get what they need. Deprived children keep returning to the parents, in the futile and pathetic hope that this time perhaps they will get what they need. The same dynamic is found in other animals, including the rat. The failure of attachment produces dependence, not autonomy.

Individuation also takes place differently in hunter-gatherer societies. Separation-individuation was brought into the mainstream of clinical psychology by Margaret Mahler, the revered grande dame of the object-relations school. According to Mahler, human children go through a specific "separation-individuation" stage between the ages of 18 and 32 months, when children begin to take their first steps away from mother. In the process of moving away from her and exploring the environment, they begin to realize that they are separate from her, and that they can do things without her. Prior to that time, Mahler thought, children experience themselves as part of a single larger organism made up of mother and child. Mahler called this "human symbiosis." In order to ensure proper development, the mother must both encourage the child's impulse to explore and welcome the child back upon its return. If she doesn't do both, the separation-individuation process can be disrupted.

Mahler observed that there were "vicissitudes" in the process of separation-individuation: Some mothers were overprotective; they got angry when

---

[2]The concept of attachment was brought to the fore by John Bowlby, who showed that children were born with a tendency to behave in ways that secured for them the attention and protection of parents. He demonstrated that disruption of the normal attachment behaviors, including separation from and loss of the parents, had an adverse effect on subsequent functioning.

their children tried to explore. Other mothers let the children go, but were cold and hostile when they came running back. These mothers seemed to want to punish their children for having left. Mahler argued that such mothering produced children who grow up having trouble with intimacy and with independence. Children who are not encouraged to explore, or who are punished by rejection when they return from exploration, often seem to develop a crippling fear of both of exploration and of return. They have learned that they might be abandoned if they leave, but they have also learned that if they stay, they have to give up their impulses to grow and develop. To go is to die, but to stay is to be smothered. Hence, fear of abandonment goes hand in hand with fear of engulfment. Both independence and intimacy become impossible. Panic at the prospect of either impels the sufferer back and forth from one pole to the other in a frantic search for safety.

In hunter-gatherer bands, the nature of adult work and group life operate so that individuation proceeds largely without actual (physical) separation. Infants and toddlers have constant access to their mother or to some other adult. There is of course the crisis of weaning which can be a rough experience, but otherwise all separations from the mother are buffered by the constant company of familiar people. There are always other adults around when the child explores. If the mother is in a bad mood, someone else will generally pay attention to the child. Children who move away from the mother do not find themselves alone.

We conclude that the "vicissitudes" of separation-individuation in the West are a consequence of our particular way of life, not a universal characteristic of the human species. In our world, a child's emerging need to explore can't develop quite as smoothly as it might. Children can't extend their interest in the surrounding world gradually and without excessive restriction. They are not free to roam at will and strangers cannot be trusted. Responsible mothers can't really tell when it is safe to let a child go and when it is more prudent to hold on. And, in nuclear families, the number of supportive adults who might help children explore is sharply reduced.

Since, as mentioned before, mothers who stay home to take care of the kids are often isolated, some of them inevitably come to resent the children, and yet their overdependence on children for self-respect and company means that they might have a hard time letting go. If children are the mother's only source of self-esteem, she is likely to get angry when those children do begin to move away, and cannot really show joy when they return.

The conditions under which modern parenting has to operate produce a variety of problematic family structures. One of them is enmeshment. Enmeshment can best be understood as a failure of both autonomy and intimacy. Enmeshed family members cannot get away from each other, they cannot stand on their own, but they cannot get along with each other either. They are dependent but dissatisfied or hostile. Typically, the children from enmeshed families have trouble establishing intimate relationships with potential sexual and marriage partners.

"Be neither too close nor too distant" is the biological rule. The natural environment virtually compelled parents to maintain the optimal distance. It is difficult to construct rational substitutes for the natural regulation of distance.

In the family, deviance varies in severity and individuals vary in their vulnerability. Some children survive unscathed and even thrive. Others develop serious psychopathology. Still others, the majority perhaps, come away with a vague but pervasive self-doubt.

Problems of identity and integration

Children today do not grow up with the clear sense of identity and belonging that results when one can say: "I am the daughter of X, the sister of Y and a member of band Z." Indeed, at least in American society, people

---

FREUD, WISHES, AND REPRESSION

Freud believed that the repression of unacceptable wishes was one of the prime causes of psychopathology. Children had to repress their wishes because the wishes involved unacceptable fantasies such as sleeping with mother and killing father.

It is easy to see that such wishes are the natural outgrowth of the changes described in this chapter. If the sexuality of children were encouraged, if it had other outlets, there would be no need for fantasies about parents. If children were not subjected to endless artificial constraints, they wouldn't generate such anger, and would probably not generate fantasies of violence and revenge. If their upbringing made sense to them and was appropriate to their own personal stage of development, they would experience life as a series of successes and would not need to escape from an intolerable reality by withdrawing into fantasy. The human brain is obviously capable of repression, but the excessive development of repression derives from the way children are brought up.

tend to see this sort of identity as simpleminded—something inferior that ought to be "transcended." Most thinking people take for granted that everyone needs to fabricate an identity based on some sort of uniqueness: "I am, because I am special."

Quite naturally, when creating an identity, people tend to choose traits that are most highly valued by their society. In our society, the traits that people tend to choose, when they are choosing who to be, usually have to do with the rational and/or spiritual aspect of the personality: "I am a good/intelligent/moral/talented/successful person." Many people can, in this way, successfully construct an acceptable identity. Others, however, and especially those who begin with low self-esteem, create an idealized, perfect, or grandiose self to compensate themselves for the unpleasantness of real life. The idealized self serves as protection against failure: "I am not really the person who failed; I am really terrific (even if it doesn't show)." This leaves the person with two incompatible self-images, the ideal self and a negative self based on real defeats and self-castigation.

Always, on some level, the individual knows that the ideal self is not real. This knowledge leads to a pervasive sense of phoniness. There is no "real" self that includes both the good and bad aspects of the personality. Successes feed the ideal self; failures feed the negative self. The individual never experiences the self as a complete entity, one which possesses value as well as shortcomings.

Note that grandiosity is also promoted by indulgence and the child-centered ideology of some parenting and of the schools. Children who are constantly the center of attention naturally come to feel that they are more important than anything around them. In the hunter-gatherer environment, the mother's need to collect food and perform her chores provides the child with a realistic assessment of his position in life. He is dragged around while she fulfills her tasks. He is a witness to her life, not the object of her adoration.

The split self-representation we have described here is a well-known aspect of borderline and narcissistic personality. We feel that it can be found, with lesser severity, in many other people who come in for psychotherapy. Judging from the prevalence of journal articles on this and related themes, and on the conversation of clinicians, we think that split self-representation may be one of the most common ailments seen in psychotherapeutic practice.

Confusion, Idiosyncratic Rules, and the Family

As children grow up, they tend to learn rules that help them get along in their families. These rules mark the children deeply. Indeed, Robert Hinde and his collaborator Joan Stevenson-Hinde (in press) suggest that natural selection has operated to produce children who shape their adult personalities to suit environments that are "predicted by" conditions in the family of origin.

Children reared in idiosyncratic families learn rules that may contribute to getting along in their particular home but don't help them relate to outsiders. If what children learn is too different from what they will encounter later on, they are put at a great disadvantage. In particular, deviant rules make reciprocity difficult. People who have been scapegoated and have low self-esteem tend to undervalue their contributions or overvalue the contributions of others. If they create compensatory fantasies of superiority they may operate according to an inflated sense of their worth. Or, they may shift between idealization and devaluation of others. The rule for these children is, "I'm not worth much." The compensatory rule is, "I am a uniquely valuable person, though not yet appreciated as such."

One needs a word here on the concept of "rules." We are not using the term to refer to conscious, moral precepts. Rather, we are using it to describe generalizations, assumptions, and operating procedures that are part of a person's world-view. Some rules are innate. For example, newborn human infants would rather look at certain types of objects than others. They favor designs that resemble a normal human face over any other shape. Obviously, this rule has survival value; it serves to intensify the interaction of infants and their caretakers.

The preference for faces is one of the cornerstones of the infant's cognitive framework, leading, under normal circumstances, to a very important rule: large oval objects will protect and nurture me. But this rule operates effectively only in particular types of environments — environments where there are trustworthy caretakers. What if the large oval object is a face that belongs to someone who is abusive? What will the child do with its preference for face-like shapes? It may generate another, contradictory rule: those who are close are dangerous. Such a rule generates fear of intimacy, and would undermine anyone's ability to engage in social relationships.

Children are capable of learning all kinds of different rules, but only certain rules work properly. Some rules, such as the those governing reciprocity, *must* be learned if the child is to grow up with a reasonable measure of inner peace and successful interpersonal relationships.

A small number of incorrect rules can generate a wide variety of disturbed behaviors. The following are some key incorrect rules that are often learned in modern society:

1. There is something wrong with me. (This of course is the master rule. It is enough to incapacitate a person in every situation that s/he faces.)

2. Beware of your sexuality. There is something evil about it.

3. Don't take. You might have to give too much in return.

4. Don't give. Nobody ever gave you anything.

5. Don't show kindness. You may let yourself in for more of a commitment than you want.

6. Don't get close. You might get smothered.

7. Don't assert yourself. You will set yourself up to be attacked. You will make others angry. They will leave (punish) you.

8. Beware of women. They are all just like your mother. They will smother you if you give them a chance.

9. Beware of men. They are just like your father. They are distant and might leave you (hurt you) at any time.

Children who grow up operating according to one or several of these rules are in trouble. Their ability to pursue a career and make a living will be affected, so they are likely to have trouble with autonomy. Their ability to establish relationships based on reciprocity will be affected, so they will have difficulty with affiliation. Their ability to trust will be affected, so they are likely to have trouble sustaining intimacy. Finally, their chances of developing an integrated sense of self will be affected; there will be too much failure and too much isolation. A negative self-image is likely to develop, and once this is formed, an unrealistic, idealized self-image is likely to follow.

Summary and Conclusions

In summary, what does the evolutionary perspective suggest to us about the origins of psychological distress in our society? First, it affirms some widely held views. It clearly supports the notion that psychotherapy should focus to some extent on the exploration of childhood issues. The rules learned in childhood, in the family of origin, are crucial for subsequent development. Furthermore, it supports the views of those who argue that self-esteem and identity are the issues most crucial to therapy.

Beyond this, there are other conclusions which we put forward as very likely. We will summarize them here.

1. One of the major problems with modern upbringing, at least in the dominant culture in the United States, is excessive emphasis on the values of individuation and independence, at the expense of community and social relationships. Autonomy and self-reliance are important in any culture, and particularly important in ours, if only because everyone must, throughout life, make enormously important decisions

about the group(s) to which they will belong. But most of life is lived within groups. Children need training in relationships and reciprocity. The family is a kin-based system that once prepared children for a world based on reciprocity through exchange. Now that system has to prepare children for a world based on exchange without reciprocity. Not suprisingly, it often fails.

2. Modern upbringing does not, as a rule, facilitate the development of identity and self-esteem. In a band, these qualities would be acquired automatically; in our society, they must be invented by each individual, and only some people manage it well.

3. Today's children suffer from what might be called, to paraphrase Herbert Marcuse, "surplus conflict"—conflicts that are caused by social and economic pressures on parents. Parent-offspring conflict (see Chapter 4) is inevitable; the interests of children and parents don't coincide completely. So there are conflicts in hunter-gatherer families too. But these conflicts take place in a context of basic interdependence and agreement about what the world is like. The hunter-gatherer lifestyle minimizes parent-offspring conflict; our lifestyle exacerbates it. Our conflicts involve basic disagreements over values, such as those which arise between parents of different cultural backgrounds, or those that derive from conflicts that are a product of isolation, poverty, inequality, aimlessness, parental indifference, or even excessive privilege. The resulting clashes of interest, divided loyalties, irreconcilable value systems, and contradictory messages are too complex for many children to deal with successfully.

4. The difficulty of raising children exists at all levels of society. If a family is rich and provides too much, the children may lack challenges. If a family is poor and provides too little, the children will almost inevitably feel inferior. In the absence of obvious dangers, parents can hardly avoid being either too indulgent, pretending that the world is safe, or too strict, seeming to the children to be the inventors of dangers. Given the competitive nature of life today, parents feel they have no choice but to push to give their children a head start over other children. This can make them seem like oppressive disciplinarians. Parents loom too large in their children's lives. The triviality of some of the events that cause trauma in our patients' lives is disturbing. It serves to remind us that the upbringing that has long been considered normal in our society—two loving, attentive parents raising several children in their own home—diverges dramatically from the natural environment, the environment in which our genes were formed. Our ideal family is problematic. There is a need to reconsider theories of

child-rearing from the point of view of human evolution.

5. The relative absence of effort and danger in daily life may be related to the purposelessness that plagues so many people, and which is so prominent in the experience of rich children. For most people, there is now no clear relationship between daily activities and survival. We work to eat, but the path between the office and the supermarket is not as clear as the trail that leads to a wild animal's lair catch or a grove of fig trees. This explains the success of program such as Outward Bound, and argues for a greater use of such programs.

Some Objections

We would like to take up two reasonable objections to what we have written in this chapter. One concerns the issue of evidence, and one concerns the question of individual differences.

The first objection is that we have not presented "evidence" in favor of our views. We do not disagree. The evolutionary, paleontological and biological views we are presenting are well supported by evidence, evidence that we present in only a cursory way. We have, instead, attempted to provide a framework for the interpretation of the data.

Scientists studying the child-rearing practices of a given culture could work forever, generate a mountain of incontrovertible data, and still fail completely to understand the effects of those child-rearing practices. Behavioral science cannot proceed without some standard of comparison, some yardstick by which to evaluate data. The evolutionary perspective can serve as such a yardstick. And, as a yardstick it is unique in that it allows one to make some attempt to evaluate the consequences of the *absence* of some environmental factor, such as the absence of clear dangers in the surrounding environment.

The second anticipated objection relates to the question of innate personality traits. We have stressed the role of the environment, but nothing in our account argues against the obvious fact that children are born with widely different temperaments and different predispositions.

Each temperament interacts with the environment in a different way. If temperament and environment are reasonably matched, development should proceed normally. If not, there will often be trouble. In contemporary society, there are problems with this "matching." One example is particularly telling. Researchers such as Jerome Kagan at Harvard and Frank Farley at the University of Wisconsin have developed strong evidence indicating that there are innate differences in the propensity to take risks. Some children are born with a tendency towards extreme physiological arousal in

A Note on Freud

Freud, basing his work on the skimpy anthropological data available in his time, believed that a primary cause of an adult male's ills can be traced back to a particular, fateful, universal experience—the Oedipus complex. The complex involves the shattering, by fear of castration, of a small boy's dream of making love to his mother, and the formation of the superego (the voice of conscience), control and repression, as a permanent memorial to his dread.

If one were to write a recipe for a full-blown Oedipus complex, here is how it would read:

Isolate a child in a private home with a mother who spends her entire day watching him and taking care of him. Provide the child with an authoritarian father who is responsible for discipline when he comes home from work. Don't allow the mother to let the child out of her sight. Deprive the mother of all other activities so that she is driven to try to get affection from the child to bolster her self-esteem. Have her be ignorant of childhood sexuality so that she is free to overstimulate him without restraint. Deprive the child of the constant company of other children and the availability of other adults who can be there for him when the parents are angry or otherwise occupied. Punish the child for masturbating and otherwise expressing his sexuality. Keep him from seeing the naked bodies of other children, girls and boys. When the child's maturing sexuality begins to creep into his expressions of affection for his mother, punish him.

Oedipal complexes, we conclude, are particularly the outcome of this kind of family system, which is our kind of family system. Is the Oedipus complex universal? There is room for doubt. But as we said in Chapter 4, Freud deserves credit for being the first to glimpse the fact that some degree of conflict between parents and offspring *is* universal.

the face of novel situations; they will probably become shy and cautious. Other children, called type-T (for Thrill), show much less arousal. Danger doesn't deter them. They will probably be risk-takers and thrill-seekers.

In our society, type-T children often grow into troublemakers, but this doesn't imply that they were born troublemakers. Their problem may be that they aren't given proper outlets for their energies and needs. Sitting in school all day may be particularly difficult for them. But with the proper stimulation and channeling, they might well become productive citizens. It goes without saying that in the natural environment, where development proceeds at a pace dictated by the child, and where imitation is the dominant mode of learning, both types of children, type-T and the shy cautious types, would have little trouble finding appropriate stimulation and suitable roles.

One last note on the subject of inborn traits. Two innate factors, sensitivity to social signals and ability to give off proper social signals, have powerful effects on an infant's social relationships. For example, infants who smile easily are likely to get more attention from their mothers than children who don't, all other things being equal. We appreciate how important, for better or for worse, these kinds of variation in children are. When children have troubles that derive from such variation, early intervention with parents to encourage special ways of parenting can often help. Once again, we want to make it clear that we do not imagine that the modern environment is the cause of all the problems children experience.

CHAPTER 6

On Gender

> The woman thou gavest to be with me, she gave me fruit
> of the tree, and I ate.
> — Genesis 3

PSYCHOTHERAPISTS ARE BEING PRESENTED with some pretty strange ideas about gender. Take for example a 1981 book edited by Sherry Ortner and Harriet Whitehead called *Sexual Meanings: The Cultural Construction of Gender and Sexuality*. The first article in the book is entitled "The gender revolution and the transition from bisexual horde to patrilocal band." The author, Salvatore Cucchiara, affirms that "like other social organizing principles, such as class, gender made its appearance on the human stage at some point in the past. . . . " Unabashedly, he simply postulates—he doesn't even pretend to discover—"the existence of a non-gender stage in human cultural evolution. . . . " So much for gender. With another swipe of the imagination, he disposes of kinship. In the non-gender stage, he declares, kinship was not an organizing principle of society! He thinks he can describe a "thoroughly human social system that operates on principles other than what we have come to think of as the very essence of being human—kinship." Finally, he affirms that sexuality in this pre-gender society "is both bisexual and unrestrained."

Like the authors of the Bible, Cucchiara has devised his own creation myth, his own private version of human evolution. Why? To prove the following assertion:

Human sexuality is innately plastic—bisexual. Exclusive heterosexuality is therefore an institutional restriction on sexuality, an incest taboo that runs counter to our biology and part of the structure of the gender system (sic).

91

The moment one stops to reflect that humans evolved out of another species, the absurdity of Cucchiara's scenario becomes clear. What creature is he talking about? An australopithecine? *Homo erectus*? The Neanderthals? Preposterous. Gender is clearly a major organizing principle in the societies of all our relatives on this planet. Do the chimps "construct" their gender? Is gorilla sexuality a matter of culture? Are the langurs of Abu bisexual?

Cucchiara's fable was not placed at the head of the Ortner and Whitehead book by chance. If one wants to believe that humans "construct" their gender, one is obliged to "construct" an evolutionary scenario to explain how bisexuality could have evolved. Cucchiara's version of human evolution is crucial to the constructivist enterprise (if they acknowledge the importance of evolution at all).

What are the facts? Gender is something we share with myriad other creatures that inhabit earth. Our ancestors were males and females long before they were human. Gender predates the mammals and even the reptiles. It goes back to the early days of multicellular life on earth.

Gender is our most precious possession. It links us to each other and provides us with our most exquisite and powerful experiences. William Blake, whose painting adorns the jacket of this book, understood it well:

> What is it men in women do require?
> The lineaments of Gratified Desire.
> What is it women do in men require?
> The lineaments of Gratified Desire.

He also said:

> Love seeketh not itself to please
> Nor for itself hath any care
> But for another gives its ease
> And builds a heaven in Hell's despair.

But what about gender as an organizing principle of society? If anything, the transition to humanity made gender even more fundamental than it was before. The hunting and gathering society is based on a division of labor by sex. It was hunting and gathering that gave men responsibility for their offspring. In most vegetarian primate species the male is nothing but a semen donor. Man the hunter became much more: a member of the family. This is one of the most profound genetic differences between men and their ancestors.

Gender implies difference. In some species, the differences are small; in

---

What Is a Female? Or a Male, for That Matter?

An individual can either make many small gametes (sex cells) or fewer but larger gametes. The individuals that produce smaller gametes are called "males" and the ones that produce larger gametes are called females. The small ones are designed to fuse with a large one, and the large ones are designed to fuse with a small one. The female strategy produces gametes that are large, and have a high rate of survival and fertilization. The male strategy is to produce as many as possible, to increase the chances of finding a large one.

An individual must either invest in a few large eggs or in millions of sperm. Thus, there will always be many times more sperm than there are eggs. Consequently, sperm must compete for access to those rare eggs. Most of what is masculine is determined by the quest for access to eggs.

These two strategies appear to be stable over time. In the jargon of evolutionary biology, they are called evolutionarily stable strategies. Neither one can out-compete the other. Any intermediate strategy does less well, which is why virtually all sexually reproducing species have two, and only two genders (Adapted from A. Forsyth, *A Natural History of Sex*)

---

others, they are great. With respect to anatomy, humans are somewhere in the middle. We are moderately "dimorphic" (having two shapes). For example, men are bigger than women, but the size disparity is not nearly as great as that between male and female chimps.

With respect to behavior, the situation is not so clear. The first task is to identify the differences. This itself is a perilous task. Those who talk about male-female differences are often accused of being reactionaries, even fascists. And, indeed, it is true that in the past the notion that the sexes are different has been used to justify social inequities. We hope that we will be able to avoid this pitfall.

How are men and women different? Since we—the authors—are both men, we have tried to keep our description of women close to what women say and write about themselves. We have relied especially on the writings of Jean Baker Miller and the second generation of feminists—Carol Gilligan, Carol McMillan, Judith Jordan, Alexandra Kaplan, Irene Stiver, Janet Surry, Betty Friedan (at least the Betty Friedan of the second stage), etc.

Carol Gilligan has perhaps been the most explicit in affirming that men and women are different. She has shown, conclusively we believe, that women and men think differently about moral issues. Women, she says, are more concerned with the personal and the social, less with achievement and abstraction. In *Women, Reason and Nature*, Carol McMillan writes that the cognitive styles of men and women are different. Each sex takes different elements of a situation into account. In *The Second Stage*, Betty Friedan, in a rather drastic shift of position, writes that women have a special role in the family: "to deny the part of one's being that has, through the ages, been expressed in motherhood — nurturing, loving softness, and tiger strength — is to deny part of one's personhood as a woman."

Jean Baker Miller and the group of women around her at Wellesley College's Stone Center for Developmental Studies and Services have focused on the emotional differences between men and women. Taking aim at psychological theories that emphasize separation, individuation and autonomy, they argue that women are more concerned with connectedness and caring. For women, relationship is primary. The apex of development is to be woven into a web of close, cooperative relationships. A girl's self-esteem develops out of a feeling that she is a involved in relationships and able to nurture them. Women are attuned to the inner life of other people, and they expect others to be tuned into them. Their sexuality can be fulfilled only through emotional contact.

Traditional psychological theories describe these qualities pejoratively, as dependence and immaturity. But these theories, it is argued, arose out of the experience of men, and are not applicable to women.

We agree. Male developmental theory should not be applied to women. We add only that one should not make the reverse error, by applying female developmental theory to men. Men are different. The traditional theories describe them fairly well. For men, separation and autonomy have special importance. Thought tends to be rated more highly than feeling. Control and power are essential elements of the psyche. Men feel best when they are being protective, a stance which requires feeling strong. Male sexuality, while it can be enhanced by relationships, is independent of them and has a compelling logic of its own.

One must not exaggerate these differences. As we discussed in Chapter 2, the transition to hunting and gathering required that males cooperate with each other and share food with women and children. Furthermore, females selected men who were good providers, i.e., who would stay with them for long periods of time. As a result, the genes that enable men to cooperate with each other and establish permanent relationships with women spread through the population. Modern men have these genes. They do need relationships. They are not incapable of empathy. Their sexuality is often informed by emotional commitment. The differences between men and women are *relative* differences. Women are more like this and less like that. Men are more like that and less like this. Furthermore, statements about sex differences refer to statistical *averages*. Individual men and individual women differ. Some men have more of the qualities that are quintessentially female than many women, and vice versa. Nevertheless, the generalizations are important and useful. One has to know the theme to appreciate the individual variations.

The traits of each gender are not always pleasing to the other. Women don't particularly like the fact that men are so eager to jump into bed. They often experience men's sexual advances as intrusive, threatening, and at the extreme, akin to rape. Men find this puzzling at best and often annoying. Why so much fuss? Men are quite frequently turned off by the emotional intensity that women bring to relationships. They experience it as cloying and deplore the responsibilities which the "dependence" brings. The incompatibilities extend to the sexual act itself. Women are generally less than pleased by the quickness with which men reach orgasm, a touchy subject for men. Men, on the other hand, are often not motivated to put out the energy and effort necessary to provide satisfaction to their sexual partners. On the other hand, most men are able to appreciate women's talent for empathy and connection, while most women appreciate male strength when it is joined to commitment and constancy. Our goal is to enhance the appreciation of difference.

Reciprocity and Gender

We hope that a better understanding of male-female differences will serve to enhance male-female reciprocity. If men and women understand how they are different, they will have a better idea of what they can expect from each other. We can no longer rely on chance and tradition to bring about understanding. Because society is so complex science must play a role. In hunter-gatherer times, reciprocity was relatively straightforward: men exchanged meat for other goods and services. In the present environment, such simple-minded exchanges are not possible, but reciprocity is still essential.

The expectation of reciprocity leads each individual to do what he or she does best, in exchange for something of fair value. It leads each individual to seek out a partner who is different—a partner with complementary virtues. It keeps men and women from trying to force each other into an alien mold. It causes people to think about their own uniqueness and to ask themselves: "What can I do for you that you can't do for yourself as well?" It helps to keep people from trying to beat each other out for the same prize. It prevents people from seeking for an ideal that cannot be realized. "Why can't a woman be more like a man?" is a wonderful song but it is a poor guide to successful relationships.

Why are males and females different? Why are women the way they are and men the way they are? In the next four chapters, we will show how this came about. We will describe femaleness and maleness as they have come down to us from our remote ancestors, many millions of years removed. We will highlight the different selective pressures that have molded male and female behavior over the ages. Note that we touched on this theme in Chapter 2, where we described the different roles of the sexes in hunter-gatherer society.

We will also talk about the conflict between our sexually-based predispositions and the current environment. Because we inherit our gender and much of the behavior that goes along with it from prehuman species, much of what we are predisposed to do is not particularly appropriate to modern life. Hence many people have trouble learning to adjust to the requirements of our society. When culture makes demands that biology is reluctant to meet, the result is often serious internal *conflict*. Hopefully, an understanding of this conflict will help to mitigate it.

Reproductive Strategies

The heart of the evolutionary approach to gender is found in the concept of "reproductive strategy." The male and female body and brain have been shaped by their roles in the process of reproduction. When these roles are understood, the details of the morphology and behavior of the sexes begin to make sense. We will be discussing reproductive strategies in the next four chapters, but before we do so we must clarify the sense in which biologists use the word "strategy."

On the concept of "strategy" in biology

In standard English language usage, a strategy is a plan that is worked out consciously. In evolutionary biology, it means something entirely different. A strategy is simply a characteristic way of doing something. The term "standard operating procedure" is probably the best approximation of the biological meaning of "strategy." But even that term isn't adequate, because a "strategy" can be anatomical as well as behavioral. For example, the long neck of the giraffe can be considered a strategy for getting to leaves that are high on the tree. The hump of a camel is a strategy for storing water. Big leaves are a strategy for using all available sunlight. These traits are strategies in the same way that hunting in packs is a strategy used by social carnivores (animals that hunt in packs like lions, wolves, and wild dogs) to bring down game that is bigger than any individual in the pack. In sum, virtually any trait can be looked on as a strategy. The word does not imply any conscious intent or awareness.

Every species has a characteristic set of "reproductive strategies" — ways in which individuals of that species succeed in passing their genes on to the next generation. These reproductive strategies include both anatomical and behavioral features — the tail feathers of the peacock, the teats of a goat, the mating dance of the goose, etc.

Within each species of sexually reproducing organism, the characteristic reproductive strategies of males and females are often very different. The interests of males and females sometimes overlap, but are never identical. Therefore, at any time, the reproductive strategies of males and females of any species may be in conflict. What's good for the goose is not necessarily good for the gander.

In chapters 7 and 9, we discuss the most typical reproductive strategy of humans. It bears many resemblances to the reproductive strategy of all mammals, but also differs in some ways. Many permanent anatomical and behavioral features of humans are related to our reproductive strategy. These features appear, in one guise or another, in all cultures at all periods of history, and at all levels of economic development. In this sense, every culture, like every individual, represents a variation on a species-specific theme.

We certainly do not mean to imply that individuals are bound to follow the standard human reproductive strategy. Indeed, we urge therapists to pay particular attention to individual differences — to the ways individuals deviate from the statistical norm. Specifically, male traits are not confined to men and female traits are not confined to women. Traits are distributed on something like a bell-shaped curve. Some men are intensely nurturing, some avoid nurturing. Some women are intensely competitive, some much less so. The differences in traits between men and women are average differences. We would be very disturbed if an increased awareness of what is typical served to blur the vast amount of variation that exists.

We also want to stress that the existence of a standard strategy does NOT imply that most people in current society are actually following it. What we define as the human reproductive strategy is the strategy that worked best for most individuals of the human species *in the natural environment*. We are fairly sure that in the *modern* environment, most people are *not* maximizing the number of their offspring or their inclusive fitness. Certainly, few people are consciously attempting to do so. Most people, when given a choice, prefer immediate gratification. Many choose not to have children and to devote their energies to getting rich, enjoying leisure, or other pleasures. But some of those who do so find themselves suffering from serious inner conflicts. The predispositions—"the whisperings within," as David Barash called them in his book by that name—that once led us to follow the typical human reproductive strategy are still very much alive in most people. To take but one example, when women who have chosen career over family approach the end of their child-bearing years, they often find themselves experiencing an intense desire for a child.

"Reproductive strategy" in psychotherapy

The concept of reproductive strategy will prove valuable to psychotherapists, but it must be used with caution. It is not predictive; it cannot tell us how modern humans *will* behave in any given situation. And it must not be used to tell people how they *should* behave. No moral obligation is implied. Individuals, who vary in all things, vary to the degree to which they are predisposed to follow the modal (typical) strategy. Therapists cannot assume that clients are so predisposed.

The greatest value of the concept lies in its ability to shed light on internal conflict. In our society, people are being driven in several directions at once. Biology pushes them to maximize inclusive fitness. Culture pushes in other directions. Culture often condemns what feels natural. People often behave in ways they don't understand, or feel bad about behaving the way they want to. An understanding of human reproductive strategies throws light on the conflicts people are likely to encounter as they try to cope with the industrial world. This insight can help men and women to devise ways of being and behaving that will maximize their satisfaction.

The role of a psychotherapy based on evolution is not to push people into roles they find uncongenial, but rather to produce liberation through self-acceptance. The genes whisper to us. We must learn to hear what they say, so that we can choose when to listen. We must discover when to be more of a man, when to be more of a woman, and when to borrow characteristics most often found in the opposite sex.

CHAPTER 7

The Reproductive Strategy of the Female

Naked came I out of my mother's womb and naked shall I return thither.

—Job I, 21

LIKE OTHER MAMMALS, humans bear their young alive and nourish them with milk. These inescapable facts have profound consequences for gender. As we shall see later on in this chapter, humans have some features that make them very special among the mammals, but they cannot ignore their mammalian heritage.

In almost all species of mammals, the females not only bear the young, but also rear them. After conception, the fertilized egg lives and divides in the female's womb. After birth, the offspring live almost entirely off milk, which females secrete from specialized glands. The young spend virtually all of their time near their mother, who both protects and shelters them. For contrast, one can look to the fishes. In many species, female fish deposit their eggs on the floor of whatever body of water they inhabit, and then leave. A male comes along and deposits sperm on top of the eggs, and then he leaves too. Both sexes contribute (relatively) equally to the process. Parenting ends with conception. There is no "rearing" and no family life whatsoever.

Carrying the fertilized egg (the zygote) within the body can be understood as one solution to some of the problems of living on dry land. The womb is an improvement on the sea; it contains life-sustaining liquids, and is much safer than any harbor a fish has ever known. But this solution has consequences. Having to keep the fertilized egg in the womb greatly reduces

99

the number of eggs a female can bring to the point of conception (compared to fish). Consequently, the eggs that do get fertilized—and thus the off-spring that emerge—are much more precious. Armed with milk and womb, females become "mothers"—adults who shelter and nourish their offspring, instead of leaving them to fend for themselves.

Mothering had a consequence of its own: it facilitated the appearance of species whose young are helpless for long periods of time. Helpless young have to be taken care of.

Prolonged helplessness and dependence played a crucial role in the series of events which led to the emergence of the human species. To a large extent, we owe our intellectual capacities to it. The long period of dependence favored the emergence of higher and higher degrees of intelligence. This is because learning new things requires the kind of openness to experience that is characteristic of immature organisms. Animals that rely heavily on learn-ing tend to be helpless when they are born. Conversely, animals that can take care of themselves at birth don't have as much behavioral flexibility. Thus, the "invention" of milk set the stage for species that live by their wits.

The mammalian mother is one of the crowning achievements of evolu-tion. Outside the mammalian order, motherhood does not have the same meaning. In particular, it does not involve the long period of intimate con-tact between a female and her offspring.

With some notable exceptions, the mammalian "family" is made up of the mother, her young, and perhaps some of her female relatives. The males are peripheral. From these ancient roots spring the female predisposition to nurturance and affiliation.

But there is a cost to all this. Mammalian females have to bear virtually all the consequences of the sexual act. Copulation is likely to involve them in pregnancy, which can be dangerous, and in nursing, which takes time and energy. This is time that she does not have to devote to herself. And, if resources are scarce, nursing can adversely affect her health. This leads us to the concept of parental investment, another brilliant idea that we owe to Robert Trivers. In most mammalian species, the female provides virtually everything the offspring need. She "invests" more, in time and energy, than the males. Indeed, most mammalian females supply virtually all of the parental investment that is needed to produce adults of the species.

Male mammals of most species contribute little to the young except their genes. Once insemination has occurred, the male is free to go. In most cases, he will not provide his offspring with food or other special benefits. His level of investment is very low.

Male mammals do have certain uses. In many species, they play a role in defending the females and their young from predators. Baboon males have even been known to sacrifice their lives fighting off leopards that were threatening their troop. But such acts are unusual and the males of many species will abandon the young and the females rather than endanger their own lives.

Some exceptions to the rule

There are some exceptions to the rule of low male parental investment, and they are instructive. The males of social carnivores (animals that hunt in groups) do allow the young to eat of the kill. It is also true that social carnivores, like hunter-gatherers, need to work together to hunt successfully. Hence, when an animal is brought down, all members of the pack share in it, including adults who didn't participate in the kill and young who don't hunt yet. Among social carnivores, the male contribution to the support of the young derives from the requirements of the hunting way of life.[1]

Males of monogamous species also provide high levels of parental investment. The gibbons are the best-known example. Alone among our close relatives, these Asian apes mate for life and are not known to conduct what we call extramarital affairs. Hence every male can be sure that the offspring of his mate are his as well. He can be sure that his "investment" will go only to his own offspring. Monogamous, faithful females are common where paternal investment is high. This can best be seen in birds. Male birds generally invest heavily in their offspring, as anyone familiar with the heart-warming photos of male birds bringing food back to the nest can attest. Not surprisingly then, 90% of bird species are monogamous; females will copulate only with their mate. Avian monogamy is probably due to the high metabolic requirements of birds. The young, which are born helpless, have voracious appetites. The combined efforts of mother and father are usually necessary to keep the young alive.

Nonhuman animals do not "understand" parenthood, but natural selection causes them to behave as if they did. Where social arrangements such as monogamy make it likely that the infants of a male's mate are really his, males tend to invest heavily. Where the likelihood is that the female has mated with more than one male, the males generally do not invest very much.

[1]Specialists believe that the reason male social carnivores invest and other male mammals don't is because meat is a compact, highly nutritious food that can be easily transported. How can a grazing animal such as a zebra provision a female? Bring a tuft of grass? So the argument is that most male mammals don't provision their families because there is no energy-efficient way for them to do so. Be that as it may, the fact is that they don't.

Female mammals, of course, always "know" who their offspring are because they give birth to them. Therefore, they generally invest heavily in their offspring, even after birth. Furthermore, they have their secret weapon: milk. They can nourish their young by themselves. Not surprisingly, in most mammalian species, the females are not faithful; they don't need males nearly as much as birds do.

Female choosiness

Because female mammals provide so much parental investment, they are the more "valuable" gender. Males provide nothing but their semen, and since a small number of males can impregnate many females, most species can get along with few males. But half the animals born are male—far more than enough. As a result, almost every female can find a male to impregnate her, but not every male will manage to reproduce. Consequently, males compete for females (by fighting, showing off, developing spectacular antlers, etc.).

Because the males are competing for them, the females get to "choose" which one(s) they want. They can accept or reject the offers they get. (Here again, a word of caution is necessary. The word "choose" does not imply consciousness. It simply means that there will be many available males, and that females will be drawn to one, or one type of, male over the others.)

On what grounds will they choose? Since the only thing a male is good for is his genes, the best female reproductive strategy is to try to choose good genes. If a female chooses unwisely, she may conceive offspring who are not healthy. She may make an investment of months in offspring that will die or fail to reproduce. This would be a terrible waste of her energy. Females with a tendency to make mistakes in this matter will have fewer offspring than females who don't. Mistake-prone females will not be represented as heavily in the gene pool of future generations. They will, in other words, be eliminated by natural selection. Hence, most animals in any given generation are liable to be carrying the genes of females who chose wisely.

How does an animal that can't think or reason choose good genes? She has to be differentially attracted to signs. What signs indicate good genes? Some are physical: health, strength, size, agility, and vigor. Often, however, behavior—the ability to do the right thing or make the right move at the right time—is equally important. Proper behavior indicates a well-functioning, intact organism. So both appearance and behavior can indicate—as well as anything can—the presence of good genes.

What are "good" genes? They are the genes that promote survival, reproduction and/or the reproduction of relatives (inclusive fitness). Good genes enable the offspring to perform all the functions that are necessary to stay alive, to reproduce effectively when mature, and (in some species) to conduct proper relationships with relatives.

In the struggle for access to females, males develop all kinds of signs indicating that they have good genes: horns, manes, elaborate mating dances, and complicated displays. In some species, possession of these apparently useless, but seductive, traits becomes more important than strength and fighting ability. For example, the oversized antler racks of certain species of deer are not useful in combat; they serve no purpose except as advertisements to females. The point to remember is that the characteristic traits of males get transmitted from generation to generation because females choose males who have those traits.

In the competition among males, some win big and some lose out completely. The "best" males are attractive to many females, and thus pass along their genes in large numbers. But many males never get to reproduce at all. They have no offspring and will not be represented in the gene pool of the next generation. In the jargon of evolutionary biology, variation in reproductive success is much higher in males than in females.

Just how deeply choosiness is embedded in the female reproductive strategy is highlighted by what might be called "the case of the hermaphroditic worms." As David Barash tells the story, primitive turbellarian worms have both male and female sexual organs. However, they don't inseminate themselves. They mate with both the male and female parts of their fellow creatures. Amazingly enough, each worm is very willing to impregnate others, but quite coy about allowing itself to be impregnated. As males, the worms are magnanimous about spreading their genes around; as females, they seem to act in such a way as to make sure that they are getting only good genes.

The explanation is simple. It costs very little for a male to engage in copulation. If he lucks out by chancing on a good female, so much the better. If he makes a mistake, little is lost but some sperm, which is a renewable resource. But the female will have to carry and nourish eggs, so *she* does what she can to avoid making a bad investment.

There is no "determinism" here. Not every female will follow the best reproductive strategy of the species. But females who don't, on the average, won't leave as many offspring. Thus, natural selection favors certain strategies and eliminates others. The tendency to behave according to the reproductive strategy is passed along from generation to generation.

Females and aggression

In most species of mammal, males tend to be bigger and more aggressive than females. This makes them potentially dangerous. Hence it doesn't pay for females to challenge them physically. Males respond aggressively to signals given by other males of the same species. Hence, it is advantageous for females not to give off these same signals.

Under these conditions, an ability to inhibit male aggression is also a valuable trait. Signals which do so exist in many species. These signals are often related to sexuality. Female monkeys who fear being attacked by a male turn around and "present" their rear. In many species, male monkeys use this same signal to avoid being attacked. In general, males will not commit acts of violence against a creature of the same species who, in one way or another, indicates a willingness to copulate. These traits are passed from generation to generation because females who can find ways to control male aggression survive better than those who can't.

This doesn't mean that females are never aggressive. It has long been understood that females are in competition with each other for scarce resources. Female monkeys of various species have been known to kill the offspring of other mothers, presumably to maximize the resources available to their own offspring. Nevertheless, it remains true that overt aggression plays a relatively small role in the female reproductive strategy.

Human Variations on Mammalian Themes

In many ways, humans are different from other mammals. As our ancestors increased their consumption of meat, the sexes specialized. Men hunted, women gathered. The male contribution to the upkeep of the children became as important as that of the females. As we described in a previous chapter, a "contract" between the sexes came into being. The human male was woven tightly into the fabric of the social order. Males established special relationships with their offspring. Male had become man. And man was on his way to becoming Daddy.

As men began to be valued as much for their paternal investment as for their genes, a variety of changes in the female personality began to occur. For one thing, choosing a mate became more complicated. In addition to assessing a man's strength, health and status (his genetic viability), females had to calculate whether a given male would be a good "provider," i.e., whether he was likely to make a significant investment in the offspring of the coupling. If he wasn't the type to stick around, her children's chances would be diminished. Thus, the criteria females used to choose their mates changed significantly.

Since males had become a valuable resource, females found that they had to "compete" for them. Unlike most of our closest relatives among the monkeys and apes, human males will not mate with any sexually receptive female. They are a bit more choosy. They are even more choosy about whose children they will invest in. The early females were in a position to benefit from ways of attracting, and holding, men. They needed something more subtle than pheromones (odors that have the power to arouse the opposite sex) and brightly colored sexual swellings.

Various new traits with effects on men came into being, including beauty, breasts, emancipation from estrus, and the female orgasm. We suggest that these traits became part of the reproductive strategy of the human female. We will briefly discuss each of these features.

The importance of what we call beauty in humans probably derives from the fact that our species relies more heavily on vision and less heavily on smell than most other species. Beauty may be only skin deep, but it is not something to be despised. Its presence in human culture is an expression of a major difference between us and ancestral species. Beauty is truly human. When Keats said that beauty is truth and truth beauty, he spoke better than he knew.

The forces leading to the evolution of the breast are less clear. Some investigators feel that it evolved because it was attractive to men. If men started to prefer women with protuberant breasts rather than women without them (sexual selection), women with breasts would begin to have more offspring, and the trait would spread throughout the population, until most women had breasts. Other authorities, taking a more functional view, suggest that the breast exists only because it can sag. Because humans stand upright, sagging facilitates nursing. The nipple would be more difficult for a baby to reach if the breast didn't protrude and, with time, elongate.

There is a problem with this last line of reasoning. Since bipedal mothers are able to pick up their children to hold them to their breasts, it is difficult to see how sagging could be much of an advantage. Still, we cannot choose between these two hypotheses and indeed they are not mutually exclusive. Whatever their origins, breasts have become a universally appealing sexual symbol.

Perhaps the most important development in the reproductive strategy of the human female was her emancipation from estrus. Apes and monkeys go into heat seasonally; the rest of the time they are not available for sex. The human female is sexually receptive all year round. As a result, a single female can meet a male's sexual needs throughout the year, making it unnecessary from him to seek other sexual partners. Her availability tends to bind him a bit closer to her and to her children. Emancipation from estrus also brought a woman's sexuality under conscious control. A female in estrus is dominated by her hormones. She will respond strongly to simple biological cues. By contrast, a woman is able to choose her sexual partners on the basis of a variety of physical, psychological and moral factors.

Discrimination and control make it possible for human females to offer a male a guarantee of sexual exclusivity; faithfulness, a rarity among primates, was added to her reproductive strategy. Over time, this "moral" dimension of the female strategy began to take on more and more importance. Culture made it "right" for a female to be coy and chaste.

As Masters and Johnson have described so eloquently in *The Pleasure Bond*, the female orgasm, when it happens, plays a significant role in forging intense bonds between contemporary men and women. Did it evolve for this purpose? Was the female orgasm shaped by natural selection? Did it spread through the gene pool because males sought out females with this new trait? We tend to think so. But some authorities disagree. Indeed, one of our friends, a prominent female evolutionist, asks wryly: "How can something that happens so infrequently be an adaptation?" In response, we would ask: Can something that is now so important be an accidental side effect of some other selective force? But one thing is clear. No matter how it came into being, the female orgasm is now a major factor in male-female relationships.

One can speculate about other methods of inducing men to stick around. It is well-known that there is something very compelling to men about displays of vulnerability and helplessness in women. This is somewhat of a puzzle. Hunter-gatherer women are very self-reliant and work very hard. Why are men so susceptible to the appearance of vulnerability? We think it likely that an old trait was put to a new use. Human males inherited from ancestral species a tendency to protect the group and to protect helpless children. When paternal investment increased in importance, females who could elicit this response from males might have been able to gain protection, affection, and hence resources. So, males who responded to vulnerability might have been selected.

The constant presence of the male in the family may also have put a premium on displays of vulnerability. Human males were still bigger, and still somewhat dangerous. The ability to inhibit male aggression and avoid conflict remained important. Here again, a childlike helplessness could well have been useful. It could keep a women from becoming the object of a violent attack.[2] Obviously, this reconstruction is purely theoretical, but what other explanation can be found for the phenomenon?

---

[2]It is noteworthy that in our culture submission sometimes fails to turn off male fury. Family therapists have described what they call "complementary escalations," in which the battered partner, usually the wife, placates and apologizes, hoping to calm an angry man. He responds with greater fury and eventually attacks. In those couples, it turns out that violence is less likely when the women stands up to the man and threatens effective retaliation. It is likely that this is the exception that proves the rule. Most men can be placated. It is only when the usual strategy fails that the opposite strategy is called for.

Reproductive Strategies in the Alcoholic Family

In recent books on alcoholism, family therapists have observed that alcoholism creates a family structure in which individuals take on certain roles. The alcoholic, sometimes called the Dependent, is the most visible member of this constellation. Next to the alcoholic, one often finds the Enabler. The Enabler is a person who makes it possible for the alcoholic to avoid experiencing the full consequences of the disease. The Enabler calls work to make excuses, takes on the tasks that the alcoholic fails to accomplish, provides emotional support, creates the illusion of normalcy, and generally holds the family together.

The alcoholic is generally a man and the Enabler is generally a woman. Is this a social accident, with the roles parceled out that way because men have the jobs and women must help the men to continue earning? Certainly, that is part of the story, but it is superimposed on a larger pattern. The role of the Enabler is one that would be familiar to most mature chimp or baboon females. The person who plays Enabler to an alcoholic is a peacekeeper in a deranged environment. The woman who takes on this role is using deeply-rooted temperamental and intellectual predispositions to enhance her survival (avoid violence), retain her male's paternal investment, and protect her reproductive investment (the lives of her children).

Vulnerability can be simulated, and a successful simulation is just as good as the real thing. But simulation is difficult, and might be detected. A person who really does have a trait can project it more easily than someone to who has to play a role throughout a lifetime. Thus, there may have been some positive selection for females who were truly predisposed to letting themselves be taken care of.

Continuity amidst change

Despite all the changes, there was a great deal of continuity in the evolutionary history of the human female. Like females of ancestral species, hunter-gatherer females and their children had primary responsibility for the offspring and comprised the heart of the family. The males hunted their spectacular animals and performed their dramatic rituals, thus monopolizing the spotlight, but the women and children were the true core of society. Men could come and go, despite the fact that their value had increased. Without fathers, infants were disadvantaged; without mothers, they were dead.

Being important in the family brings on certain responsibilities and generates certain interests. Chimp and baboon females play an important role in maintaining order and peace within the troop. They conciliate and appease, deflect aggression, form long-term relationships that constitute the structure of the group, and help to determine which male(s) will attain a dominant position. They dominate the politics of the family. The rise of paternal investment, with the concurrent need to keep males contributing to the family, could only have intensified female specialization in personal politics.

The special abilities of women

The selection pressures that shaped the female psyche are evident in the special abilities of women. Intuitive observation and psychological testing lead to the following conclusions: Women are, on the average, superior to men in certain verbal skills; they possess greater emotional and social sophistication; they can read the emotional content of faces better; and they have a greater sensitivity to nonverbal communication. These abilities are precisely those which would help them to carry out the tasks that the hunting-gathering lifestyle required of them.

We can be sure that the traits that best fit the new reproductive strategy were not equally distributed among early human females. But as the importance of paternal investment increased, these traits began to spread through the gene pool. In time, they came to characterize most, though certainly not all, females of the our species.

The evidence indicates that many of the differences in the way the genders behave are related to structural differences in male and female brains. It would be hopeless to try to review all the data on this issue, but when any region or circuit of the brain is subjected to close scrutiny, sex differences are found. We will mention only a few.

The hypothalamus, which is often referred to as the organ of mood, is perhaps the most significantly different anatomical structure in the brain. For example, differences in the male and female hypothalamus determine whether an individual will menstruate or not. The mood changes associated with the monthly cycle are due to chemical substances whose presence or absence is determined by the hypothalamus. In the final analysis, therefore, the overall emotional climate of men and women is different because the genders have different hypothalami, and hence different brains.

Here is a short list of other differences. The size and shape of the left and right lobes of the cerebral cortex are different. There is less lateralization in the female brain (Inglis and Lawson, 1981), probably due to the fact that the corpus callosum, which transmits information from one hemisphere to the other, is in women larger and wider at one end (Lacoste-Utamsing and Holloway, 1982). The organization of the speech centers is different (Kimura, 1985). Perhaps most important of all, the brains of males and females are differentially sensitive to sex hormones, due to gender-specific distribution of receptors (Ehrhardt and Meyer-Bahlburg, 1981).

Keep in mind that these are average differences. Some male brains may have a preponderance of "female" qualities and vice versa. Therapists must not try to impose a way of thinking or feeling on anyone, just because most individuals of that gender feel or think that way. By the same token, however, therapists ought not to assume that someone's way of feeling is the product of conditioning—and therefore the proper target of counter-conditioning. Sensitivity to the predispositions of the genders is sensitivity to the innermost core of the self.

The sex differences in the brain make males and females differentially receptive to certain stimuli. The result is that males and females are each more prone to certain reactions and behaviors.

Most if not all of these differences are due to events that occur while the infant is still *in utero*. All mammalian infants start out in life on a basically female plan. In those infants who are carrying a Y chromosome—the males—the onset of testosterone production induces sexual differentiation of the brain approximately three months after conception (McEwen, 1981).

Child rearing practices can modify an individual's behavior, but have no effect on these underlying structural differences. These differences are permanent characteristics of the human species. Nevertheless, early experience and conditioning can override or otherwise modify the expression of many of these abilities and predispositions. Also, it isn't so much that males and females are "better" or "worse" at doing something, but rather that they are more or less likely to find that they enjoy a particular action or situation.

Note that we are not suggesting that all differences in behavior that are observed in any given society are influenced by genetic factors. Over the past 10 or 12 thousand years, cultures have invented all kinds of customs, rules and institutions. These often have nothing to do with biological traits. While biology can easily explain why men specialize in hunting and women in gathering, biology cannot possibly justify the extension of this division of labor to law or medicine, for example. Nor, as we argued in Chapter 5, is there any basis in evolution for having women do nothing but take care of children all day.

Biology does not provide any support for any of the sociosexual relationships that have been prevalent in modern societies, communist or capitalist, developed or undeveloped. Only those social arrangements that can be traced either to ancestral species or to the evolutionary pressures that brought *Homo sapiens* into existence can be presumed to be based on genes.

In the next chapter, we will look at what happens when a primate female with a big brain finds herself in an environment to which she is not adapted.

CHAPTER 8

Women on the Contemporary Scene

Every mother is a working mother.

— Anon.

DILEMMAS. THAT'S WHAT THE CURRENT environment presents to women. Contemporary women live in a drastically altered environment, one that is not supportive of their biological predispositions. First, the female predisposition toward nurture and affiliation is in conflict with the dominant values of our culture. Second, the female need for full participation in socio-economic life is not being fully met. In this section, we will look at some of the dilemmas that are created for women by modern industrial society.

Some Current Dilemmas

Career vs. home

In the natural environment, women did not have to choose between career and childcare. Since children were brought up by the working group of adult females, mothers did not have to give up their economic activity nor their social lives. A society in which this choice has to be made is not well suited to the genetic characteristics of women.[1] The consequences of creating such a drastic choice is now becoming clear: more and more women are

[1] Judith Brown (1970) concluded, on the basis of an analysis of George Murdoch's *World Ethnographic Sample* (1957), that the degree to which women participate in subsistence activities is dependent on the compatibility of that activity with simultaneous childcare. The modern industrial pattern is perhaps the first in which women are expected to participate in subsistence activities *instead of* childcare.

110

deciding not to have children. In general, the higher the social class and educational attainments of women, the less likely are they are to reproduce. This means that the most intelligent and successful women will have the least children.

Women who try to have both career and children must pay someone else to take care of their children. The person hired may be a competent professional, but might also be an unskilled stranger who resents the fact that she is forced to accept a "menial" position. The child will have an absent mother to go with the absent father, and the mother will have to cope with a burden of doubt and guilt.

Interdependence vs. independence

The baseline female mammal is almost totally independent. As primary caretaker of her children, she is essentially responsible for her own survival as well as that of her young. She provides all her own food and all of theirs as well, until they are weaned. Finally, she protects them from others of her own and different species, with a ferocity that is proverbial. Since humans are mammals, human females tend to have the psychological equipment to carry out this task: motivation, drive, skill, and what Betty Friedan called tiger-strength.

However, as the importance of paternal investment increased, the human female also developed the capacity to enter into an interdependent relationship with a male. Independence was no longer a viable strategy. No one in a relationship based on reciprocity can be independent. New emotional responses were required. This is the true origin of what Colette Dowling called the "Cinderella Complex." Dowling thought that women behaved in a "dependent" fashion because they are brought up to have a hidden fear of independence. We disagree. A woman's reluctance to be independent is not based on pathological fear; it is, rather, a genetic strategy designed to enable her to bond with a provider of meat. The strategy is mediated by the emotions: women get a feeling of discomfort or dissatisfaction when faced with being totally on their own. In a hunting-gathering environment, these emotions would have induced her to do what would enable her and her offspring to survive.

One can look at this trait negatively, as the "price" a woman has to pay for paternal investment, but one can also look upon it as one of the genetic achievements that makes possible the intensely cooperative, intimate social life of humans. However one looks at it, the trait won't go away.

Humans are complex organisms, genetic mosaics made up of bits and pieces that have been fitted together to create a creature that can survive in a certain range of social circumstances. On the average, human females are adapted to work independently part of the time and to cooperate the rest of the time with the man who is helping take care of her children. Women are not adapted to living like idle drones, nor are they adapted for head-to-head competition. Nature lies somewhere in the middle.

Unfortunately, many women today have been subjected to highly polarized forms of socialization. Some were raised to be helpless and subordinate; they picked up the message that they had to stay at home because they didn't have the capacity to do anything "better." Others, at the opposite end of the spectrum, grew up under the influence of the slogans of radical feminism: intercourse is rape, heterosexuality is treason, wives are prostitutes, motherhood is slavery, etc. Ideologues on both sides demand that women choose between the two poles of their nature, not realizing that a woman who does so probably will have to betray a part of herself.

There is another major source of confusion. The incredible wealth of the American economy makes it possible, for the first time in the history of our species, for large numbers of women to support themselves and their children without the aid of any one man. To the "logical" mind, looking only at contemporary society, and lacking awareness of our evolutionary history, there is absolutely no reason why any woman should make sacrifices just to get paternal investment from one particular male. There are police to protect women, jobs to provide them with food and shelter, and government transfer payments such as welfare for those who don't have jobs. Women and their children can now survive without a "father." Biologically, however, women are set up to attract paternal investment. Logic and emotion don't fit together, and the result is psychological distress.

Rationally, then, independence is a viable strategy, even if it means hardship for those in the lower socio-economic strata. But emotionally, the members of our species are adapted to living together. Hence the conflict and the pain.

Let us hazard a dictum: When culture strays too far from biology, it also moves away from sanity. We will return to this theme in Chapter 11.

Choosing a mate

A typical dilemma: go with an attractive, seductive man who promises excitement, or with a solid, career-oriented man who offers the promise of stability? Some women choose excitement; others choose security. The important point is that the choice almost always has to be made. The problem arises because in human society males are a source not only of good genes but also of paternal investment. Few women have a chance at the men who offer both glamour and reliability. Many women don't have much of a choice at all. A recent film, *Crossing Delancy*, illustrated this classic dilemma very well. A young woman from New York's lower east side, enamored of a wild and crazy writer, is maneuvered into seeing an old-world style matchmaker, who sets her up with a business man (a pickle vendor). At first the young woman balks, but then the voice of reason takes over and she chooses stability over glamour.

Here again, the logic of paternal investment is important. As we mentioned in the previous chapter, when the contribution of the male becomes significant, competition between females comes into play. Consequently, not all females find mates and some have to settle for mates of low desirability. The existence of a trade-off between physical attractiveness and paternal investment may help to illuminate infidelity in women. Since they don't necessarily find stability exciting, there is a temptation to find excitement outside the marriage.

Sexual freedom, fidelity, and the double standard

The evolutionary reasons for many of the best-known characteristics of the sexual behavior of women should now be almost self-evident. Since women have to bear the consequences of the reproductive act, they tend to be more careful than males about having sex. They require romance (courtship displays, prenuptial gifts, mating dances, etc.) and foreplay before they are ready for intercourse, and they resent being treated like "sex objects," i.e., not taken seriously as candidates for long-term relationships. Girls, according to the old saw, give sex to get love; boys offer love to get sex. Women can get money and favors for sex; men have to give money and favors for sex (unless, significantly, they are willing to engage in homosexual acts with older men). The situation is the same in virtually every culture that has ever been studied.

Throughout history, socialization and culture have tended to reinforce these innate tendencies. Wise parents, knowing that their daughters will have to bear the consequences of copulation, teach them to be careful. Naturally, carefulness comes in different varieties. In societies where children are raised communally, such as those of hunter-gatherers, sex is relatively easy to come by but parents won't give a girl in marriage until a man has proved himself worthy.[2] In societies where individual fathers invest only

[2]These marriage practices help to explain why so many women are attracted to older men. In general, only older men had access to women, while girls got men not too long after puberty. The older men were the more valuable ones. Women who accepted them got the better deal, in terms of ability to protect and provide. Presumably, some women refused older men, for reasons of preference. The children of the women who took the older men survived better than the others, and thus women today are descendants of women with a preference for older men.

The Wrong Strategy?

Adele, an attractive, intelligent woman of 26, had three illegitimate children, and was living with her parents and the children in a three-room apartment. The first child was fathered by a man she fell in love with during her senior year in high school. When she went away for the summer, she cheated on him. When they got back together, she told him about it. He left before she knew she was pregnant.

She conceived the second child during a trip to California. She had a passionate affair with Mark, a drug-user and dealer whom she really liked, but she also let Allen sleep with her once. She was convinced that the one-night stand was responsible for the pregnancy, but she didn't like Allen, so she told Mark the baby was his, hoping he would marry her. Not surprisingly, Mark didn't jump at the chance to do the right thing, so Adele went home. There, she sued Allen for paternity. Then Mark came to visit her, wanting sex and a place to stay. She took him in but, after some weeks, proceeded to tell him that the baby was Allen's. Mark became abusive, and this is when Adele came for therapy. She said she wanted to "work out some problems in her relationships with men," but she really wanted to know how to work things out with Mark.

The therapist questioned whether such a man could reasonably be expected to be a good husband to her. She was adamant. "I know he's not perfect, but he's better than nothing." She could not see that her having had a child with another man while she was with Mark was a crucial factor in the situation. Shortly thereafter, Mark left for a neighboring state. For a few sessions, Adele talked about looking for someone else, but soon she reported that she was traveling back and forth to see him. They were having sex. She kept finding him with a woman, usually, but not always, the same one. But she refused to give up hope that he would marry her. She could not see that she was making herself cheap. Several times, Mark told her he didn't want to see her anymore. Finally, he announced that he was returning to California to take up with a woman who was carrying his child. Adele, in tears, asked why he preferred that woman. He replied: "If you had my baby, I would stay with you." Adele promptly went off birth control. After one month, Mark left. When Adele came home, she was pregnant.

Human behavior is diverse. But beyond a certain point, variation brings problems and becomes, in effect, deviation. Adele could not follow, or even understand, the female reproductive strategy, and she paid a terrible price.

But . . . Adele was living on welfare, which was paying for the children. Some biologists might argue that her behavior was a strategy, i.e., a way of coping with the existing environment. We don't agree. If strategy it was, it was a bad strategy. It created extreme psychological distress.

in their own children, daughters are taught to withhold sex until the man makes a commitment. This often means that men have to wait for sex as well as marriage.

Much of human culture, in other words, is an elaboration on the reproductive strategies that are natural to the species. Socialization is used to strengthen the prevailing genetic predispositions — or to substitute for them in an individual who doesn't have them. The double standard echoes, elaborates on, and rigidifies, often to the point of parody, an element in the conflicting reproductive strategy of males and females.

Among hunting and gathering peoples, the double standard exists, but isn't particularly rigid, at least when compared with the patriarchal cultures of later history. Among the !Kung, men do fight and kill each other over the infidelity of a woman. But among the Inuit (Eskimo), wife-swapping is common. More significantly, we know of no hunter-gatherer culture where virginity is prized or considered a precondition for marriage. We know of none where there is a systematic attempt to control and/or denigrate female sexual expression and behavior. Hunter-gatherer women manage to carry on their affairs, not without incurring ill-will, but yet without risking life, limb, or access to resources. Remember Nisa's sly remark about the one in the hut and the one in the bush.

Most other societies are less tolerant. Why? There are probably many reasons, but the invention of private property surely played a role. Hunter-gatherers don't have property, except for a few personal possessions. Property didn't became a major factor in human life until the invention of agriculture. The essence of private property is that it can be passed from parent to child. Male sexual attitudes haven't been the same since.

Being able to transfer the fruits of one's labor to an heir provided an incentive to accumulate more than was needed in a lifetime. Thus was born the notion of work and sacrifice. Not long afterward, no doubt, the first parent said, "You ungrateful wretch, I've devoted my whole life to giving you a better start than I had."

For mothers, having heirs didn't present any new problems. Mothers know who their children are. But men don't. They have to take paternity on faith. Once they got involved in a system which caused them to spend their lives working for their children, men needed something more than faith. Their stake in paternity rose dramatically. A man who was slaving away for his children wanted to be very sure that they were his. The cult of virginity, the practice of ritual cliterodectomy, *purdah*, and similar attempts to control the sexual behavior of women owe their origins to the concern of men for the future of their property.

The great monotheistic religions have been put into the service of this rather mundane goal. They make the sexual behavior of women a moral, rather than a practical matter. The creator of the universe himself is said to take an interest in sex. The fear of God helps to make sure that men pass their worldly goods to those who carry 50% of their genes. That the sexual behavior of men also came under restriction is, we believe, an ironic turn of the screw.

Notice that concern about legitimacy is a cultural phenomenon that is superimposed upon a biological pattern. Mammal males generally attempt to monopolize access to ovulating females. Males who don't will not reproduce as often as those who do. The interest in not passing an inheritance to the child of another man maps onto that predisposition. Combined, these forces lead to the elaboration of cultural practices that seek to control female sexuality.

One might ask, why didn't men evolve to let women have sex with other men when they aren't ovulating? One possible answer is this: since females emancipated themselves from *estrus*, men can't tell when they are ovulating and when they are not. To be effective, control has to be exercised almost constantly. The price of year-round access is year-round vigilance.

We have to this point explained why men evolved to be jealous, but why are women jealous? After all, most mammalian females are not. The answer, we believe, is again parental investment. If a human male becomes interested in a new woman, he might shift his investment to her. Hence, human females do have something to lose if their men consort with other women. One should expect, therefore, that women would be more tolerant of male sexual infidelity if it did not involve the risk of losing resources. Various lines of evidence indicate that this is so. For example, in many French villages, married men used to visit bordellos with the knowledge of their wives. The wives could be pretty sure that the men would not abandon them for one of the prostitutes. Folk wisdom taught that it was better to let men stray where it was safe, rather than risking a strong emotional attachment. One cannot imagine the average man in any society allowing his wife to be "serviced" in a similar manner.

Contraception, abortion, and the new morality

In the age of contraception and medical abortion, the consequences of copulation are far less severe for females than they used to be. Disease aside, careful women can have sex with as many men as they like. In this sense, the genetic predisposition to coyness has become anachronistic. However, as we pointed out before, predispositions don't go away just because their original function disappears. Most women still find less satisfaction in "promiscuity" than do men. On the average, women still prefer to be loved and kept rather than loved and left.

Furthermore, women have to deal with men, and men haven't changed genetically either. They tend to be jealous. Given the high degree of paternal investment in humans, plus the cultural overlay of property consciousness in post-agriculture society, male jealousy is inevitable; men who aren't jealous risk investing in children who aren't their own, and such males will not attain high levels of inclusive fitness. Of course, inclusive fitness is irrelevant to personal motivations. Still, humans continue to act as their ancestors have acted for hundreds of thousands of years. Jealous males make sure that their wives don't copulate with other men and, given the chance, they make love to the wives of the men who aren't jealous. Genes that promote jealousy spread through the population. Hence, most of the men who are alive today are descendants of a long line of jealous males.

A man betrayed by a woman is a pitiful figure. The immensity of his pain is somewhat ludicrous, which only makes it worse. Yet while the cuckold is a figure of fun, the man who murders an unfaithful female is often forgiven and always understood (at least by other males). These opposing attitudes seem to reflect differences between the rational and the emotional brain. Viewed dispassionately, adultery is trivial — what has been lost? But the pain doesn't go away for all that. While many males are currently trying to accommodate themselves to the sexual freedom now enjoyed by women, and are quick to appreciate the advantages it offers in the form of readily available sex, most men don't want the woman they are with to bed down with other men.

The more women emancipate themselves from restrictions on their sexual freedom, the more difficult will it be for them to elicit paternal investment from individual males. The next generation of males may be more tolerant of female sexual infidelity, but these "new men" are not likely, on the average, to become model family men. Socially, the breakdown of the sex contract leads to unstable marriages, the single-parent family, the meat-market ambiance of the dating bar, delinquent fathers, the feminization of poverty, and the swelling welfare roles. Again, one cannot say if such a society will prove emotionally satisfying in the long run. For the moment, it is undeniably creating widespread psychological distress.

Changing behavior is relatively easy. Predicting all the consequences of a change is more difficult. Reproductive strategies are there for a reason, at least an evolutionary reason, and the human species has been shaped by them, emotionally as well as physically. When we change one element of such a system, we are bound to run into all sorts of side effects, and some of them are likely to be unpleasant.

Permission to initiate sex

Logically, there is no reason why sex shouldn't be initiated by either sex, as advice books for the modern women claim. But what does "initiate" really mean?

Among nonhuman mammals, the first step in the complicated series of moves that leads to intercourse generally doesn't happen until a female indicates her readiness. Her entry into estrus is heralded by smells, sexual swellings, or other clear signals. These signals, which reach the brains of all the males in the vicinity, trigger hormonal changes that lift the males to higher levels of arousal. The aroused male is then motivated to "initiate" copulation. But who really initiated the process?

Human females, like other mammals, send signals, but they rely much less on smell. As a result, their signs of readiness can more easily be directed towards one single male, rather than broadcast to the community at large. Monica Moore of the psychology department of Missouri University did some research on how women make their availability known. She developed a catalogue of behaviors that succeeded in attracting men. Her list of 52 behaviors included the darting glance, the head toss, the eyebrow flash, the hair flip, the lip lick, and the neck presentation. By watching women in a variety of contexts — singles bars, snack bars, libraries, and women's groups — Moore was able to ascertain that women exhibited these behaviors much more often when they were interested in attracting the attention of men. She didn't say whether women did this consciously or not, but it doesn't make any difference.

A man who receives these signals is shifted to a higher state of arousal, just like males of other mammalian species. He is ready to make moves, to swing into action, to take risks, to fight off other males who might have picked up the same signals, and finally, to engage in sexual intercourse. Readers who are interested in this topic might read Timothy Perper's book, *Sex Signals: The Biology of Love*.

When a woman interrupts the normal sequence of moves, by actively making a proposition instead of eliciting it, a male is likely to be taken aback.[3] If he takes the proposition to indicate readiness, he will find it flattering, and therefore stimulating. But he may also find it disruptive to his own erotic response. Why? Because by catching him off balance, it takes away the move that his hormone system prepares him to make in such circumstances.

Why do males respond in this way? Several possible explanations exist. We first surmised that because a male who is preparing to make a sexual overture is vulnerable, an unexpected move could cause him to feel that the situation is getting out of control, creating fear, which would inhibit the expression of his sexuality. However, the reason could be that natural selection has shaped males to be "investment coy," i.e., suspicious of an apparently promiscuous woman, who might entrap them into taking care of another man's children. The two explanations are not mutually exclusive.

Fear is the likely response if a man takes a woman's initiative as a demand rather than an offer. Erections, after all, are not subject to voluntary control—the penis has a mind of its own. Hence, a demand is a challenge, and a challenge is something to be met with caution. The line between indicating accessibility and making a demand is quite fine. On either side of that line, there is a no-man's land, and in that ill-defined region, the sexes destroy each other with discouraging frequency. Therapists may need to help their female clients understand the effects their new freedoms can have on their sexual partners.

On competition

The dilemma: In any industrial economy, women must compete to earn a greater share of the resources. In the absence of a division of labor by sex, they must compete with men. This creates a problem for male-female relationships.

As we shall see in Chapters 9 and 10, natural selection has created males who respond aggressively to competitors when the circumstances are appro-

---

[3]As is well known, sexual and aggressive behavior patterns are closely linked, but more so in some animals than in others. The geese studied by Konrad Lorenz (1967) can mate only after a long series of dance steps, each of which has to be carried out exactly by both partners. The steps help the goose and the gander to recognize each other as potential sexual partners, rather than as rivals. If either goose or gander make a mistake before the dance is completed, the outcome is aggression rather than copulation. Human behavior is obviously not as rigidly programmed as this, but the story can serve to help us understand some of the constraints within which our behavior operates.

Clinical Vignette: The Caspars

This case illustrates the delicate balances that have to be maintained if people are to enjoy satisfying personal and familial relationships. In this case, the evolutionary perspective guided the therapist through the maze of competing interests and needs and suggested that attention needed to be paid to the balance between assertiveness-individuation and conciliation-reciprocity. When opportunities presented themselves to intervene in these areas, the therapist was prepared.

Mr. and Mrs. Caspar came into therapy for two reasons. First, she was afraid her marriage of 10 years was going to break up. Second, her children were becoming discipline problems. Her husband was threatening to leave, and she wasn't sure she wanted him to stay. She loved him, but she was increasingly dissatisfied with their relationship.

In her first real act of independence, Mrs. Caspar had gone back to school several years earlier. (She had married young and moved from parentified child to homemaker with virtually no transition.) Her husband supported her decision to go to school, and had become much more helpful around the house than he had been before, but he seemed to have reached his limits in this respect quite early. She wanted him to do more, especially now that the kids were becoming a problem.

Mr. Caspar's major goal was to have his wife become more independent of her family of origin. In his opinion, this was her problem. As soon as he saw that she was working on it, he dropped out of therapy.

Work with Mrs. Caspar focused at first on making her more assertive. Despite her decision to go back to school, she was still trying to be the perfect housewife, mother, and family matriarch. She was forever taking people places and doing favors for them. She didn't see how she could stop.

(continued)

priate. Normally, a male's competitors are other males, but if a female becomes a competitor, a male may still respond aggressively (in spite of some inhibitions he may have). The resulting interaction will contribute to the ill-will that already exists between males and females. Women in business often interpret such responses as hostility to women, when in fact what is involved is the normal male response to competition.

Can anything be done to solve this problem? We aren't very optimistic. Even if women behave in ways that are on the surface noncompetitive, the

Clinical Vignette: The Caspars (*continued*)

A combination of psychotherapy and assertiveness training soon caused her to insist on reciprocity in all her relationships.

Mr. Caspar was delighted to see his wife become assertive with other people, but he had a hard time when she made demands on him. Because he was strongly motivated to preserve the marriage, he tolerated her demands and began to spend more time in the house, with her, and with the children. Things went better for a while. But after some months, he asked to be seen privately, and announced that he had reached the end of his rope. He was beginning to feel defeated. No matter what he did, his wife demanded more. He didn't feel she was showing any appreciation for the changes he had already made. The therapist sensed that if this kept up, he would leave.

The therapist raised the issue of his feelings with Mrs. Caspar, and she began to explore the reasons why he was feeling that his efforts were unappreciated. She discovered that she didn't really know how to express approval effectively, either with him or with the children. She was making demands but not providing emotional feedback when her demands were met. Her lack of responsiveness, unnoticed when she was busy doing favors for everyone, became blatant once she stopped.

Overall, her new assertiveness had really gone farther than her social network would support. She had gone from one extreme to the other. As this subject came into clear focus, she realized that if she wanted to maintain her family, she would have to moderate her assertiveness, find different ways of expressing it, and discover new ways of giving to others. This approach provided fruitful material for subsequent work with her, with the couple, and with the family as a whole.

This example illustrates how an evolutionary approach can help psychotherapists to find the middle ground. Individual goals have to be attained without sacrificing social relationships, lest therapy promote alienation and loss. The skill of the therapist lies in helping each individual to identify the center.

fact that men and women are competing for the same positions pits the sexes against each other. For example, women have been shaped (by natural selection) to be sensitive to interpersonal situations. They often bring these skills to the business world, and when they do, they may feel that they are *not* being competitive. But objectively, they *are* competing, because if they are good, they will get positions that might otherwise have gone to men. Men, faced with competition of a type they understand only dimly, may respond with *their* style of competition, leaving women confused and angry. In the current environment, there is no really good solution to this problem. Hopefully, the more individuals understand what is going on, the more effectively they will be able to deal with it.

To reproduce or not to reproduce

There is inescapable inequality here. Women bear the brunt of reproductive costs, because females are the ones who get pregnant, suffer the adverse health effects that pregnancy entails, take the risks of birth, and nourish the young. Today, some women seek to "equalize" this situation by demanding that fathers do more child-rearing. A measure of success here seems possible to us. Men in America traditionally spent less time with children than hunter-gatherer men, so a movement toward more male involvement in child-rearing can be considered "natural." However, we don't believe that men will, on the average, be willing to devote themselves to children the way women do. They simply don't get the same rewards from it. Furthermore, each child is more "valuable" to a mother than to a father, because fathers can engender new children at a much lower cost. Hence men are, on the average, much more able, emotionally, to walk out on their children than women are (as welfare agencies around the country know to their chagrin). We predict, therefore, that women who want to have children will have to continue to be the primary caretakers. The inequality will remain.

A woman can of course choose not to reproduce, but if she does, she will pay a greater psychological price than a man who makes the same choice. It's quite a dilemma.

Some Characteristic Problems of Contemporary Women

Depression

Women are more prone to depression than men. The biological basis for this finding is now beginning to emerge. Men respond to stress differently than women. In men, excess stress tends to produce physical ailments such as heart disease, high blood pressure and lowered resistance to infection. In females, it tends to produce depression.

Why should this be so? The answer isn't clear, but may be found in the differing evolutionary pressures that formed the male and female psyches. Men, the hunters, were more likely to have benefited from fast-acting stress mechanisms which would enable them to cope with danger. Women, the nurturers, were more likely to have benefited from a response to stress that either caused them to conserve energy or made them more sensitive to the people around them.

Ultimately, of course, the differences are caused by the differing effects of testosterone and the estrogens on the organization of the brain/pituitary/adrenal system which mediates the response to stress. It follows that *vulnerability* to depression is biologically based. We believe, however, that current social conditions precipitate more depressions than would occur in the natural environment. Depression, one can assume, results when a vulnerable person encounters adverse social circumstances. Adverse circumstances are unfortunately quite common in today's environment.

Let's go back a few years to the days of the typical suburban housewife. She had to do her mothering without benefit of nature's support system — the group of adult females who take care of children while working and socializing. As Americans got wealthier, more and more people achieved the American dream: a house for every family and a room for every individual. Luxury, privacy, individualism. And isolation. The white picket fence kept people out and misery in. The typical suburban home was a great place to go back to in the evening, but was too isolated a place to hang around in all day. It is not surprising that many of the women who lived there got depressed and began to seek ways out.

Other historical developments contributed to women's dissatisfaction with the role of mother and homemaker. One of them was the population explosion. Reproduction has become a bad word. There are too many people already. Society does not admire the woman who contributes a hefty batch of children to the already crowded generations of the future. Furthermore, as discussed in Chapter 5, children are no longer economic assets. In the old days, healthy children ensured their parents a comfortable old age. Today, with social security in place, many children contribute almost nothing to the economic welfare of their parents, except through the tax system. The return on parental investment is not what it used to be.

Since children brought neither glory nor gold, the prestige of the homemaker declined. Few women want to be a "mere" housewife or "just" a mother. Women who chose these roles began to be looked on as failures by many of their contemporaries. Small wonder that they got depressed.

The result was that women turned to the labor market as a source of satisfaction as well as income. Here too there were adverse circumstances in abundance. First of all, many of the available jobs were dead ends. Secondly, the jobs that did offer opportunity for advancement often required women to make unhappy choices. To be, for example, successful corporate executives, women generally had to make rather extensive sacrifices. They often

DEPRESSION AS A STRATEGY?

In January, Inuttiak, the man of the igloo, had left on a long trip, leaving his wife, Allaq, their two daughters, and Jean Briggs, an anthropologist they had temporarily "adopted," alone for a month. The cold, says Briggs, "had an aching, relentless quality . . . that I felt as a physical weight." In the absence of Inuttiak, his wife

> became a different person; her passivity was beyond belief. She never boiled fish, rarely brewed tea, and never lit the lamp to dry clothes — any of which activities would have heated the igloo. Neither did she go out to warmer igloos to visit. She just sat in her corner . . . waved her feet, blew on her hands, and endlessly observed that the igloo was cold. . . . But when the dogs' howling signaled Inuttiak's return, bleak passivity vanished in a flash . . .

> Briggs doesn't say so, but to us Allaq sounds depressed. Her mood changed, she reduced her movements, and she slept 16 hours a day. These reactions would be expected to reduce her caloric requirements and indeed she ate less than she normally did. Was Allaq a weak woman who barely managed to cope with the challenge of winter alone? Or was her depression an adaptive response, one that enhanced her chances for survival?

> The study of the biology of depression may eventually help us to answer this question. There is evidence to indicate that depression is related in some ways to hibernation. Although human beings evolved in a climate in which there was no winter, we do turn down the metabolic furnace — the consumption of energy — at night, during sleep. The same mechanism could be used for other purposes, i.e., energy reduction during times of famine when activity is useless. It is possible that people in difficult environments, such as the Inuit, can shut down on purpose.

> Whatever benefits it may confer on the Inuit under cold weather conditions, depression is not much of a strategy in the modern environment. At best, it is, like the appendix, something that has outlived its usefulness.

had to put their family life in second place by delaying pregnancy, shuffling their kids off to someone else's care, and/or paying less attention to the man in their lives.

To really go far, say the management books for women, they have to learn to play by men's rules. They should demand to be treated as if they had no gender. They should reject all references to their sexuality and deflect the sexual interest that they arouse. They should, says Jeannette Scollard in *No-Nonsense Management Tips for Women*, talk tough and use the language of war and sports. They should learn to bluff and threaten and to treat men as competitors and subordinates. They must understand that "lawful deception is admirable," says Betty Lehan Harragan, in *Games Mother Never Taught You* (900,000 copies in print!). And, says Harragan, they must understand that behind the facade of decency, men are "crude, illiterate, sexist, mentally-deficient smut peddlers and voyeurs."

If a woman really gets into this mode of thinking, she will find it difficult to carry on a relationship with a man outside her work. To do so, she would have to lead a dual life. She would have to treat this man differently than she treats all the other men she deals with. Eternal watchfulness would be the price of domestic peace. This may be possible for superwomen, but not for anyone else.

Obviously, most women don't have to go this far to hold their jobs. Nevertheless, it remains true that the model for success that is being presented to women today is based on masculine values. When males behave like males, they get deep satisfaction from it. A male who out-bluffs another one gets a powerful emotional charge. His status among males rises and he becomes more attractive to women. To top it off, his sexuality is aroused as well. Males need to feel powerful in order to function well sexually. It is no accident that our language speaks of the "lust" for power.

When women behave in the same way, the results are different. One set of rewards—money and fame—is obtainable, for those who are talented or lucky. But other rewards—personal satisfaction and appeal to the opposite sex—are more elusive. Certainly, women who achieve fame and money get pleasure from their achievements and this pleasure may be highly motivating. But even successful women are becoming acutely aware of the sacrifices they have had to make, at least if one can believe such recent books as *Success and Betrayal: The Crisis of Women in Corporate America*, by Sarah Hardesty and Nehama Jacobs, and *Women Like Us*, by Liz Gallese. For the vast majority, who will achieve nothing more for their efforts than a place in an office hierarchy somewhere, the costs of the struggle may outweigh the benefits.

Women don't, as a rule, get the same thrill out of winning a fight or staring down an enemy. Why is this? Culture no doubt plays a role, but there is a good evolutionary explanation. In the course of human evolution, winning fights was not the way females enhanced their reproductive success. Females who acted aggressively towards males weren't attractive to them, and therefore didn't have as many offspring as females who avoided competition. Women today, being descendants of females who did not behave competitively towards males, have the genes of those ancestral females, and tend to behave in a similar manner. Women can of course *learn* to behave like men, but it leaves many of them feeling lonely, confused, and turned off. Such feelings breed despair and depression.

Frigidity

The characteristic female sexual dysfunction is frigidity—a failure to respond. Why this should be so is now easy to understand. In the transition from ape to human, female sexuality was put into the service of securing paternal investment. To enable females to bond with one single male, the natural impulse to mate with any healthy, powerful male had to be curbed. Completely spontaneous responses were incompatible with the new reproductive strategy. This meant that inhibitions had to be developed.

The study of the evolution of the nervous system has shown that many, if not all, higher mental functions are achieved by adding new inhibitory circuits to the nervous system. Such circuits enable the organism to delay, modify, and modulate acts that were previously "instinctive" or "involuntary." Control is a mixed blessing. The individual's behavior can be more finely tuned, but the response becomes vulnerable to suppression. The inhibitory circuits can become too powerful, or too prone to fire, either through conditioning or due to some genetic imbalance between excitatory and inhibitory pathways.

Something like this clearly happened to the sexuality of the human female. It is easily inhibited; any disturbance in a relationship can make it impossible for her to experience orgasm or even sexual pleasure. This failure to respond is now most often dysfunctional, but one should keep in mind that the ability *not* to respond originally served an important purpose. It allowed the human female to direct her sexuality towards the male who was going to provide paternal investment. In investigating frigidity in psychotherapy, one should always be alert to the function of frigidity in withholding bonding.

"Masochism"

Technically, the word masochist means a person who derives sexual pleasure from pain. More commonly, it is used to describe a person who remains in an unpleasant situation for no apparent reason. In our opinion, the latter behavior has little or nothing to do with the enjoyment of pain. The tendency to remain in an unpleasant situation is in part a function of the human female's need for paternal investment. As we described previously, the female tendency to enjoy being taken care of serves to awaken the protective tendencies of the human male. As a result, women tend to have "dependency needs," needs which make them less likely than males to strike off on their own when in a bad situation.

In today's environment, there are two problems with this tendency: one, it is in conflict with society's emphasis on self-gratification; two, it doesn't guarantee women a decent family life, because men leave anyway. The resultant mismatch between genes and environment creates the illusion of masochism.

Gender and Therapy

In trying to sum up our approach to gender, and indeed to people in general, the phrase "respect for the innate" came to mind. One could do worse as a guideline. The idea behind the phrase is admittedly difficult to implement, since there will always be questions about what is, in fact, wired in, but the effort must nevertheless be made.

Acceptance of gender and acceptance of self are inseparable. Humans are quite capable of thinking of themselves as beyond or above gender, but this is an illusion, a symptom of alienation from the self. People who don't accept their gender are divided against themselves.

Acceptance of the predispositions that go along with gender and sexual orientation is as necessary for the statistically "average" as it is for minorities. It is as true for homosexuals, transsexuals, and transvestites as for the average heterosexual. Just as we now recognize that homosexuality is not a disease, and should not be "treated," we must also recognize that having predispositions towards gender-specific attitudes and behaviors is not something that can be ignored. Just as the homosexual individual must be helped to accept his or her predispositions, rather than being conditioned to conform to an alien norm, so the heterosexual must not be conditioned to accept a social or political ideology that does not recognize biological realities.

It follows that in dealing with the conflicts described in this chapter, psychotherapists should not cling to the myth of gender-free behavior. Rather, they should help each individual woman to understand the roots of her conflicts, so that she can deal with the trade-offs she must inevitably make.

What is the effect of this kind of intervention? Is it to make women accept the status quo? Give up their efforts to improve their lot in life? Are we proposing some kind of biological fatalism? Quite the opposite. When one validates a woman's desire to be taken care of, one doesn't increase her need for protection; rather, one decreases the degree to which she condemns herself for having such feelings. When one explains to a woman why she isn't comfortable with a corporate rat-race, one improves her ability to deal with the corporate environment — provided she chooses to do so. Like other types of insight, insight into biological realities provides greater freedom and more options.

It can also improve relationships. People need to understand that there is an underlying conflict between the male and female reproductive strategies. A conscious awareness of the biological basis of the war of the sexes helps depersonalize the conflict and allows people to stop blaming each other for behaviors that are natural to their sex. Thus, if a woman knows that men aren't (on the average) as good at talking about their emotions, she will be less likely to criticize her less-than-articulate husband. At the very least, she will realize that it is farfetched to expect him to "grow" to be just like her. He, on the other hand, finding himself off the hook, may become willing to risk more self-exposure.

We would like to go back to a point we made in Chapter 6. When thinking about a relationship, use reciprocity as a guideline. Think about exchange of value, not equality. Find someone who has something different to offer. Do what you do best, and let your partner do what s/he does best. Don't try to measure each other by the same standards.

Overall, we think it advisable to help women to understand that when they demand to be treated like men, accept the superiority of male values, and try to behave like males, they are devaluing their gender. It is for example true that "worth in American society is measured by money," and we would agree with those who argue that this is essentially a male system of values. Why then should women be encouraged to accept it? On the evolutionary scale of values, the reproduction of life and the training of children are far more significant than the status games men play to amuse themselves and make themselves feel important. After all, men are predisposed to play these games largely because success makes them attractive to women. We hope that women will reclaim their basic values, if necessary by working towards a change in America's priorities.

Therapists who confront these issues may sometimes find themselves supporting positions that conflict in some degree with the values that a client brings into therapy. Such situations must of course be handled carefully, so as not to compromise the therapeutic alliance.

Obviously, the guidelines outlined above should not be used to impose alien behavior on women who for whatever reasons, genetic or other, are not predisposed towards biologically typical female behaviors. As always, awareness of the existence of individual variation is important, but, in turn, the appreciation of individual variations is no excuse for ignoring the species-specific traits of human behavior.

The Gender of the Therapist

The gender of a therapist is a much more important issue than previous theory suggests. Attitudes towards the therapist can be expected to reflect the gender makeup of the treatment situation: male-male, male-female, female-male, female-female. In each of these four possibilities, individuals have a natural (biological) way of relating that precedes the establishment of the therapeutic relationship. This mode of relating depends in turn on age: older female-younger male is different from older male-younger female. Theories that don't take these factors into account do not provide an adequate theoretical basis for understanding and interpreting transference. For example, Freud developed his theory of transference in part because he felt he wasn't young and attractive enough to "really" be a love-object for his female patients. He simply did not realize that because of the importance of paternal investment, young human females are naturally attracted to older men of substantial position.

We might make another point about Freud. He thought that girls fell in love with older men because they loved daddy. The study of evolution suggests that girls love daddy because they have a yen for older men.

Since there are few if any human neuters, humans have no mode of relating that is not gender-based (unless it is the mode that we use for things or for other species). Hence, there is no reason to expect, or for that matter to want, the treatment situation to be gender-independent.

Once one takes into account the effect of the gender situation on the client's behavior, one is able to notice deviations from the expected. For example, a male client can be expected to treat an older female therapist like a mother, and a younger one like a potential lover. A female client can be expected to treat an older male therapist with deference, and a younger one with a mixture of condescension and flirtatiousness. Expected gender-based responses should not be treated as "transference." Deviations from the expected behavior are probably significant. They may reflect vicissitudes of childhood, but could also represent alternative biological predispositions (e.g., homosexuality).

There is no reason to believe that any particular set of gender arrangements is therapeutically superior to any other. We are simply saying that one must be aware of the influence of gender before making inferences about individual behavior.

CHAPTER 9

The Reproductive Strategy
of the Male

Access is all.
— Adrian Forsyth,
A Natural History of Sex

THE BASIC THEMES OF MALE BEHAVIOR are more elusive than those of females. Male animals come in bizarre shapes and engage in behaviors that at first seem wasteful or perverse. Still, there is one iron law of maleness: males who can't find and impregnate at least one female will not transmit any of their genes to the next generation.

Consider the anglerfish *Ceratias holbolli*. Males of this species don't get any bigger than two inches long. The females, by contrast, can grow up to 26 inches long, an astounding degree of sexual dimorphism. The disparity is so great that, when originally encountered, the males and females were classified as members of different species. The truth was discovered quite by accident. A male was found with its mouth embedded in the flank of a female. At first, observers thought that the small fish had been eating the big one. But then they realized that the little fish was the male *holbolli*, and that he was permanently attached to his mate.

How could such a system have evolved? Apparently it is an adaptation to life in the trackless ocean. Finding a mate out there is not all that easy, so when a male *holbolli* does find a female, he makes sure he doesn't lose her. He bites his way into her body, and then hangs on until his lips fuse around a wad of her flesh. The boundaries between the two fish eventually disappear. Their vascular systems become continuous. He no longer feeds as an individual. His eyes disappear. Her blood flows through his veins, and he simply

130

absorbs the nutrients that come his way. His testes, however, enlarge, and he devotes himself entirely to one single function: the provision of sperm. He becomes, in the words of Stephen Jay Gould (1982), a sexual appendage of the female, a kind of incorporated penis. This is monogamy on a truly heroic scale.

The males of certain mantis species go even farther. They often give up their lives for the transmission of their genes. Female mantises are dangerous predators who will eat anything they can reach. The males have to sneak up on them from behind. But even if a male succeeds in mounting a female, his troubles aren't over. His mate will sometimes twist around and bite off his head while he is in the act of copulating. Mantis males have adapted well to this contingency; they can continue to copulate for up to 20 minutes without their heads. The payoff is that the sperm of the dead male will fertilize all the eggs the female lays. Thus, willingness to lose one's head is transmitted from one mantis generation to the next.

Among our fellow mammals, however, male reproductive strategies are somewhat less diverse. There is a more or less typical mammalian pattern, which we humans share to a certain degree. Therefore, if we wish to understand the human male, we must begin with the themes that are common to the mammalian male. While some of the material in this chapter may at first seem remote indeed from the behavior of our fellow men, the connection will become clear later, when we discuss human males specifically.

The Strategy of the Mammal

Male mammals tend towards promiscuity. They seek to spread their sperm around to as many females as possible. The reason is easy to understand. Sperm is cheap. The average male makes millions of sperm every day, at very little cost in time or energy. Each tiny, mass produced bullet of DNA can engender one entire offspring. Hence, evolution favors males who mate with as many females as possible.

Of course, there are some inherent limitations on a male's capacity to deliver sperm. First of all, it comes in packets. The packets are more "expensive," in time and energy, than single sperms; there is a limit on the number of packets a male can deliver. So even though there is enough sperm in the ejaculate of one man to inseminate all the women in North America, no single man can enjoy that degree of reproductive success. Nevertheless, even a packet of sperm is cheap when compared to the parental investment made by female mammals. Secondly, in species where males must protect and/or provision the young in order to ensure their survival, the value of mating with other females will be reduced by the potential loss of ability to provide for the offspring he has already engendered. If his philandering jeopardizes the young he already has, his reproductive success will not increase.

The existence of potential rivals also limits male freedom of action. If a male leaves his mate, other males can take his place. In species where males must actively keep other males away from their mate (or their harem), they may have to forego other sexual opportunities.

Given these limitations, the strategy of males of most mammalian species is to spread their genes around. This strategy helps to account for many features of the male body and behavior, several of which will be discussed below.

The Coolidge Effect

When a sexually receptive female mammal meets an aroused male, there is a flurry of copulation. This activity eventually subsides, but if another receptive female appears on the scene, the male frequently begins to copulate again. Each new female is capable of producing a new burst of sexual interest.

The rearousability of males has become known as the Coolidge Effect after an oft-repeated story told about Calvin Coolidge. The President and the first lady were given separate tours around a model farm. Mrs. Coolidge, noticing an active group of chickens in the yard, observed that the rooster was being kept quite busy. She suggested that her husband might be interested in the matter. When Mr. Coolidge arrived at the chicken yard, the guide duly relayed the message: "Your wife wanted me to point out how frequently the rooster copulated in a single day." The President thought awhile. "Same hen?" he asked. "No sir," replied the guide. "Well," said the President, "tell *that* to Mrs. Coolidge."

The number of times a male can be aroused differs of course from species to species; in the end, every male will reach the point of exhaustion and become unresponsive. But until that point is reached, novelty will repeatedly rekindle his ardor. The Coolidge Effect has a clear evolutionary purpose; it serves to decrease the probability that a male will continue to copulate with a female whom he has already inseminated, and thus increases the probability that he will seek additional females who might increase his reproductive success. Males who are subject to the Coolidge Effect tend to transmit their genes more frequently than males who aren't (all other things being equal). The Coolidge Effect thus puts sexual boredom in the service of the male reproductive strategy.

Sexual jealousy

From all of the above, it should be clear that sexual jealousy is a natural consequence of the male reproductive strategy. Under most circumstances, a tendency to restrict the sexual activity of his mate(s) will help a male to increase his reproductive success. Hence, in most mammalian species, the presence of a rival usually triggers some kind of preventive action. What kind and how much usually depends on the reproductive status of the female. Male jealousy is conditional and carries the clear mark of its evolutionary purpose: males are most vigilant when their females are in estrus. At other times, they are much more tolerant.

Mountain gorillas are particularly discriminating. A dominant (silverback) male keeps a constant vigil on the movements of his mates as long as they are not *pregnant*. However, once a female has conceived, he becomes incredibly tolerant. He may watch, from a distance of several feet, while the future mother of his offspring copulates enthusiastically with another silverback. A female may well indulge in more sexual acts, sometimes including homosexual mounts, during the early months of her pregnancy than during her estrus period. A pregnant gorilla can quite literally do no wrong.

In only a few species does male jealousy seem to go beyond concern for paternity. Among hamadryas baboons, a dominant male keeps the females in his harem under very strict control at all times. If one of them strays, or lags behind the group, he will harass her, threaten her, and even bite her until she conforms to his sense of what is proper. He seems to want to control her life as well as her reproduction. But hamadryas baboons are notoriously despotic. They are not typical of primates.

Competitiveness

The roots of the competitiveness of male mammals are found in the imbalance between male and female parental investment. Females invest more, and are therefore more valuable. They are also choosy; it is to their advantage to mate only with males who have the very best genes (otherwise they risk wasting their investment on nonviable offspring). Consequently, males have to prove themselves; they must demonstrate that they should be chosen above all other available males.

Males seek to mate with as many of these valuable creatures as possible. Obviously, the excess reproductive success of any one male has to come at the expense of others. If one individual monkey sires all the offspring of 25 females, 24 males won't reproduce. This set of circumstances leads evolution to select males for traits that lead to success in competition. Males who don't outdo others fail to gain access to mates and don't transmit their genes.

The competitiveness of males takes two principal forms: anatomical and behavioral specializations, and aggression. We will discuss them separately.

Anatomical and behavioral specializations. Various male traits serve to "advertise" the qualities of the male who grew them. This is called epigamic

ANATOMY AND JEALOUSY

Riding herd on females is not the only way males express their jealousy. For example, the males of certain acanthocephalan worms secrete a cement-like substance, known as a copulation plug, which they insert in the female's sexual opening after they have deposited their sperm. This plug, David Barash tells us, serves a dual purpose. It keeps the sperm from leaking out and keeps other males from getting in. In some cases, these plugs are even used as weapons against other males. When one male gains an advantage over another in a struggle, the victor applies his cement-gland to the victim's sperm opening, and seals it, thus neutralizing a potential competitor.

Incredible as it may seem, such plugs also exist in at least one primate species, the Japanese macaque. Macaque plugging was discovered, totally by accident, by anthropologist Jeffrey Kurland. Kurland had noticed that male macaques occasionally went out of their way to scare females for no apparent reason. The females generally responded with fearful cries of the kind that might have given pleasure to a mischievous boy. At first, Kurland assumed that he was watching a form of play. But one day he noticed that something popped out of a female's vagina while she was being "teased." Kurland eventually realized that it was a copulation plug. Apparently it had come out because of convulsions of her muscles. With the plug gone, she became available again . . . perchance to the male who frightened her, perhaps to one of his pals.

Is it too farfetched to see the copulation plug as a forerunner of the chastity belt?

selection. In this category one finds, for example, the fabulous antlers of deer and antelope. Impressive as they seem, these antlers are often of little or no value as weapons. They serve only to impress the hinds. The hinds are indeed impressed, but not because they are stupid. The large antlers carry information; they signal that the male has the skill to forage effectively and a metabolism that functions efficiently. A beast that can grow huge antlers has energy to waste, a sign that it is good at foraging. This trait will be valuable to its offspring.

Aggression. The second type of competition involves direct male to male interactions of a hostile or aggressive nature (agonistic encounters). This is called intrasexual selection. In many species, males who want to mate must emerge victorious from physical and/or psychological combat with other males, because females prefer winners. A male must either acquire a territory and defend it from other males, defeat rivals in combat, subdue them in trials of strength, or cow them into submission. Under these conditions, evolution tends to favor males who are aggressive. In cases of actual fighting or trials of strength, the more ferocious animal has a big advantage. But more significantly, an animal that makes itself *seem* aggressive, by threatening, making menacing gestures and indicating readiness to fight, can often drive away rivals without having to risk actual combat. The result is selection for males who look and act aggressively.

(Note that the term "aggression" lends itself to misinterpretation. In the context of international relations, it means an unprovoked attack involving violence. This is not what is meant here. Wherever possible, we hope to avoid the confusion by substituting the word *aggressivity*, which can be defined as follows: the tendency to respond in a competitive or hostile way to a provocative stimulus.)

There are genetic differences in the degree to which animals respond aggressively. Furthermore, the tendency to respond aggressively has a high degree of heritability; aggressive parents tend to have aggressive offspring. However, this does not mean, as ethologists such as Konrad Lorenz (1967) once seemed to imply, that organisms are born with, or generate during the day, a quantity of aggression that has to be discharged in one way or another. Aggressive acts are elicited by events in the environment; in the absence of the eliciting stimuli, normal individuals will not act aggressively.

Note that "aggressive" is not the same as "violent." Whether aggressivity leads to violence depends on circumstances, the most important of which is the response of the other animals involved in the aggressive encounter. Furthermore, the degree to which a given individual responds aggressively to a particular stimulus can of course be modified by prior experience. Aggressivity can be shaped and channeled, intensified or controlled, by learning. However, an animal that cannot respond aggressively cannot survive in competition with those who can.

Dominance

Males who have emerged victorious and who have gained access to females are said to be dominant. One can often tell the dominant male in a group by the way he holds himself. For example, a dominant rhesus monkey keeps his head and tail up, and his testicles down. His movements, as primatologist Stuart Altman puts it, "are slow and deliberate and accompanied by unhesitating but measured scrutiny of other monkeys that cross his field of view."

Dominance is linked to aggressivity. In many species, it has to be reaffirmed constantly, by bluffs and threats, if not by actual fighting. But this isn't always the case. The leader of a wolfpack, for example, can usually control his subordinates without any overt display of aggression. His status, visible in the way he holds his head, ears and tail, and by the confident, face-forward manner in which he approaches other members of the group, is all he needs to maintain his position.

Dominant males tend to play specific roles in group life. They are the defenders, the coordinators, the initiators and the policemen of the group, where such roles exist. They are also the males who reproduce the most.

Failure to achieve dominance has profound physiological effects on males of many species, a phenomenon which has given rise to the term "psychological castration." Subordinate male monkeys tend to have smaller testes, lower sperm levels and lower levels of androgens than do the dominant ones. Observers once believed that these traits were the *cause* of low social status, but experiments have shown that this is not always the case. In some species, when dominant males are removed from a group, so as to allow a previously subordinate male to take over, the new leader's testes enlarge and his production of sperm and androgens rises dramatically. Room at the top means room for growth.

The physiological basis for the connection between dominance, aggressivity, and reproductive success is well established. The same hormone, testosterone, is involved in the expression of both sex and aggression. Experiments have shown that increases in testosterone generally tend to bring about an increase in aggressive behavior *and* an increase in sexual behavior.

This makes good evolutionary sense. Males get sexually aroused when a receptive female is in the vicinity, and the resulting aggressivity helps them to keep other males away from her. The connection between sex and aggressivity plays an important role in the social life of many species. For example, the great British primatologist T. Clutton-Brock and his collaborators discovered that during most of the year male red deer browse quietly alongside other males, but during the mating season the peace is dramatically interrupted. The males become aggressive and begin to fight. Successful stags acquire, and have to defend, harems of up to 30 or more hinds; those who lose out don't get to mate at all.

Where aggressivity plays a smaller role in determining access to females, other forms of competition are likely to be prominent. This is the case among the chimpanzees, whose intelligence most closely resembles our own. Dominant males do try to monopolize estrus females, but they meet with limited success. Because chimpanzees live in fluid, shifting bands, males have a hard time trying to ride herd on the females. As a result, even subordinate males get to mate, and females may well mate with more than one male during an estrus period. So evolution provided male chimps with an anatomical specialization: huge testicles. Chimp testes are almost twice the weight of those of gorillas, despite the fact that gorillas are bigger animals. The anatomical *strategy* of the chimps enables them to produce huge quantities of sperm. In addition, their sperm is unusually motile. These characteristics increase a chimp's chance of producing offspring in the matings he does achieve.[1]

Dominance hierarchies

In many species, the aggressive interactions between males lead to the formation of dominance (status) hierarchies. Where such hierarchies exist, each male has a place and knows who is above him and who is below him; each defers to his superiors and can intimidate his subordinates. These hierarchies serve to reduce the havoc that males might otherwise wreak. Status formalizes and reduces aggression. Very often, the hierarchies determine which males will have access to females. Hence all males must seek to establish a position.

Once established, dominance hierarchies tend to be very stable. Individuals of virtually all mammalian species seem to have a knack for avoiding unequal combat. With uncanny skill, they can judge who is likely to win an agonistic encounter. Often a smaller animal can be seen sizing up a rival and then sidling off without making a challenge. In other cases, a few trials of strength suffice to indicate to one party that further effort is worthless. Protracted struggles usually occur only among animals that are roughly equal. Real battles don't usually occur until some event, such as the aging of a leader, creates a window of opportunity.

As a result, dominant males usually manage to keep other males away from their females without having to resort to violence. Among animals as clever as chimps, only a trained observer can detect what is going on. In his delightful book *Chimpanzee Politics: Power and Sex Among Apes*, Frans de Waal recorded a particularly subtle interaction between two males, Luit and Nikkie. Luit, who ranked lower than Nikkie, was making advances to a female in what he must have thought was a safe place. Unfortunately for him, Nikkie, the Alpha male, caught sight of him.

[1]The chimp sperm was analyzed by Anders Moller of Uppsala University. He also found a strong correlation between testes size, sperm motility, and percentage of mobile sperm across 25 species of primate. Male-male competition will come out, in one way or another.

When Nikkie looked up and got to his feet, Luit slowly shifted a few paces away from the female and sat down . . . with his back to Nikkie. Nikkie slowly moved towards Luit, picking up a heavy stone on his way. His hair was standing slightly on end. Now and then Luit looked around to watch Nikkie's progress and then he looked back at his own penis, which was gradually losing its erection. Only when his penis was no longer visible did Luit turn around and walk towards Nikkie. He briefly sniffed at the stone Nikkie was holding, then he wandered off leaving Nikkie with the female.

Luit is known, in scientific parlance (believe it or not), as a "sneaky fucker," a male who tries to mate behind the back of the dominant animal(s). There are sneaky fuckers in many species, and they have all kinds of tricks. For example, some elephant seals "disguise" themselves as females. They do this by "hiding" their noses. The fully-grown dominant males of this species all have the large proboscis which gave the species its name. The bulls, as they are called, are very aggressive, accumulate large harems and are very intolerant of other adult bulls. In contrast, the young males have small noses, like the females. For a bull, anything which doesn't have an enlarged proboscis is not a threat. So some youngsters sneak into the harems, and sometimes even manage to reproduce themselves. One is reminded of the false eunuchs who, in times gone past, used to trick their sultan.

Social subordination

In many species, males who do not become dominant over other males do not even try to mate. They abandon their attempts to reproduce themselves in the presence of males who rank higher than they do. This is something of a puzzle. One would expect every animal to go to any lengths to reproduce. Why do some of them give up so easily? Part of the answer is fear. Fear inhibits male sexuality. A male who is frightened in the presence of other males will not be able to mate successfully; a male who is afraid of a female will not be able to approach her successfully.

But fear is not the whole story. Another mechanism apparently leads individuals to abandon their competitiveness in the presence of others who are stronger, bigger, or simply well-established. This mechanism is called social subordination. The males of many species seem to accept their subordinate status and clearly signal it. Rank is indicated through posture and also by specific behaviors directed towards the dominant animals. Chimpanzees "greet" the dominant males by uttering a series of short grunts, assuming a position which forces them to look up, and making a series of deep bows. Sometimes a greeting chimp will bring along a gift — a leaf or a stick — which is presented with outstretched arm. Greeting chimps also have been known to kiss the feet, neck and chest of dominant animals.

Why doesn't natural selection favor individuals who are driven to fight to the death for reproductive success? Why do these internalized curbs on aggression exist? The answer is probably that there exists an optimum level of aggressivity. Both too little and too much can reduce an individual's reproductive success. At least four different factors limit the increase of aggressivity in a species' behavioral repertoire:

1. An individual who attacks a rival with intent to destroy is likely to incur a violent counterattack, raising the possibility that both will be injured or killed. The optimum level of aggressive behavior is the one that leads to victory with the least amount of danger to the self.

2. Time spent in aggressive behavior is time taken away from foraging and courtship. A male that spends too much time fighting or jousting with other males may well reduce his reproductive success. In economic terms, this is a matter for cost/benefit analysis; gains must be weighed against losses. Evolutionary gains and losses are measured in the number of surviving genes. A male who does not defend a territory probably will not be able to mate, but a male who dies in combat before the mating season will certainly not mate. Evolution tolerates suicidal genes only under very special circumstances.

3. Killing or maiming relatives can have a negative effect on inclusive fitness. When inclusive fitness is taken into account, it is easy to see why individuals might carry a tendency to avoid violence. Fighting for mates usually involves animals that belong to the same group. These animals will probably be related to each other. If an overly aggressive animal kills a brother, for example, his inclusive fitness declines (because some of the genes held in common by the killer and his brother have been eliminated). Since these genes probably include the ones responsible for aggressivity, such a reduction in inclusive fitness works against aggressive behavior as well; the number of genes favoring aggressivity in the next generation will also be reduced.

4. Males who avoid violence when they are young may outlive the dominant older males and become dominant in their turn.

For all these reasons and perhaps others as well, the males of most species do not engage in indiscriminate violence.

Signals that inhibit aggression

As noted earlier, the aggressive behavior of males is dependent on circumstance. Certain male traits elicit aggressive responses from other males of the same species (the big snouts of elephant seals, the bright colors of birds and fish, etc.). To the extent that females don't give off these signals, they can avoid arousing the hostility of the males. In many species, mere recognition of the sex of an approaching individual is enough to switch a male from aggressive to mating behavior.

Furthermore, the females of many species have developed specific signals to inhibit male aggression. For example, in many primate species, a female who presents her rump can stop a male in mid-attack. Ultimately, this gesture derives from the fact that a female who is willing to copulate must be mounted from the rear, but it has become "ritualized." It is not normally followed by copulation at all; it has become a signal, and nothing more. The signal has been adopted by subordinate males of many species, and they can use it as successfully as can the females.

One must keep in mind that mechanisms inhibiting aggression are effective only under conditions that are normal for the species (the natural environment). When a change in the environment brings about a breakdown of social order and communication, rape and other acts of violence become common.

For most species, there are two essential preconditions for normal social behavior:

1. the availability of adequate resources for the number of individuals who are competing for them, and
2. the presence of sufficient space.

Changes in the environment such as crowding, famine and drought routinely produce an increase in antisocial behaviors such as murder, infanticide and rape. Once again, the principle holds: the behavior of a species is adapted to a particular environment. If the environment changes, the outcomes of the genetic programs that activate the members of the species will change as well.

Signals, sex, and recognition

Mechanisms that inhibit aggression highlight a very important fact. In addition to being able to distinguish between members of their own species and all others, mammals must also distinguish between individuals of their own sex and those of the opposite sex. Individuals who can't make these distinction will not be able to survive and reproduce. They will not be able to survive if they can't distinguish between predators, prey and conspecifics; they will not be able to reproduce if they can't tell one gender from another.

Almost Human? The Case of the Olive Baboons

Before we go on to the reproductive strategy of the human male, we want to devote a little attention to the olive baboons. Baboons are significant because they are the only living primate except humans to have forsaken the trees for the African savannahs. It is therefore interesting that some of their behavior is similar to that of humans.

As we mentioned before, Barbara Smuts, who stayed with the baboons of Kekopey in Kenya for several years, discovered that male and female olive baboons form friendships — long-lasting relationships marked by some degree of reciprocity. Smuts also found that the male dominance hierarchy (which is based on aggressive encounters between males) was not the sole determinant of access to females. Some sexual encounters were based on friendship — free choice and preference.

As friends — why not call them lovers? — the females seem to prefer older males. The older ones are calmer and less inclined to fight than the more aggressive youngsters. Indeed, older males will often get out of the way of younger, more boisterous males who are threatening and bluffing.

Shirley Strum, author of *Almost Human*, another fine book on the olive baboons, seems to believe that the importance of friendship indicates that "dominance" is not the key to sex among olive baboons, but this conclusion is open to dispute. We think it would be more accurate to say that social skills and aggressivity are both components of dominance among these baboons. Female olive baboons are attracted to wiser, more reliable males who know their way around and who can be depended upon for protection in case of need. Such males are so self-confident that they cannot be bothered with the frantic posturing of the young males who are seeking to establish themselves. The older males who are successful with females are invariably big — twice as big as the females — and they are quite willing to fight if necessary, but they avoid it.

Boldness remains a useful trait and powerful males who are not "friends" also obtain many mating opportunities. So one cannot really argue that "dominance" does not play a role in olive baboon society. What is true is this: dominance among olive baboons had somewhat unusual characteristics. We shall see, in the next section, that it bears many resemblances to dominance in human society. Apparently, our relatively close genetic relationship and the similar environment in which our genes evolved produced species with many behavioral traits in common.

The Human Male

The human male is a mammal and a primate, and much of what he does is clearly an expression of the basic reproductive strategy of the mammalian male. No one should be surprised that such a being should show aggressivity, competitiveness, a tendency to bluster, the desire to possess many females, jealousy, and possessiveness.

However, in the transition to humanity, the character of male behavior underwent a tranformation. Males began to rely much less on threats, bluffing, aggressive displays, and violence. Discussion, negotiation, compromise and consensus became crucial. Conflict resolution became a major activity. And family life became a priority.

What forces changed the human male? We believe that two requirements of the hunter-gatherer way of life were crucial: the increased importance of paternal investment and the increased need for cooperation between males.

Paternal investment

Evolution endowed the human male with a tendency to provide support for his offspring because, in the natural environment, human children need the care of more than one adult to survive. The contribution of the males is essential; they provide much of the food that the children eat. As we have already seen, high levels of male parental investment are rare among mammals and among our primate cousins. No one ever saw a chimpanzee or olive baboon male feeding one of his offspring. At best, a youngster may gain a small piece of meat, if game has been killed—a relatively unusual occurrence.

Hunter-gatherer boys also need male role models. Children have much to learn before being able to function as adults, and the male and female roles are different. Most of the learning is accomplished through imitation. If the child is male, there must be a man around to imitate. It doesn't have to be the biological father, but it does have to be someone who acts like a father.

As we mentioned before, hunter-gatherer men not only provide meat for their families, but also spend a lot of time around the children. They play with them, tolerate their interruptions, allow themselves to be mauled, and virtually never rebuke or punish them, except when the children do something stupid that exposes them to danger. Obviously, human males have been endowed with a capacity to get pleasure from home life, stability and permanent attachment. How did this come about?

The mechanism that seems to have been responsible is sexual selection — female choice. Once paternal investment began to be important to the survival of young hominids (prehumans — see Chapter 2), females began to *select* males for their potential paternal investment. In order to choose such males, females had to find ways to uncover the qualities which attach a male to a family. These qualities are emotional: a taste for children, an ability to control or repress the tendency to philander, perhaps an interest in the female as an individual. Also required is what might be called a "feel" for reciprocity — a willingness to exchange things of value (meat for other kinds of food). Eventually, these qualities came to characterize (the majority of) human beings. But the old impulses didn't disappear. Human males did not lose the drive to maximize reproductive success by mating with as many females as possible. The new emotions were simply added onto the old ones.

The result was a blend, or a mosaic. Human males apparently follow a mixed strategy, one which might be called "partial adaptation to paternal investment." Men carry within them a bundle of complex impulses and needs. They are attracted to the family and yet can often be found seeking sexual excitement outside of it. They are not completely monogamous, yet they don't do well without a family. They waffle, investing heavily in the offspring of one woman (or at most a few), but also seeking sexual opportunities on the side.

Let us look at how this mixed strategy gets expressed in an individual case. Werner, a very young, very good-looking executive on the threshold of success, prided himself on being unlike the "typical male." He wasn't out to have sex with every possible female. He wanted his sex in the context of a relationship. He didn't turn on until he felt affection.

The consequences were strange. In the initial stages of a relationship, he was very thoughtful, very considerate. Sincerely so. He genuinely wanted his girlfriends to be happy. Naturally, the women he dated were appreciative. Indeed, his problem was that women were always falling in love with him. He loved the intensity of these relationships, but had never found the woman he wanted to spend the rest of his life with. Eventually, he would find it necessary to break off the relationship, in order to continue his search for Ms. Right. He genuinely felt that each relationship was a trial. He entered each one sincerely, and gave it his best shot.

He never wanted to hurt the women whom he had outgrown, so he generally waited until he could pick a fight of some sort. Then he backed out quickly, satisfied that he had stayed with her until she demonstrated that she was not the one.

CLINICAL VIGNETTE: SHERMAN

This vignette illustrates the use of the concept of female reproductive strategy in the treatment of a man.

Sherman had a history of brief, highly-charged relationships with women. He was an emotion junkie; he got high on interpersonal interaction. But when the women began to talk marriage and commitment, he invariably fled. He explained this as follows: "When they start to lay a guilt trip on me, I have to get out of it." He didn't feel responsible for their desires and couldn't understand why they always had to "spoil things." On the other hand, he professed a desire to establish a long-term relationship and to have children.

About six months after entering therapy, he revealed that he had met a wonderful new woman: open, fresh, free-spirited. The therapist said: "I'll bet you're attracted to her because you think that she's different. She's going to want to have an intense relationship with no strings attached." He admitted, somewhat shamefacedly, that the therapist had guessed right.

The therapist took this opportunity to explain to him the elements of the female reproductive strategy, then added:

I would bet that even if she starts out by wanting a casual affair, she will change her mind if you open up to her emotionally. You will have to choose. You can keep some distance and maintain a casual relationship. Or you can open up the way you've always done and then suffer through the pangs of leaving her. The choice is yours, but you can't have it both ways.

(continued)

He was somewhat confused by the reactions of these women. They didn't seem to understand his sincerity: "I know a lot of guys who don't have this problem. All they want to do is screw around. They seem to get a lot of sex without all this hassle. I don't understand it. Women never just jump into bed with me."

After some discussion of reproductive strategies, Werner perceived that he was putting out a mixed message. He was indicating to women that he was interested in a long-term relationship. He was advertising himself as a potential source of paternal investment, but was not delivering on his promise. What was happening? Unlike his friends, who clearly indicated that they were just out to have some fun, Werner consistently elicited a deeper reaction from women. As a result, they felt betrayed when he failed to deliver what he seemed to be promising.

CLINICAL VIGNETTE: SHERMAN *(continued)*

He was chagrined, but he said he could now understand how and why he was triggering the reaction he so detested. However, he said he might be "falling in love" and wouldn't be able to help himself. "Are you falling in love with a real person, or with your fantasy about what women want?" He couldn't answer. A few sessions later, the subject came up again. "What do you want, a long-term or a short-term relationship?" He replied by affirming that the lady was too young, and had too many things going for her, to be interested in settling down.

This apparently evasive response was actually very significant. Sherman's fantasy about what this woman wanted was crucial to his behavior pattern. As long as he could believe that the woman didn't want a long-term relationship, he could be as intense as he wanted without taking any responsibility for the consequences. If she started to get involved, he could accuse her of breaking their bargain. He could then leave with a (relatively) good conscience. He saw this as soon as it was pointed out, and immediately realized the implications. He didn't like them: "I don't want to give up these emotions. They get me through the hard times."

From that point on, therapy focused on getting him to accept women the way they are. As often as necessary, the therapist stressed the need to accept that the probability of finding a woman who would enjoy an intense emotional experience without wanting it to continue was low (unless he wanted to spend his life with borderline personalities).

Note that the concept of reproductive strategy, like all other concepts described in this book, is used not to prescribe behavior, but to clarify options. Therapy never tried to induce Sherman to choose one type of behavior over another. Rather, it clarified the consequences of different types of behavior. The choice was left up to him.

What we have here seems to be self-deception in the service of deception. Werner clearly believes in the purity of his intentions. He genuinely craves affection with his sex. He does not mean to injure or deceive. But in effect, he is gaining access to females by simulating something that they value.

We believe that Werner is "normal." We did not find any evidence to indicate that his pattern is due to some abnormality in his upbringing, although psychoanalysts would obviously argue otherwise. Furthermore, we find this pattern in far too many men to believe that it is pathological.

To us, it seems that evolution has acted to create males who will be both good family men and successful seducers. Werner needs the kind of affection and commitment that one gets from a wife, but he also needs to seek out and mate with many women, and the women he will find will generally be interested in paternal investment. Hence he has an innate capacity to appeal to their desire for commitment, as well as an innate capacity to propel himself out of a relationship when it suits his purposes.

Now let us look at a passage in Patrick Carnes' book *The Sexual Addiction*:

> Del [a brilliant, charming and witty lawyer] would initiate relationships with women, feeling that he was "in love." After the initial sexual contact, he would desperately wish to be free. These relationships became characterized by his ambivalence. He wanted to be sexual, but he did not want the relationship. Yet he couldn't say "no" clearly without fear of hurting the woman's feelings, so he never quite broke off the relationships. Instead he hoped their frustration would force them to give up. The result was that he had a series of relationships at the same time in various stages of initiation and frustration.

Carnes fails to see significance in the fact that Del doesn't want to hurt the feelings of the women he has affairs with. Unlike Carnes, we believe that Del does "want" (crave) a relationship, but is unable to manage his ambivalent feelings. Like Werner, Del is only partially adapted to paternal investment. Why was Del unable to balance his conflicting impulses? We suspect that his ability to do so was impaired by some aspect of his upbringing. But he may also have been born with a weaker predisposition toward family life.

Cooperation

Unlike most other primates, human males are able to work together in teams on a semi-permanent basis. This is almost certainly a result of the switch to hunting. It was teamwork that enabled our ancestors to bring down the huge animals that they began to hunt around one and a half million years ago. Cooperation became essential to survival.

As excessive competitiveness became a liability, humans developed various means for controlling aggression. Hunter-gatherer men tend to seek consensus. People who give orders or act superior become the object of ridicule. Decisions seem to emerge without anyone making them. In addition, the men have all kinds of methods for resolving disputes. A common element is the tendency to diffuse hostility between individuals by involving the group as a whole. Of the endless examples in the literature, we'll give only one:

Mating and the Incest Taboo

The reluctance to mate with familiar females goes deep and is very probably connected to the incest taboo. Data from many sources, including Israeli kibbutzim and the marriage records of China, where there was once a custom of raising betrothed children in the same household, show that children who are raised together in their early years almost never mate or marry successfully. The critical period appears to be around age four to six years. The point is that familiarity is crucial in keeping brothers and sisters from mating. We believe that the same mechanism makes it difficult for men to sustain sexual interest in familiar women.

This helps us to understand the conditions under which the incest taboo is most likely to be breached—when fathers are away at war or work when their daughters are little, or when siblings are raised apart. Adoption researchers also know the sexual passions that often flame up when sons who were given up for adoption are at last reunited with their birth mothers. (Many of the mothers have had their sons when very young, and so are still at an age when they would be expected to be attractive to young adults.) Interestingly, the almost subliminal sense of recognition that these dyads experience upon being reunited seems to add to the passion.

The existence of a familiarity barrier has profound consequences for our culture's current idea of marriage. While it is true that a certain amount of closeness and involvement promotes sexual interest, as in office romances, more and more closeness may be a turnoff. The ideal of a spouse being lover *and* best friend may lead, in time, to sexual cooling, no matter how well the spouses get along. Naturally, the inevitable resentments and conflicts of marriage further contribute to sexual difficulties.

We would expect that on the average males will be more inhibited by closeness than females. Nevertheless, beyond a certain point, females will also find themselves turned off by the familiar and tempted by novelty. Hence, in any normal twosome, one will eventually want more distance and pull away.

Most therapists, acting intuitively, advise the partner who wants more closeness to refrain from pursuing, in hopes that the distancing partner will turn around and come back when the need for closeness has returned, a tactic which is fully in accord with our analysis.

If the question is one of marriage, and a father announces that he does not like the girl his son has chosen, his son can call on all his friends to help him. If he is strong and holds out, the whole group will be assembled to discuss the case. If they agree with the father, then either the boy has to give up his talk of matrimony, or else make up his mind to marry the girl anyway. In the latter case, he would probably go and live with her hunting group . . . (Turnbull, 1962).

By bringing in the group, the hunter-gatherers allow everyone to save face, and thereby to remain "undefeated."

The ability to cooperate is what made it possible for humans to formulate the idea of "equality." One cannot accept equal status if one feels that one is "losing" whenever one is "not winning" (not defeating someone).

Note in passing that Freud's bizarre notion, elaborated in *Totem and Taboo,* of the revolt of the brothers against the father could, by stretching it, be taken as a metaphor for the ancestral transition from reliance on dominance hierarchies to the collegiality of hunting and gathering.

The changed nature of dominance

One might easily conclude that dominance plays no role in hunter-gatherer society, but we think this would be a mistake. We believe, rather, that new ways of expressing it came into being. Men changed, but they did not change altogether.

Hunter-gatherer customs contain elements of ritual combat not unlike that of other mammalian species. Witness this passage from Asen Balikci's account of the Netsilik Eskimo:

Any man could challenge another to a fist fight for any reason. Usually, they stripped to the waist and the challenger received the first blow. Only one blow was given at a time, directed against temple or shoulder. Opponents stood without guard and took turns, the contest continuing until one of the fighters had had enough and gave up. *This seemed to settle the quarrel, for as one informant put it: After the fight it is all over; it was as if they had never fought before* (italics added).

The Netsilik also had "song duels," which Balikci describes as a semiritual form of conflict resolution. But, says Balikci, these bouts of ritualized aggression had a "dyadic, contractual character creating special reciprocal bonds." In other words, *men walked away from these affairs without feeling humiliated and ashamed*. They may have lost a round, but they were not defeated.

We believe that this points to the new and special character of dominance among human males: *men could win without defeating others.* Dominance became more of an internalized sense than a matter of interpersonal display. This meant that a man could be dominant if he felt dominant. He didn't have to put anyone else down. Indeed, to be an accepted member of a group, a man had to have the capacity to forego the struggle for power and attention at least *some* of the time—without experiencing a sense of defeat.

We argue—and we know we are taking our lives into our hands—that human males naturally seek dominance, and must achieve it or pay a high price. The new kind of dominance—flexible or shifting dominance—doesn't involve defeating others, and *certainly does not involve pushing women around; pushing women around is an unquestionable sign of weakness.* "Dominance" in humans is not the same as "domineering" or "domination." Indeed, even in other species, the dominant male is often a peacemaker and a protector.[2]

The new kind of dominance is closely connected to what is generally known as self-esteem. But the term self-esteem does not adequately convey the combination of strength, self-control, mastery and sexuality that dominance implies. Furthermore, the notion of self-esteem does not provide a link to other species, and we feel very strongly that the study of human behavior must emphasize our links with the natural world. Hence, despite our misgivings, we have found it necessary to attempt to restore some respectability to the notion of dominance.

Dominance today is known by other words: charisma, prestige, leadership, power, mastery, control, autonomy, self-confidence, etc. The search for dominance can take the form of striving for excellence, boasting, and especially outdoing other people in the performance of a useful task. It has been put to new uses, but it is still there.

Dominance now has many disguises. Take for example the concept of "cool." The cool man does not show fear, demonstrates benign indifference, and appears at ease in unfamiliar surroundings. He appears to have the ability to cope with any challenge. This is behavior that any mature olive baboon would understand. Dominance sometimes appears as "inner-directedness," as personal vision or conviction, as integrity, or as commitment to a cause. All of these attributes are sexually attractive to some women.

And what about elections? The "wimp factor" has now become a cliché. Successful candidates must appear calm and masterful. The appearance of

[2]We would like to acknowledge here the contribution of John Price and Leon Sloman, who for quite a few years have been developing an approach to human problems based on the notion of dominance.

weakness must be avoided. A shrill voice can lose many votes. What the pundits call leadership is just another disguise of dominance.

What is not dominant? Again there are many forms: neediness, dependence, refusal to take responsibility, being apologetic, desire for mothering, a supplicatory attitude, fear of giving offense, unwillingness to make decisions or to initiate, always asking how others feel, saying, "Was it good for you, dear?" etc. Women who complain that their men are weak or are acting like little boys are really complaining that their men lack the attributes of dominance.

As an example of nondominance, we offer the following dialogue with a woman client who was blaming herself for problems in her marriage:

T: Is there anything about your husband that could connect to the terrible arguments that you have?
C: I don't know, it's hard for me to go back and get in touch with what is going on in my mind at the time. But now that I think about it, it may have something to do with his trying to be so nice to me. I mean, I like his being so considerate and all, but sometimes he tries so hard to, I don't know, please me, I guess, that it seems to get in the way. He keeps on doing it and finally I just want him to go away and let me do it by myself. Sometimes I think he just does it out of guilt or something. It makes it seem like he's giving up all responsibility, you know? It's like he's a little boy. He's so passive, I want to choke him or something just to get a reaction out of him.

Clearly then, achieving dominance in human society is difficult to manage. It requires great flexibility. The overbearing, tyrannical man is not dominant and neither is the weak, fearful man. The dominant man can make concessions, achieve compromise, and allow others to have their say and their opinions. In the hunter-gatherer system, most if not all men managed to achieve dominance. We shall argue that in our society, most men don't, and thus may suffer psychological distress.

In summary: The human male was reshaped, physically and mentally, by the needs of females and their offspring. The result was a creature with an unlikely combination of traits. He is driven to maximize his reproductive success by mating with many females, but is also disposed to invest heavily in a family. He responds to many women—the Coolidge Effect—but is bound by his children to one family. He has been selected for his ability to ejaculate swiftly and move on, but now has to cope with the sexual needs of females who have developed a capacity for orgasm and who have a need for extended foreplay. Understandably, these diverse impulses create a good deal of inner conflict.

As might be expected, individual males respond very differently to their multiplicity. Some become Don Juans; they actually seek to live out the old mammalian strategy of mating with all the available females.[3] Most, however, just fantasize about it, and cautiously accept the few opportunities that present themselves. At the other end of the spectrum, some men allow their sexual activity to diminish steadily over the years, accept sexual boredom as a fact of life, and fail miserably to meet their spouse's undiminishing need for affection and pleasure.

The social arrangements of our species also seem to reflect the mixed heritage of the human male. George Murdoch's monumental *Ethnographic Atlas* clearly shows that most known human societies were polygynous (i.e., allowed marriages involving one man and several women). This arrangement would seem to be a cultural response to the male reproductive strategy.

With this in mind, one can perhaps understand the ambivalence of modern men. They complain bitterly about the bondage of marriage, but surprisingly, they find it harder to adjust to being single than do females. Research indicates that single men have more physical and psychological problems than women. Why then do men so often seek to escape from their marriages? If our analysis is correct, the "commandment" to be faithful is the culprit. Men did evolve into creatures who need marriage, so being married is better than being single. But married men retain the desire for more women. Polygyny seems to have been one common consequence of this duality. In our society, sequential monogamy seems to be the most common response.

Sequential monogamy has ancient roots. Hunter-gatherer marriages, writes Helen Fisher in the October 1987 issue of *Natural History*, often ended in divorce. Of 331 marriages reported by !Kung women to sociologist Nancy Howell, 134 ended in divorce. Some men and women had more than four consecutive spouses. Sequential monogamy may be an institution that surfaces whenever strict social enforcement of marriage weakens. But however ancient, serial monogamy is a major problem for women in a society such as ours, because more often than not it results in a loss of income for

---

[3]Interestingly enough, many homosexual men actually live out the male dream of promiscuity. This is probably because a major limiting factor on the sexual contacts of male heterosexuals is female choosiness. Since male homosexuals are not any more choosy than male heterosexuals, there is no built-in limitation on promiscuity.

THE PLAYBOY PHILOSOPHY

Playboy magazine seems to us to play on a fundamental wish of men that women, at least some women, especially some beautiful and sexually desirable women, want the same thing men want—to just get together and have terrific sex without fussing much about relationships. We doubt if many *Playboy* readers take this seriously, but they sure do enjoy the fantasy.

The men are out of luck, of course. The *Playboy* women want sports cars, film contracts, and eventually, good husbands, but they don't generally want the kind of commitment-free sex that men want. It goes against their biology.

Ironically, some feminists have argued that women *are* like men in this respect. Or even more so, since women can have more orgasms. Some theorists of this persuasion even get offended when someone says that women aren't as naturally promiscuous as men. Equality über alles?

women. The standard of living of women generally drops after divorce, while that of men rises—a phenomenon which is contributing strongly to the feminization of poverty.

A final word. We are not of course advocating the restoration of polygamy or the acceptance of serial monogamy. Ours is a work of analysis, not social reconstruction. Nor can we help it if the needs of males and females are different. In this chapter and the next, we are simply trying to account for the trouble men have dealing with existing institutions and mores. There is no solution which is optimal for everyone.

In the next chapter, we turn again to the modern world, where we will look at some of the problems experienced by human males as they try to make their way in an environment to which they are not adapted, an environment in which their natural moves do not produce the results they expect.

CHAPTER 10

Men on the
Contemporary Scene

It's a wise man who knows his own son.
—Folk saying

A MAN IS A MOSAIC. He is a primate, the descendent of males who organized themselves in dominance hierarchies and who gained access to females by competing with and outdoing other males. Yet he has been reshaped by the need to get along in bands where cooperation and reciprocity were essential for survival and reproduction. A creature that complicated will have some problems getting along in any kind of society. When he is obliged, once again, to live in a society that is organized along formal hierarchical lines, all kinds of troubles can be expected. It is to this subject that we now turn our attention.

Some Current Problems

The effects of hierarchy

A hierarchical society is one in which there are official positions which carry with them higher or lower status. Such societies are usually characterized by specialization, bureaucracy, social classes, and inequality.[1]

[1]Many of the problems that are associated with hierarchical societies were first identified in "capitalism," a fact which has given rise to a vast body of anti-capitalist literature. Capitalism, however, is only one form of hierarchical society. Communist and socialist societies, whatever their utopian illusions, are also organized on a

In hierarchical societies, most men are under the control of someone else. They must submit to the will of an authority. They must follow instructions, obey orders, and operate according to rules that they didn't make and that they don't always understand. Most men, most of the time, do not feel in control of their destiny. In our terminology, they do not experience themselves as dominant.

In a sense, hierarchical societies are a reversion to a prehuman type of social organization.[2] As we saw in the previous chapter, the male dominance hierarchy plays a crucial role in the social life of virtually all primate species, but the role of the hierarchy declined during the transition to humanity. In hunter-gatherer life, talking took over many of the functions of threat displays. Most of the time, adult males were not subordinate to anyone, and no one ruled over anyone else; the band was composed of autonomous, cooperating individuals. True, in some hunter-gatherer societies, one can find forms of leadership which are semi-institutionalized; the power of the elders among the Australian Aborigines is a case in point (Elkin, 1938/1964). But nowhere do we find anything comparable to the highly stratified, rigidly hierarchical systems that characterize so many agricultural and industrial societies.

Most people don't like living in hierarchies based on strength or power, and we think this dislike is innate. It is embodied in the notion of "bully." Children hate a boy who tries to get his way by force. The tactics of the bully may succeed for a time, but eventually a coalition tends to form against him and he is forced to back off.

Life in a modern hierarchical environment places some unique strains on the psyche. It requires the capacity for conformity and cooperation that

---

hierarchical basis, as are most "pre-capitalist" systems, such as the city states of Greece, the Roman Empire and the latifundias of Latin America. In fact, for all intents and purposes, all societies that have moved beyond slash and burn agriculture have been hierarchical in nature. All of them add a new dimension to male-male competition, because in all of them the distribution of resources other than females (which males already compete for in most species) depends on the outcome of competition.

[2]There's an interesting sidelight on the issue of hierarchical societies being a "throwback." Psychiatrist Lial Kofoed of the University of Oregon and his collaborator James McMillan recently argued that "social dominance behaviors such excessive bragging, arguments, bar fights, arm wrestling tournaments, etc., are exaggerated in social settings where alcohol is consumed." If they are right, and common sense indicates that they are, then it would seem that threat behaviors remain a part of the human male's repertoire, ready to come out when "released" by the appropriate stimulus.

once served to unite a hunting and gathering band, but does not not necessarily provide the equality, mutual respect, and support that once was the payoff. Most people are able to "go along to get along," but many people pay a high price. The adverse effects range from irritability, chronic dissatisfaction and lack of initiative, to physical disability, addiction and depression.

Hierarchies, dominance, and sex

As we have seen, subordinate mammal males generally reproduce much less successfully than their dominant brothers. However, in the current human environment, the connection between dominance and reproduction has been broken. In modern societies, ambitious and successful men, foregoing inclusive fitness to personal satisfaction, often limit their reproduction, so that they have fewer offspring than men who are poor and unsuccess-

---

CLINICAL VIGNETTE: THE TROUBLE WITH SUCCESS

Sean was a simple technician when he started therapy. He was confused about a lot of things, but he knew he wanted to get rich. His mind was always turning over money-making schemes, and he worked himself hard to get ahead, at considerable sacrifice to his health and his personal development. He knew that this concerned the therapist, but he thought it was because the therapist had "hippie values." Whenever the subject of his lifestyle came up, he accused the therapist of trying to keep him poor.

After a few years, he went into business for himself, and soon began to hit the big money. But he approached his first million without showing any signs of enjoying life more. When the therapist began to pressure him about his compulsive behavior, he gave this answer:

I can't just enjoy myself. When I sit around without thinking of money, I start to disappear. I become nothing. I feel my life slipping away. I reach out for gold, for expensive things. If there aren't any new ones around to make me feel that I've accomplished something, I start to go crazy. So I go back to thinking about business again. I know it's a vicious circle, but there it is.

This passage provides a somewhat unsettling image of the force that drives many of the people who rise to the top of our hierarchies.

ful. What remains, however, is the connection between dominance and sex.

Human males with low self-esteem and little sense of power, i.e., who lack an internalized sense of dominance, often suffer from sexual dysfunctions: impotence, lack of desire, inability to experience pleasure (anhedonia), and/or ejaculatory incompetence (premature and retarded ejaculation). Hence, the hierarchical, competitive system that we live in has an adverse effect on male functioning. Even the men who "win" may develop sexual problems, because the demands made on them force them to sacrifice their personal lives. Rising in the hierarchy does not automatically convey dominance. Far from it. The top is always elusive, and the stress of getting there is inimical to sexuality.

The workplace and the home

Chronic subordination in the workplace produces different reactions in different men. Some become passive, watch television, and leave their wives to manage the house, the kids and all the other details of life. To escape their woes, some immerse themselves in sports, particularly TV sports, and identify with heroes such as Larry Bird and Magic Johnson. A substantial number slide into heavy drinking or drug abuse. Still others try to compensate for their lack of status in the workplace by turning their homes into barracks. They become martinets, giving orders to their wives and dispensing punishment to their children. In the worst cases, this ends up as wife-beating and child abuse.

The problem with success

Men who manage to rise in hierarchical societies are not immune from its adverse effects. Because most business hierarchies promote the tendency to think in terms of winning and losing, rather than survival and pleasure, they stimulate competitiveness and devalue the cooperative, affiliative traits that humanity acquired in the last phases of its evolution. The competition never stops. There is always another round to fight, another rung to climb.

Even reasonably successful men can develop the emotional coldness that women frequently complain about—an opaque "front" which walls them off from other people. They seem to be doing just fine, but in reality have cut themselves off from ordinary emotions. As husbands, they may become impassive and remote. Some may act despotically around the house, but most are more likely to leave domestic affairs to their wives. As fathers, they tend to be stern and distant, taking an interest in the doings of their children only when there are successes to be praised or infractions to be punished.

They forego friendship and disparage love. They feel they have to prove themselves constantly, so they treat all other men as if they were potential rivals. For the most alienated—those for whom everything in life depends on their ultimate "success" (final position in the hierarchy)—family life becomes a simple matter of convenience, sexuality a matter of stress reduction, and leisure a preparation for tomorrow's battles.

Both winners and losers are subject to excessive levels of stress. Anxiety and tension are intensified by the constant need to impress superiors and keep ahead of subordinates. There is constant pressure from above and from below. The stress is inimical to health, sex, marriage, and social relationships. Perhaps this is what Thoreau had in mind when he wrote: "The mass of men lead lives of quiet desperation."

Devaluation of the male role

The problems of men in modern society are aggravated by the increasing devaluation of two traditional male activities: provisioning and defense.

Provisioning. Ever since high levels of abundance made it possible for women to provide for themselves and their children without help from a man, the importance of having a male in the family has been diminishing. Furthermore, while most men still bring home the bacon, they no longer go out to hunt for pig. Most men make their living in ways which do not allow them to experience the thrill of the chase and the joy of the successful hunt. Neither shuffling papers in an office nor lifting crates on a dock seems to be a truly satisfactory substitute.

Men need people to provide for, but the processes they use to fulfill this need are becoming trivial. Here is modern man singing of his role:

> Sleep my wife sleep
> the taxes have been paid
> in full
> and the car
> was inspected for the winter.

This fragment from a poem by Amos Naor, an Israeli-born psychiatrist and poet, captures the essence of the male's plight. Man's protective impulses have become anachronistic and comical. There is a mismatch between genes and environment. Some men can easily adjust; others cannot.

Defense. In modern industrial societies, defense has become the province of specialized functionaries (police and military). Individual males no longer have to protect themselves and their loved ones. In fact, they aren't supposed to. There are laws against the possession of weapons, and in some states, the law requires that a man flee, rather than fight, if his house is invaded. Furthermore, technology has created weapons that simply cannot be used. Aggression, which was once a survival mechanism, has become a threat to survival. Instead of being able to take pride in their power, men must be wary of it. This does not enhance their self-esteem or their sexuality.

Other contributing social factors

The problems of men in this society also must be understood in the context of two other important social institutions, one old and one new: religion and the women's movement.

The problems of males (and females, of course) are exacerbated by religions which equate sexuality with sin. The effects of repressive sexual doctrines are well known. Otherwise normal men become obsessed with sex and suffer deeply from the belief that they are dirty and that their desires are shameful. This self-hatred results in sexual dysfunction and in hostility towards women, since women are responsible for evoking the feelings that are labeled shameful.

The women's movement, with its emphasis on on competition and independence, has further complicated the situation. Competition being what it is, men now lose not only to other men, but also to women. This is certainly no better, and probably more confusing, than losing to other men. But if men don't want to lose, they must learn to treat women the same way they treat men—as competitors to be defeated at any cost. This goes against the grain. Like many other mammals, human males have inhibitions against aggression towards females. They have to train themselves—steel themselves, in many cases—to fight with women.

One result is that even when men are not in direct competition with women, they must often fight against their impulses to treat women protectively. Many men are afraid to open doors, to pay for dinners, and to be romantic, for fear of giving offense. And many are hurt and confused by this. Some women might reply: "Learn new behavior." Good advice, but often easier said than done, when a behavior has biological roots.

Men must learn two modes of relating to women: one for social settings, and one for business. Some men find it difficult to develop two entirely different and conflicting approaches to the opposite sex. How does one know when to be cognizant of gender and when to pretend to ignore it? How does one learn to shift back and forth with ease? Some men have the flexibility and the self-awareness to modulate their behavior with sufficient precision; others don't.

At worst, men in therapy today are caught between two sets of conflicting expectations. They are attacked for being patriarchal brutes, and scorned for being weak. Their tendencies towards protectiveness are mocked while at the same time they are asked to be more involved with their families. They are expected to be better lovers, while at the same time having their power and authority challenged. This is not a comfortable situation.

Alternative Reproductive Strategies

An objection may at this point be running through the reader's mind: "I know many men who aren't like that at all." Quite right. As we have often repeated, there is substantial genetic diversity in the human population. Some men are less predisposed than others to compete with other men and to engage in typical male display behaviors. Such men welcome the opportunity to cast off tradition. They are delighted to have the freedom to express themselves emotionally, to act in more nurturing ways, and to express "female" aspects of their nature. For them, the "new masculinity" has been a godsend.

Such men may be predisposed to what is called an alternative reproductive strategy. One example is the "sneaky-fucker" strategy, which we described in the previous chapter. Sneakers, as they might be called in more genteel parlance, are found among mammalian males of many different species. They don't attempt to out-compete other males. Rather, they exploit opportunities to mate with females who are not being monopolized by the dominant males.

The reader no doubt winces at the use of such a term to describe human behavior. We suggest the term "opportunist." Opportunism can be used to describe a wide variety of heterosexual behavioral styles: nondominating, nonthreatening, affiliative, emotional, cuddly, etc. (We specify "heterosexual" here because homosexual men are not seeking access to women.) While the development of such a style can be affected by learning and culture, there is evidence that strong stylistic preferences emerge very early in life. Some boys, for example, show a spontaneous interest in competition; others don't.

We suspect that the importance of paternal investment has heightened the effectiveness of the opportunist strategy in humans. Since women attach great weight to a man's potential as a provider and family member, men who are not particularly powerful, magnetic, charismatic, or physically imposing, i.e., men who do not have the appearance of dominance, can (more easily) find mates. Indeed, some women feel that the less-dominant types are preferable as husbands. This makes it easier for human males to succeed, sexually and reproductively, without male-male competition.[3]

Now to the question of flexibility. Natural selection seems to have favored primates who can adjust their behavior to meet different situations. Humans are an extreme example of that trend. Thus, individual humans can be expected to display different behaviors in different situations. This means that men can be expected to have some ability to shift from one reproductive strategy to another, depending on circumstances.

Many people have used this fact to argue against the notion that humans are genetically predisposed to *any* particular strategy or type of behavior. We of course are not convinced. Some people are indeed very flexible and can adjust easily to all kinds of situations, even if they have a built-in preference for one style or another. Thus, some men without any genetic predisposition to an alternate strategy find themselves perfectly comfortable in situations which put a premium on connectedness. Other men are less flexible. For whatever reason — usually a combination of genetic and environmental factors — they find it difficult if not impossible to change strategies effectively. They will require help.

Alternative strategies in the workplace

In the workplace, noncompetitive behavior can often be an effective strategy. In many organizations today, the best jobs are often offered to men who have not challenged their superiors and who have made no enemies in the course of undistinguished careers. Government bureaucracies are, of course, notorious for rewarding sheer durability. As in other mammalian

---

[3]Homosexuality may also be an alternative strategy for the promotion of inclusive fitness (Trivers, 1974; Wilson, 1975), but is too complicated a subject to be treated here. No one has as yet succeeded in teasing apart the role of biology and socialization in the genesis of homosexual behavior. We do think that homosexual men who are experiencing psychological distress require a different treatment approach than the one described in this chapter. This is because homosexual men do not seek access to women, and it is not clear that homosexual pairing is an entirely apt parallel. We might also point out that one of the main ideas in this book, namely, concern about the mismatch between genes and culture, also applies to homosexuals. Western society has not managed to develop a way to appreciate the special strengths of homosexual men without stigmatizing them as deviants. As anthropologist W. Williams showed in *The Spirit and the Flesh*, many other societies accord them special status and provide them with appropriate roles. The absence of such a role probably contributes to the psychological distress American homosexuals currently experience.

societies, if one waits long enough, the old leaders are bound to die off, leaving room at the top for those who have stayed out of battle. Indeed, natural selection has probably acted to favor primates who strive for high status (dominance) if they are likely to succeed, but who bide their time if the situation is not favorable.

The avoidance of competition has many advantages. If fighting is likely to lead to injury or death, it's better to avoid fighting. If aggressivity is likely to call up the wrath of stronger beings, it's wiser to hold one's peace. If the attempt to acquire more resources is likely to endanger what one already has, it may pay to moderate one's desires. Hence the timeless expression of folk-wisdom: discretion is the better part of valor.

Enzo and Injustice

Enzo was an experienced craftsman who took a great deal of pride in his work. He insisted on doing the job right or not at all. He could not compromise. As a result, he was in constant conflict with his supervisors, who were concerned primarily with profits and customer relations. The stress had produced a variety of symptoms, including insomnia, lack of appetite, and an obsessional concern with the minutiae of his interactions with his boss. His wife was threatening to leave him because he kept going over and over the same ground.

His problems came to a head when he was obliged to take a job in a small, owner-operated shop specializing in the quick and dirty. For weeks, Enzo complained to me about this boss, and we had the following exchange over and over again:

C: He tells me that the work I do is great. The best anyone ever did on his machines. But he keeps shoving stuff at me, piling up the jobs, promising customers that they'll be done today, tomorrow, whenever they want. I keep telling him that I can't produce quality work under these conditions, but he doesn't listen.
T: Do you think he might be telling you that he doesn't mind if you don't do such careful work all the time?

Enzo did not seem to understand. As time went on, he began to find other problems with his boss:

(*continued*)

Enzo and Injustice (*continued*)

C: The guy's an incompetent, I tell you. He doesn't understand his own business. People come there because of the work I do. He'll drive that place into the ground. He gets the work orders all mixed up, he doesn't have supplies on hand for the jobs he books, the place is a mess.
T: I believe you, Enzo. But it's his place and he's been there a long time. Why don't you just do it the way he wants it while you're there, look for another job, and stop worrying about it.
C: There's no way I'm going to let a guy who doesn't even know the business tell me how to do my job.
T: It's tough when the guy above you really isn't better qualified than you are, isn't it?
C: You better believe it. Why the hell should he be making all the money, while I'm breaking my ass for peanuts?

The therapist tried to validate Enzo's values without encouraging the self-defeating behavior they were associated with:

T: You know, in the natural environment, things would be the way you say. No one would have to take orders from people who didn't have superior skills. You wouldn't have to follow anyone you didn't really look up to and admire. So you're absolutely right to feel the way you do. But that's the way it is in America. There are hierarchies. You've got to come to terms with the way things are now.

Enzo was a very competitive person who had neither the skills to master the current environment nor the flexibility to avoid feeling defeated by it. It took several years and a combination of exploratory therapy and cognitive behavior modification to bring about any degree of change.

Consequently, men who are predisposed to avoid competition may end up quite successful—certainly successful enough to find a desirable mate. In fact, men who don't have very strong competitive drives in the first place may even have an advantage when it comes to avoiding the worst aspects of competition in modern society. But they may at times need reassurance that their strategy is legitimate.

Men who are predisposed to be competitive can of course *learn* to avoid competition, and can even be conditioned to accept low positions. However, psychological distress is a likely outcome if such men fail to achieve objective status. Hence, they may need help becoming more assertive and competitive.

In practice, distinguishing one type of man from the other is a difficult problem for psychotherapists. How does one know when to help a man become more assertive or ambitious and when to help him become less so? There is no pat solution. One has to assess several factors, including (1) the degree of satisfaction that the client is getting from the strategy he is following and (2) the degree to which his behavior is being affected by current cultural values. And, of course, one is constrained by the need to remain close to what the client wants for himself.

Need we say again that we do not underestimate the role of the environment? No one can doubt that the way a man was raised plays a major role in determining whether he will have the attributes of dominance — the bearing, posture and mien. Children who are encouraged to take delight in their own sensory and intellectual experience are more likely to develop an outlook on the world that will enable them to achieve a reasonable degree of psychological well-being no matter what position they eventually reach. They will feel good about themselves in relation to other men and will find women to love them.

Coping with low status

Certain attitudes seem to help people cope with their place in society without suffering from the feelings that go along with social subordination. We will mention a few of these.

Some men find an activity outside the workplace in which they can achieve status. Choosing an activity in which only a few people are interested helps to make this strategy successful.

Philosophies which downplay competition and status are very helpful. So are meditational techniques. Hence, Eastern religious philosophies such as Taoism and Buddhism can function as remedies for Western social ills. Similarly, if one truly believes that one will be rewarded in heaven for one's suffering on this earth, lack of objective status can easily be explained away.

The rebellious position, in which one disparages the values of existing institutions, is also helpful. As long as one believes that "the system" is corrupt or unfair, one can avoid suffering from a sense of personal defeat. And since all modern societies have diverged considerably from the environment we are adapted to, there is always some merit in rebellion.

Weakness as a Strategy

Trevor was telling me that he was trying to make his girlfriend stop saying nasty things to him by showing her that he was hurt:

T: That strategy isn't likely to work. The chances are that it will make her mad.

C: (Surprised) It does! She says it's like a criticism of her.

T: That's probably the way she experiences it. But I think what is really happening is that she doesn't want to be *able* to hurt you. She wants you to be invulnerable, at least to her. So by showing her that she is hurting you, you're making her mad, and she does it again, because now she's really mad at you.

C: Are you suggesting that I play a role, that I should fake it?

T: No, I didn't express myself clearly enough. What I mean is, you have to reduce your vulnerability. You have to become stronger. Expressing the truth about how vulnerable you now feel isn't likely to get you the relationship you want.

C: Why?

T: Everybody knows that women generally prefer a man who is a little bit taller, why are you surprised that they might want someone who is a little bit stronger, or a little more assertive? Women have been selected to seek men who are dominant, who are able to bring them resources and to defend them. You need to find someone you have the edge on, someone who will feel comfortable with you.

Here he made an important objection:

C: But I thought that my desire to have the edge over people was part of my problem. I thought is was vanity. You're telling me it's OK.

T: Well, there's more involved there. Your problem is not that you want the edge, it's more that you are afraid to compete at all, afraid to contend for position, so you stay down with people who are really much less talented than you are. You get the edge by staying with people who are unattractive and unsuccessful, people you don't respect. You need the edge, but you also need someone who is fairly close to you in ability and desirability . . .

Obviously, this very complicated problem was not solved through discussion. It was necessary to explore the roots of his choices in detail and to go over the ground many times, but eventually he did become able to take more risks.

Some Implications for Therapy

As we argued in a previous chapter, psychotherapists should not attempt to override gender. Socialization should proceed with the grain, not against it. The unisex approach to behavior that is now presented as a way of overcoming "stereotypes" is a temporary political phenomenon from which therapists should stay aloof. Gender identity is a permanent, indispensable component of self-worth; a healthy society will do everything possible to foster it.

Psychotherapists will often have to attempt to overcome the effects of improper socialization for sex-based behavior in childhood, e.g., the absence of visible, successful male role models, of appropriate rites of passage, and of specific messages affirming the value of masculinity. We have often found it helpful to engage in an explicit discussion of the notion of reproductive strategy. Males need to have a sense of their continuity with other men and indeed with males of other species. They need to appreciate the biological context of maleness. An awareness of the male strategy helps men develop a clear understanding of their own impulses, thus making it easier for them to accept themselves as males. Once a man understands when the strategy serves his purposes and when it does not, he can modify his behavior to suit current environmental conditions.

In any case, therapists should avoid making men feel guilty for thinking, feeling and doing what comes naturally. The shame of being male should not be heaped onto all the other shames that our culture has concocted. For example, many therapists, apparently under the influence of psychoanalysis, interpret a man's tendency to desire many women as an expression of unresolved (oedipal) conflicts, hatred for mother, or the failure of his parents to provide him with love. Such interpretations do not seem justified in the light of biology. A man's impulse to spread his genes is a basic part of the male repertoire, not a sign of pathology.

We know there will be screams of outrage, because we heard some when we circulated early drafts of this book: "But aren't you encouraging adultery! What you're saying is immoral." Hardly. First, as we said in Chapter 8, validating a behavior does not necessarily increase its frequency. Helping a man to understand why he desires many women does not cause him to desire more women; it causes him to feel less self-hatred. Second, to the extent that a man's pursuit of women is the result of other factors (fear of intimacy, desire for revenge against mother, etc.), the intensity of his need for promiscuity may actually decrease. He will understand that he needn't be putting his natural inclinations to self-destructive uses. At any rate, one has to trust that increased insight into biological reality will be as therapeutic as any other kind of insight.

We close this section with a story. A man once came to a therapist with the following complaint: "I feel really bad about it but physical appearance is still important to me in a woman. I know I shouldn't feel this way, but I can't help it. What do you think is wrong?" Unbelievable? We have heard it from two different men. We hope that there are no therapists out there who would have "treated" this man for his "condition."

Heterosexual relationships

In order to maintain the respect and sexual interest of their partners, men in heterosexual relationships generally need to demonstrate self-confidence, success with other males, independent interests, and decisiveness. This does not mean they should abandon the running of their homes to their partners. On the surface, having a woman run the house might seem to put a man into a superior position, but in reality it turns him into a child, thereby placing him in a subordinate position. An absent father is a weak man, at least in his own home.

A word about fathering. In the recent rush towards more meaningful fathering, many men have looked toward women as role models. In the process, some of them have become more like mothers than fathers. It may be wiser for fathers to express their more masculine side to their children. Children learn primarily through modeling; if a boy doesn't have an appropriate role model, he is at high risk for confusion at an early age.

Communication

Most therapists today believe in fostering communication. And most therapists deplore the fact that men are so often less communicative than their female partners want them to be. Some degree of caution is necessary here. There may be good reasons why men don't communicate their feelings. One is that some of their feelings (e.g., desire for other women) would be unacceptable to their partners. Another is that certain negative feelings (e.g., fear, low self-confidence) might frighten their partners and/or cause them to lose the respect of other men.

Caution is necessary even when men come in professing a desire for a relationship based on nurturance, communication and support. Clients generally frame their behavior in terms of the usual values of their religious/ethnic group, age cohort, occupational group, etc., and communication is popular today. Many men have now been persuaded of the importance of these values, and are aware that therapists believe in them. They may present themselves to the therapist in what they think is the socially appropriate manner. But as Helen Singer Kaplan pointed out in the Spring 1988 issue of the *Journal of Sex and Marital Therapy*, some of the men who talk about wanting more intimacy may be concealing an excessive need for reassurance and mothering.

One particularly dramatic example involved an intelligent couple, both of whom claimed to believe profoundly in the equality of the sexes and in the value of communication and support. They were, however, in therapy to consider a temporary separation, at the instigation of the wife and against the will of the husband. She was tired of his failure to hold a steady job, his inability to make decisions, and his incessant need to share his problems with her.

Whenever she expressed some dissatisfaction with any aspect of his behavior, he would accuse her angrily of forgetting the "good parts" of their relationship: "Are you saying that everything we have is no good?"

At first this response made her feel guilty and caused her to back off, but as time went on, she became visibly impatient. After several months of therapy, he finally agreed to a separation. At the very next session, she announced that she had decided on a divorce. He was flabbergasted. First he blustered and threatened to fight it. She was adamant. Then he made a passionate but futile appeal: "But we love each other so much! We have such good communication! We give each other so much support!"

After the session, the therapist spoke to the man alone:

T: Tell me, why do you always go back to communication and support, no matter what is under discussion?
C: (after avoiding the question for a while) Because I didn't get that stuff when I was young.
T: Do you think it appropriate to get that from your wife?
C: Where else could I get it?

The therapist encouraged him to think about that, but never saw him again. The lesson is clear. Men should not be encouraged to reveal all their weaknesses, fears, and doubts to their wives and lovers. Some things are better left unsaid, or rather, said elsewhere.

The need for intimacy, writes Helen Singer Kaplan in the same article, can reach pathological proportions. What a woman may present as a man's avoidance of intimacy may actually turn out to be an excessive demand for intimacy on the part of his spouse. Too much closeness can create an intru-

---

Men, Women, and Deceit

Men who can conceal their emotions may have an advantage in love. Men who love too much may appear needy, and so "turn off" the object of their affection. A woman is generally gratified to feel that she is the only one in a man's life, but she may well feel uneasy if she senses that a man "can't live without her." It makes her feel that he isn't competent enough to provide her with the support and security she needs. Many men have an intuitive grasp of this fact. From high school on, males can be overheard warning each other against showing too much interest in an attractive woman.

Jack, a big, strong bricklayer from a working-class background, provided a flagrant example of this dynamic. He came into therapy because he was having trouble with his girlfriend. He couldn't understand why. He constantly bought her gifts, picked her up at work and drove her home, and even ran errands for her mother. She, on the other hand, constantly picked fights with him and was evasive about marrying him.

The reason for Jack's behavior soon became clear. His father was an alcoholic who beat wife and children. Jack was trying not to be like him. He didn't realize it was possible to go too far in the other direction. When

---

(continued)

sive, hothouse environment which is inimical to sex and which may drive the pressured partner away.

As therapists, we are all committed to promoting supportive relationships. But excess communication can be as destructive as insufficient communication.

One must avoid overstating the case. Men do need to appear strong. On the other hand, they do not need to appear omnipotent or invulnerable. As always, balance is necessary but difficult to achieve. Trying to appear strong is tricky. Being caught trying to appear strong is embarrassing. Human beings are biologically predisposed to detect faked behavior (cheating) — and usually view it with contempt.

Therapists who are truly committed to having their male clients express their emotions should be prepared to hear feelings which are neither nice-nice nor socially acceptable. What men feel most is anger, fear, and lust. Lust is complicated. It makes some men feel protective, and others violent. Many men feel wistful and disappointed about the women they haven't

MEN, WOMEN, AND DECEIT (*continued*)

he finally learned to become less compliant, his girlfriend responded immediately: "I think you're growing up." "I'm glad you're becoming more independent." And even: "I'm glad to see that you're not letting me push you around." More significantly, the frequency and intensity of their fights diminished rapidly.

Jack's case was unusually dramatic, but the lesson is clear: Be careful about letting a woman know how much you love her. Some women are liable to become suspicious.

One of our clients, a man with a history of unsatisfactory relationships with women, expressed the dynamic very well:

> I'm terribly afraid of women that I'm attracted to, and they sense it and shy away from me. Women are attracted to men who are in control, and I'm only in control with women I'm not attracted to. Which is a terrible catch, because I only get women I'm not attracted to.

This client's emotions were so strong that he was incapable of any degree of deceit. He paid the price.

It goes without saying that the man who can show that he is just a little afraid, while at the same time demonstrating that he is fully capable of overcoming his fears, will have the best of all worlds. He will be loved both for his sensitivity *and* his competence. This is the kind of man who will be most attractive to women who verbalize a demand for honest and open communication without recognizing their need for reassurance and security.

possessed. The slope of a stranger's buttocks can produce a deeply painful combination of envy, regret and bitterness. Eyeing attractive women on the street, many men feel a kind of choking longing, a yearning that goes nowhere (the emotional consequence of the inhibition of a fundamentally positive desire to approach). They are reluctant to talk about this because it makes them feel ashamed.

It is very hard, in men, to separate sex and the kind of loving emotions in which women delight. A sexually excited man tends to feel protective and giving. Men who have been sexually fulfilled tend to feel grateful and compassionate. We would even say that men, in general, tend to feel much more love toward their children with women who turn them on than toward their children with women who don't. Men who are not getting sexual satisfaction tend to have less of these rich, warm and satisfying feelings.

Even in good marriages, marriages which provide companionship, comfort and security, men often feel bored and trapped. They have no way to explain these emotions; they aren't "supposed to" feel them, and they can't justify them. So they try to conceal them.

And this barely scratches the surface of what men really feel.

Male-female conflict of interest

Both men and women need to understand that there is an underlying conflict between the male and female reproductive strategies. Unless socialization and social structures minimize the conflict of interest, male-female relationships and the family will be subjected to excess stress. This means that male-female relationships should not be conceptualized in terms of power. In power relationships, there is always a loser (if not necessarily a winner). If power becomes the issue, men will have to fight to mainain their self-respect, and there will be no end to bickering and misery.

Competitiveness in males should be directed towards other males, in socially approved circumstances, and away from females. A society which

---

THE MADONNA-WHORE COMPLEX

Are the images that men form of women merely random expressions of cultural diversity? We doubt it. All over the world, women are seen sometimes as mothers and sometimes as sex objects. The madonna-whore complex — idealization of some women and devaluation of others — is a perverse version of this duality. In its sharply contrasting images one sees reflected the dual nature of the human male's reproductive strategy. The madonna is the woman you invest in, the mother, the virgin who will bear your children and no one else's. The whore is the woman you try to have sex with, without making an investment.

Culture modifies the images men form and changes the degree to which the diverse attributes of women are split, but the underlying duality persists everywhere.

encourages competition between males and females places unnatural strains on both. The contract between the sexes is part of our biological heritage and should be defended, just like the Constitution.

Competition and conflict

Therapy must seek to balance the costs and benefits of competition. This means that therapists must help some men to strive less, and others to strive more. Interventions must be dictated by a sense of the client's personal style and needs. There is no substitute for an individualized approach.

It isn't easy to induce men to strive less. The rewards of objective status are many, and these rewards include the most important, from an evolutionary perspective: an increase in one's ability to secure the woman (women) of one's choice. The incredible "visibility" of the rewards that success brings, in store windows and advertisements, makes their attraction that much greater. Modern man knows all too well what he is not getting. This accounts for America's jackpot mentality; everyone wants to make it big. Most men don't want to hear that they might benefit from a different strategy, but therapists must sometimes try to move them in this direction.

On the other hand, men with strong competitive drives won't be satisfied with very subordinate positions and below-average access to resources. If such men are not successful, they will suffer from social subordination. Therapists must do their best to recognize this condition and find ways to enable such men to reach their full potential.

Our analysis so far leads to at least one seemingly paradoxical conclusion. Since the failure to achieve (an internalized sense of) dominance often leads to compensatory aggression, it follows that much antisocial aggressiveness can best be treated by increasing a man's sense of power. We have consistently found that restoring a man's sense of control over his life reduces his aggressiveness.

This point is important so we're going to provide three brief case descriptions.

Roddy

Roddy came into therapy complaining of a variety of stress-related symptoms: an ulcer, headaches, heartburn, and spastic colon. He was a skinny man whose hunched-over posture, tics and deferential demeanor clearly suggested that he had been defeated by life. He was currently working as a laborer, having sustained an injury that kept him out of his trade. One of his daughters had recently been raped, another was pregnant out of wedlock.

He himself, he revealed, was under a court order to stop beating his wife, Rona. She was being treated in a center for battered women. A check with various agencies connected with the case indicated that everyone thought that Roddy's drinking was the source of all the problems in the family.

According to Roddy, Rona nagged him all the time, accepted his sexual overtures capriciously, and was moody and unpredictable both with him and with the children. He always ended up doing everything she wanted. He wasn't even allowed to come home and be left alone. Rona would follow him around the house with her grievances. She was a "shopaholic" who spent more than he could afford and who wanted him to spend his leisure time traipsing around with her to her favorite stores. After an interview with Rona, and some independent investigation, the therapist confirmed most of Roddy's story. It also turned out that Roddy had never actually hit his wife. He had pushed her once, causing her to fall.

Roddy felt he was helpless to change the situation. He wanted pills for his symptoms. The diagnosis: failure to achieve dominance. The therapist set out to help Roddy take control over the situation. The first priority was to avoid any further acts of violence. Roddy was instructed never to argue:

T: Take care of your own affairs. If something you've done is brought up more than once, just agree, and then go about your own business. Always agree cheerfully, then go on with your life.
C: But she threatens to have me kicked out of the house.
T: Aren't you the breadwinner? What will she do if you leave?
C: I don't want to lose the children.
T: Sometimes you have to take risks in life. . . .
C: (at a subsequent session) I bring the check home, she wants the whole thing. I can't even get her to give me money to pay my insurance bills.
T: Do you have to bring the check home?
C: She screams if I don't.
T: Do you have to?
C: What should I do, pay everything before I come home?
T: Why not?. . . .

C: (at a subsequent session) My kid refuses to pay room and board. I've been hassling with him for months, nothing helps.
T: Arguing is no good, I thought we agreed on that.
C: What do you want me to do, throw the kid out?
T: Can he get a better deal somewhere else?
C: I don't know. Maybe he can.

T: The truth is, you want him to stay with you, don't you? You don't want him to go out on his own, even though you tell him you do.

C: Yeah, I guess you're right.

T: Well, that's a problem. He knows that, so he has the power.

C: So I encourage him to leave?

T: Try it. . . .

In approximately six months, Roddy's household was in fairly good order. Roddy reported that he wasn't being nagged anymore and was communicating much more effectively. They were having sex as often as he wanted, and he was finding it in his heart to do many of the things that Rona had wanted all along. Everybody was relieved that he had started playing a powerful role in the family.

Trent

Trent, a strikingly handsome young salesman, came in to therapy because two women had left him, fearing that he might hit them. He agreed that he might have. On several occasions, he had gotten enraged to the point of smashing up his apartment.

He felt he knew what was wrong: "I'm too domineering. I want my way all the time. I'm jealous." In therapy, a different picture emerged. Exploration revealed that Trent was still seeking approval from his parents. One of the first clues: of several different women he said, "They don't express enough affection," or "They never come over to give me a hug." These are unusual complaints from a man. It became clear that Trent was looking for reassurance—for the approval he had never had. His jealousy, it turned out, was due to fear that the women would leave him, and this was traced to low self-esteem. Trent eventually realized that the violent incidents always occurred after he had gotten scared about something—scared that his girlfriend preferred someone else or was withdrawing her affection. He would seek reassurance, there would be a quarrel, he would get mad, and his temper would get the best of him. Again the same problem: failure of dominance, loss of control. Trent's problems began to fade after his childhood situation had been analyzed in detail.

Yannick

Yannick had once been the major problem in his family system. He had come to therapy with a serious drinking problem. Alcohol changed him. Generally a quiet, sensitive man with a touch of naive romanticism, he became sullen, withdrawn and easily irritated when he drank, which was not frequently, but often enough to infuriate his wife. They quarreled over it constantly, and she often threatened to leave him. In therapy, he was able to dredge up an extremely disturbed, abusive childhood, one which had left him with a strong sense of inferiority. His self-esteem had not been bolstered by some of the things he had done in later life. He came into therapy thinking of himself as a degenerate. His behavior reflected his low opinion of self in many ways.

After some years, he was able to give up the drinking. He integrated the idea that he had been a victim, and forgave himself for the abuses he had perpetrated. Since the therapist had, with great difficulty, forced him to realize that drinking was the major problem in the family, Yannick was positive that all would now be well. He was disappointed. His wife continued find things wrong. She continued to complain, more or less at the same rate as before. Attempts to discuss it with her led to more complaints: "You don't want to know how I feel." Now Yannick began to talk of leaving, not to her, but in therapy.

The therapist felt that Yannick's failure, over the years, to play his role as the man in the family was responsible for his wife's behavior. Yannick was brought to the realization that it was his responsibility to stop the nagging — to take control of the situation. He was encouraged to devise strategies that would make complaining difficult. He made a sign with the word "complaint" on it, which he brought out whenever he felt he was being nagged; this brought home to his wife that her expressions of dissatisfaction had not abated, despite her husband's sobriety. He decided to leave the room, rather then continue a discussion, when his wife attempted to get the children to take sides. He began to take over responsibilities that he had previously left to her (paying bills, decisions about the children, etc.). Within a few months, the quarreling ceased to be a problem.

Our experience consistently indicates that when men come to understand the roots of their dominance-related behaviors, they become better able to forego the attempt to dominate others. We demonstrate this kind of liberation through self-acceptance in Chapter 15.

The Future of Female-Male Relationships

Some readers may feel that we are too pessimistic about the effects of recent changes in American society. Many feminist writers feel that as women gain more power in society, they will transform it, making it less competitive, more cooperative, promoting conciliation and affiliation, caring and reciprocity.

There is an element of evolutionary truth in this dream. As we saw in Chapters 7 and 8, women have indeed specialized in these roles and responsibilities. But we are not optimistic. Even though women probably are more prosocial and less competitive, the nature of hierarchical societies will probably not permit these predispositions to determine social relationships. The women who get ahead in hierachies will be transformed by them, not vice versa.

Reciprocity flowers only under certain conditions, not under others. It flourished in the hunter-gatherer band; we don't think it will flourish in hierarchical societies, no matter who runs them. We doubt that a change in power relationships will produce many positive results. What would be needed is a change in social organization that would enhance complementarity. We don't see that happening.

Can evolution be used to devise a better society? Perhaps, but we doubt it. Evolution is less useful in designing social policy than it is in analyzing problems. There are simply too many factors to consider and too many competing interests to reconcile. The point can most easily be seen if we take a trivial, uncontroversial example, one we have dubbed "the diaper dilemma."

In the natural environment, children don't wear diapers. They live outside and can be allowed to excrete where they will. Hence, they don't get diaper rash and don't have to be subjected to the horrors of premature toilet training. This is good for both children and parents. Obviously, we moderns cannot go back to that system. Diaper rash and toilet training, with all its pressures, are apparently inevitable consequences of modern life. There is no good solution.

How does this apply to gender? The analysis we have presented in the last four chapters indicates that social policy with respect to gender should have at least four goals:

1. women should be full participants in the economic life of their society;
2. women's special position in child-rearing should be preserved;
3. men should have an arena in which to compete with each other for access to women; and
4. men and women should not be pushed into competition with each other.

In the natural environment, all of these goals were achieved automatically. In the current environment, one is hard put to imagine how all four could be reconciled, without drastic restructuring of society. It is probably necessary to choose one goal over another. Here, evolution is no guide at all. Science can tell us about the consequences of our choices, but it cannot determine our values. Science — and psychotherapy — can help us to understand the mismatch between our genes and the current environment, but cannot eliminate the sources of the conflict.

CHAPTER 11

Psychotherapy and the Brain

Then the eyes of both were opened, and they knew that
they were naked; and they sewed fig leaves together and
made themselves aprons.

—Genesis 3

If we desire to be conscious masters of our own fates,
and if conscious effort in that direction is the most likely
vehicle of survival and happiness, then we *ought* to
study evolution.

—Richard Alexander,
The Biology of Moral Systems

UP TO THIS POINT WE HAVE been saying that people need to pay attention to their innermost feelings, their predilections and their predispositions. We now turn our attention to thinking. Our message is simple, perhaps too simple: we suggest that people need to think in ways which accord with their needs as creatures—males and females who live, age, and die. We address ourselves to those who say "you can think anything you want." We agree. You can. But there are costs. Humans are able think things which aren't good for them. They can be convinced that these things *are* good for them, and they can pursue these aims with obstinacy. Yet it is necessary to help them change their thinking.

This makes therapy complicated. One can't simply encourage people to act according to how they feel, because how they feel is often a function of how they think, and how they think is a problem. Ideas have emotional consequences, as Aaron Beck and the cognitive therapists have shown. Culture has given rise to ideas which create anxiety and depression, loneliness and confusion, rage and violence. Some ideas are better than others. Some ideas are no good at all.

We are talking about ideas that are very basic, ideas that control the way people live. "I must live up to the image my father had of me" is an idea. "I have to vindicate the honor of my family" is an idea. "I have to beware of women because they might smother me" is an idea. "I have to be the best (or

177

else)" is an idea. "I mustn't try because if I fail I will be humiliated" is an idea. "It's my fault I was abused" is an idea. Often these ideas are held unconsciously and even nonverbally, especially if they result from serious trauma early in life. But they are ideas nevertheless.

It would be nice if therapy consisted simply of helping people to get what they want. Unfortunately, what people want is often something they only think they want, something they have been induced to want by a parent, a peer group, or an advertisement. Wants have become subject to influence and distortion, to ideas about what is right and proper and good.

"Respect for the client" is a widely accepted principle, but it cannot be extended to the client's self-defeating ideas. People need help sorting out which of their ideas are helpful and which should be discarded. But how is a therapist to know which ideas to support and what ideas to combat? An individual therapist's ideas are likely to be too idiosyncratic to serve as guidelines. Cultures differ and are strewn with subcultures. Some universal point of reference is needed. Evolution can provide it. In the hands of a skillful therapist, it can help people sort out the ideas that will help them from the ideas that won't.

In place of "respect for the client" we propose what Leda Cosmides has called "respect for the natural contours of the mind." This concept moves us away from the particular to the universal. Because the natural contours of the mind have been shaped by evolution, they are very similar from person to person. Individual variation is largely the product of culture, rather than structure.

The contours of the mind are shaped by the structure and organization of the human brain. To understand the mind, we must start with the brain.

What Does the Brain Do?

When people think about the brain, they generally think about it as the organ of thinking, but thinking is only a very small part of what the brain does. The brain regulates the internal environment of the organism and controls the response of the organism to the external environment. Whatever else it does, it must assure the survival and reproduction of the organism or brains like it will not be around in the next generation. This is true of all animals, including humans.

The human brain can do things which no other animal can do, and its special powers have made us, at least temporarily, the rulers of this small planet. But the special powers of the human brain have also made us vulnerable to psychic distress. Like an exotic racing car, the human brain was designed to work under a certain set of conditions. It was designed to help us survive, get along, and reproduce, in a hunter-gatherer environment. The brain can manage under a much wider variety of conditions, but it then begins to require more maintenance. Psychotherapy is one type of brain maintenance.

For an understanding of the human brain's unique susceptibility to psychic distress, one needs to understand the evolutionary history of the brain. This history will help shed light on the relationship between characteristics of the normal brain and the problems that humans are experiencing in the current environment.

The Evolution of the Brain

The human brain wasn't planned the way an engineer might go about designing a computer. It evolved, in layers of increasing complexity. Paul MacLean, one of the pioneers of neuroscience, called the result "the triune brain." One part, the brainstem is as old as the reptiles. This part of the brain is responsible for vegetative and basic life-sustaining activities. On top of this "reptilian brain" the early mammals added a layer of tissues that mediate emotion and memory—the limbic system. The primates inherited all that, and surrounded it with an additional mass of tissue, the cerebral cortex, which specializes in language and cognition.

This arrangement demonstrates a lot about the way we came into existence. Evolution doesn't start from scratch; it tinkers. It always begins with a living organism that is complete and functional in and of itself. It can add to this, but only if the new structures are compatible with the old. The creature bearing the innovation must be able to survive and reproduce at least as well as the original animal or the innovation will disappear.

Freud, and many others before and after him, believed that our animal heritage was the primary cause of our psychological problems. According to this way of thinking, "primitive" drives and aggressive impulses inherited from lower animals threaten to burst free of the controls imposed by the higher brain elements. Dark forces lurked in the unconscious, and were tenuously held in check by socialization. This view is not supported by what is now known of the evolution of the brain. The unconscious is not a seething cauldron of rage, nor is it a primary source of antisocial drives. It is, rather, the repository of life-sustaining regulatory processes, processes that are responsible for the order that we observe in animal life.

Psychological distress cannot, therefore, be attributed to the ancient brain. Most of the conditions that can be treated with psychotherapy are due to conflicts between ideas and the needs of the organism, or to conflict between the various ideas generated by the cortex. The new brain is the source of the difficulty. The ideas it creates can be considered part of the changed environment — an environment to which we are not adapted.

The expansion of the cortex

Over the last four million years of primate evolution, the brain expanded with extraordinary rapidity. However, the expansion was not the result of an overall increase in the size of all the brain's different parts. Most of the increase was in the cerebral cortex. The cortex has grown larger relative to the size of the whole brain. This phenomenon is crucial to an understanding of human psychological distress.

The neocortex is estimated to contain 70% of the neurons in the human brain. In it are found the circuits that underlie many of humanity's most prized functions, among them the collections of neurons — Broca's area, Wernicke's area, and related pathways — that provide us with the capacity for language. Experts such as Harry Jerison and Ralph Holloway believe that these areas probably began to appear in the brains of ancestral species such as *Homo erectus*. Humans owe their superior intelligence and extraordinary behavioral flexibility to this expansion of the cerebral cortex.

The neocortex is now intimately involved in many functions that in simpler animals are carried out entirely by the brainstem. This involvement represents a new level of control. The cortex now contains the highest level of decision-making power over motor output and can override instructions issued by the more ancient brain centers.

The value of this arrangement is that much more information can be brought to bear on any action. Long-range planning can be used to design a series of coordinated steps, leading to a far-off goal. For example, a hunter can remember and analyze the habits of a deer over a period of years, to develop a hunting strategy that will minimize effort and maximize return.

But this arrangement can also create certain problems. One of these problems relates to the process of inhibition. Much of the action of the cortex is inhibitory. In all organisms, higher functions are dependent on the inhibition of phylogenetically-primitive responses — responses that are made impulsively on the basis of limited information.

Inhibition is a mixed blessing. The human ability to carry out long-range plans depends absolutely on the capacity to delay action, hence on the ability of the cortex to inhibit an impulsive response. But the cortex can also interrupt and interfere with activities that are better performed without its participation. When one wants to act impulsively or spontaneously, cortical input is undesirable. For example, in tennis or basketball, if one thinks about a shot, one is more likely to miss. Someone who is playing great is said to be "unconscious." To take another example, a woman who has bad memories of her childhood may be unable to reach orgasm with her husband. In such cases, the cortex, with its vast memory banks, reaches down to spoil the party.

Another problem derives from our cherished ability to learn. In the natural environment, learning enhanced survival and reproduction. It helped early humans cope with the complexities of social exchange in foraging bands, and with the fluctuating weather patterns, complicated landscapes, lurking dangers and physical hardships of the Plio-pleistocene era. There were woodlands and grasslands, highlands and lowlands; survival was enhanced by the ability to exploit the many different ecological niches, to predict the movement of animals and the seasonal appearance of useful plant foods.

Yet under some circumstances, learning can have unwanted consequences. As we showed in a previous chapter, children now have opportunities to learn things that don't help them or that program them to function in destructive or self-destructive ways. It is because the brain is so good at learning that human behavior can deviate very far from valuable norms. For example, individuals can learn that they will always be let down, and so find it difficult to maintain productive social relationships.

Furthermore, the flexibility of the brain has given rise to a damaging illusion: the idea that its flexibility is infinite. The brain can adjust to almost any physical challenge and to almost any danger coming from the external environment. It can develop an incredible variety of stratagems and responses. But there are nevertheless limits on what it can do.

What happens, for example, when there is no clear and present danger, no external physical challenge? Without an external challenge, the brain often turns its formidable powers of analysis on the self or on trivial matters. The tendency to scan the environment for danger can become free-floating anxiety; the tendency to analyze situations can turn into obsessions; the tendency to find one's daily food can turn into an endless search for security and wealth. Paradoxically, the achievement of wealth and security can result in a nagging preoccupation with trivialities. Most brains need concrete problems to function smoothly.

There are other problems with our vaunted flexibility. To achieve it, evolution provided humans with relative freedom from fixed, instinctual behavior patterns. Behaviors that are instinctive in other species are, in humans, subject to analysis and modification by the association cortex, which contains so much of what the individual has learned. As a result, learning is to some degree involved in almost all human activities, even down to basic physiological regulatory processes; yogis and meditators can learn to control heart beat and pulse rate. Some animals develop proper mating behavior with very little learning; humans must learn to mate. Lots of things can go wrong.

We were exiled from Eden, the Bible says, because we ate of the tree of knowledge. As it is written: "Then the eyes of both were opened, and they knew that they were naked; and they sewed fig leaves together and made themselves aprons" (Genesis 3). Perhaps we can understand this story best as a metaphor for the troubles created by our species' expanded cortex.

Model Building

The aspect of brain functioning that most conclusively demonstrates the usefulness of psychotherapy is model-building.

Animals create representations — models — of their environments in their brains. As best as can be determined now, these representations actually exist in physical form — as patterns of connections between neurons. Events in the environment create synaptic connections which provide a topographical "map" of the event. The physiological details are not important to the basic argument presented here. What is important is this: the environment makes changes in the brain. Perceptions become real entities. These entities — the patterns of connection — change the functioning of the organism.

Model-building provides the crucial neuroscientific rationale for psychotherapy. A genetically intact brain can malfunction because of the structure of the information contained within it. By altering the information — the model — therapists can improve the functioning of the organism.

Let us compare this approach to the brain to that taken by the hardliners of biological psychiatry. Nancy Andreasen, describing the symptoms of mental illness in a recent issue of *Science*, makes this statement, "Ultimately, all these types of symptoms must be understood in terms of the interaction of neural systems and neural circuits." Andreasen is almost certainly right as far as the symptoms of schizophrenia, manic depression and other serious mental diseases are concerned. We would not propose treating these conditions with psychotherapy (although therapists can certainly help clients cope with these afflictions).

We maintain, however, that many symptoms are caused, not by problems in neural systems and circuits, but rather by problems in the structure of the *information* contained in the brain. Information can be faulty even if the neural systems and circuits in the brain are undamaged. *Defective models can be formed by genetically intact brains*. No anatomic analysis of the brain would be able to identify the structure of such a model.

This distinction leads us to hazard a definition of what psychotherapy can and cannot do. It can alter the structure of the information contained in the brain. It cannot alter the structure of the brain itself. But since the structure of the information can alter the *functioning* of the brain, successful psychotherapy can be expected to improve the way the brain functions.

The nature of the information that the brain relies on to form its models is subject to some constraints. The structure of the information that is gleaned from the environment must be compatible with the structure of the brain. That is to say, the brain needs certain kinds of information — a certain kind of environment — to develop and function properly. If the organism is subjected to experiences that the brain cannot cope with, the brain may begin to malfunction. For example, if a child is subjected to abuse in the home, the child's brain may begin to produce stress-related chemicals in response to intimacy, thereby compromising the adult's socio-sexual adjustment. Social events do have biological consequences.

Let us look in some detail at the model-building process. The brain is not the passive recipient of information. It does not simply record "what is out there." Far from it. The brain actively creates (constructs) its model, using clues and cues from the environment. This explains both its creativeness and its propensity to make errors.

The brain builds its models on the basis of partial (degenerate) data. A simple example will suffice to illustrate the point: people are quite capable of recognizing the face of a familiar person when some of its features are covered up. The use of degenerate data in model-building opens up the possibility of error; one can fill in the blanks with the wrong information, jump to wrong conclusions, and develop a distorted view of the world. This is one feature of the brain which contributes to the need for psychotherapy.

Another relevant feature of the brain is its dependence on emotional states. The brain, it has been said, is a computational network, somewhat like a computer. But unlike an electronic computer, the brain is state-dependent. That is to say, the composition of the materials involved in its calculations changes constantly, altering its calculations. It is as if the personal computer you have on your desk would give different results with each minute fluctuation in the temperature of its semiconductors.

The materials in the brain are of course its neurons. They function in response to chemicals produced by the body — hormones, neurotransmitters, and a host of other proteins and peptides, any of which can alter the output of the brain's computations. Changes in state can produce, for example, optimistic and pessimistic forecasts at different times, using the same data.

This is not to say that the relationship between calculation and chemical is one-way. On the contrary, the relationship is characterized by feedback. A chemical change can bring about a change in outlook; a change in outlook, brought about, for example, by new information or by a reassessment of old information, can bring about a change in chemical state.[1]

Here again, we have a feature which helps to understand why psychotherapy is often necessary. Mood can affect the functioning of the brain, and mood can depend on social events—the traumas of childhood, or the triumphs and tragedies of today.

One other feature of the brain makes psychotherapy a logical intervention. The brain begins to form its models in early childhood, perhaps even *in utero*. Errors that creep in early can affect the *perception* of later events, preventing learning and leading to repetitive self-defeating behavior (what psychoanalysts call the repetition compulsion). Only psychotherapy offers the hope of undoing this kind of error.

Models and survival

The capacity to build models evolved in order to help animals cope with their environments. By collecting information and forming "maps" and "expectations" (or "hypotheses") animals are better able to survive and reproduce—provided the models are sufficiently accurate and complete.

The models formed by the animal brain must serve the purposes of the organism, i.e., they must enhance survival and inclusive fitness, or else the organism(s) using that model will die off. The role of model-building in promoting survival and inclusive fitness is easier to see when examining the models that are formed by simpler organisms. In *Behind the Mirror*, a fascinating account of the animal origins of human thinking, pioneering ethologist Konrad Lorenz discusses a sparrow that is being approached by a hawk. We know that the retina of the sparrow does not see the hawk. Rather, it sees a particular set of lines and edges. It also sees an object getting larger.

---

[1]This situation is reflected in the physical wiring of the brain. Take, for example, the position of the *locus ceruleus*, which produces the neurotransmitter norepinephrine (noradrenaline). Axons containing norepinephrine project to areas throughout the cerebral cortex, where they exercise an inhibitory (quieting) effect on cortical activity that has the result of making the organism more sensitive to incoming stimuli (Tucker and Williamson, 1984). Areas of the cortex, in turn, project back to the *locus ceruleus*; when these neurons fire—presumably when the novel stimulus has been checked out—the *locus ceruleus* is inhibited in its turn. Similar control systems exist with respect to the sensory modalities. Thalamo-cortical projections carrying information from the senses are invariably reciprocated. For example, the lateral geniculate nucleus, which receives and analyzes visual information, both projects to the cortex and receives input from the cortex. Thus the functional state of the cortex can influence the manner in which sensory waystations screen the flow of information (Nauta and Feirtag, 1979).

After performing what in human terms would be a series of highly abstract mathematical computations, the sparrow's brain interprets the visual information to mean, not that an object in the visual field is getting larger, but that a predator is coming closer. As a result, the sparrow flies away and lives another day. This sparrow's model was *adaptive*. It served the purposes of survival and thus increased the chances that the sparrow would reproduce.

Note the use of degenerate data here. The value of being able to sense predator or prey from a few clues is clearly high—as anyone who has ever recognized a deer by the twitching of an ear in a clump of trees can testify. In most situations, the benefits of acting on incomplete information far outweigh the costs. It is better to fly away from nothing a few times a day than it is to wait around to find out if the black dot on the horizon is really a hawk.

The human brain also forms models of the environment. In this way it is similar, not dissimilar, to the brains of other animals. But the human brain has a greatly expanded model-forming capacity. This is its glory and its weakness.

The increased model-forming capacity, like learning, to which it is related, became characteristic of our species because it provided the early humans who had it with an advantage in the struggle for survival (improved inclusive fitness). The importance of the model-building capacity to early humans can be inferred from observations of surviving hunter-gatherers. For example, anthropologist Richard Gould tells us that with the help of religious rituals and elaborate myths, the Australian Aborigines construct highly detailed mental maps of the territory they inhabit. The maps are tools which help them to remember and find scarce water sources in their desert habitat. In *The Song Lines*, Bruce Chatwin describes how Aboriginal sacred songs literally map routes across the Australian terrain, using vocal inflections to mirror the undulations of the landscape.

The models of hunter-gatherers certainly provided comfort, security, and calm in the face of uncertainty and adversity. We know, for example, that shamans believe that they have special powers, powers which protect them and their relatives from disease and danger. Similarly, contemporary beliefs about the existence of heaven provide comfort and relief from anxiety.

So, the model-forming capacity once enhanced inclusive fitness. But the human brain is now capable of forming models that have nothing to do with the needs of individual organisms. As Stephen Jay Gould is fond of pointing out, the human brain can do far more than what evolution designed it to do. In fact, it can build models of the entire universe. The problem is that when it does, it can run into trouble.

For example, the brain is now capable of forming models that compromise the existence of the species or large segments of it. Among such models one might include the genocidal program of the Nazis and the current preparations for nuclear war. On a smaller scale, there are all too many examples: the beliefs of the Skoptsi, a 19th century Russian religious cult that required ritual castration; the political and religious ideas that led people to commit mass suicide at Jonesville; and the thinking that underlies the current wave of teenage suicide. Most maladaptive models are not so spectacular; they merely diminish satisfactions and inspire self-defeating behavior.

There are many reasons why people now form maladaptive models. One of the most important is the fact that the current social system is incomprehensible to so many of the people who live in it. The rules are too complicated; understanding has become the preserve of a privileged few. All hunter-gatherers had a good working understanding of the world they lived in; our world is full of people who are confused. Many of them don't understand enough about the social system to make their way in the world. Their confusion and maladjustment can produce "symptoms" like alienation, apathy, depression, despair, alcoholism, antisocial behavior, etc.

But even those who have access to wealth and education and are better able to understand the wider world may suffer psychologically when they do not understand their fundamental human needs. As we argued in a previous chapter, the human brain is not set up to cope with wealth. Humans require a social environment in which interdependence is necessary. Affiliation and contact flow naturally from that interdependence.

The brain's difficulty in coping with abundance can be seen with particular clarity in anorexia nervosa. Anorexia is rare where food is scarce. It occurs where food is easily available. According to most authorities, it is associated with a distorted body image. The victim sees herself as fatter than she is, and wants to be thinner. We call this an *idea*. This idea, then, is capable of suppressing a physiological need. Of course, in most people, the influence of the cortex over basic functions is not as drastic as this; what people think does not cause them to stop eating. In fact, they diet with difficulty. Anorexics probably have additional biological vulnerabilities. (One possibility is that the anorexic's hypothalamus, which controls feeding behavior, is not sufficiently insulated from the influence of the cortex.)

More generally, the enormous power of the brain enables it to generate an internal world that is so vivid, so alive and so intense that it can substitute for reality, opening the way for excessive self-involvement and misinterpretation of others through such defenses as projection.

Our general point is this: the brain, influenced by a culture that is hazy about what people need, and faced with an excessively complex environment, has developed a strong tendency to develop models that create psy-

A Non-Adaptive Model

When George first came into therapy, he believed that he had been chosen to suffer. This made him very special. To live up to this image, he felt compelled to be perfect. He strove for godlike ideals. He tried to transcend his baser impulses. He professed to despise both those who worked hard for personal success and those who pursued pleasure. Pure altruism was the only trait he respected, and he had never encountered it.

During the exploration of these ideas, George discovered that he imagined himself to be on a rickety ladder, in constant danger of falling down into depravity. Whenever anything good happened to him, he would begin to get a sense that he was nearing a state of grace. But then he would be overcome with trepidation and would have to sabotage his good fortune. He also felt that other people wanted to knock him off the ladder, and thus had to be constantly on his guard. When pressed about this, he asserted: "Even if they are sometimes supportive or cooperative, they might flip at any time. When people are nice, the world seems even more dangerous."

Further exploration revealed that George was afraid to assert himself in any way, because he feared that undefinable powers in the universe would punish him for his temerity. He would not do anger exercises aimed at a cathartic experience because his model told him that if you let go once, you could never get the emotions under control. He would not do relaxation exercises because he felt that if he let his guard down, his evil inner self would take over.

He was a well-educated man of Italian origin, but at 35 was still working at entry level positions and had generated no career plans. He felt he could not commit himself to any course of action. "It might not be the right one." Another time he stated:

I don't think achievement is the issue. I think that I am waiting for my suffering to give me recognition. I know you don't think much of that idea but I can't give it up. If I admit it was a mistake, my whole life wouldn't be valid.

(continued)

A Non-Adaptive Model (*continued*)

George had never had a successful relationship with a woman. He admitted that he used fantasy to escape from this reality: "In my mind, I see myself above all this and superior to it. Nothing can touch me." When, after some time in therapy, he finally did establish a relationship with a woman, he felt he had to placate her, cater to her, and devote himself to improving her moods. Having no independent life of his own, he focused obsessively on her. She soon began complaining that this made her depressed. She begged him to pay attention to his own affairs.

George was not crazy. In fact, his ideas made perfect sense. He had been subjected to considerable psychological abuse in his family. His father, an obsessively critical former mental patient, was frequently violent toward him and his mother. The nuns in elementary school and the brothers in high school had taught him that he should be pure and perfect. Since he had never been able to realize this goal, he thought of himself sometimes as a failure, sometimes as evil. Consequently, he feared being known and expected to be judged severely. No intimate relationship was possible. No career was worthwhile because no position could give him the perfection he wanted.

After several years of therapy, George admitted that his model of how the world works was faulty but stated: "It still is appealing to me. Anything else looks shabby." The therapist replied: "Can any career match the expectations you have of yourself?" "Not really." "So why bother?" "Right."

Therapy was difficult, because he perceived any attempt to help him see that he was not to blame for the abuse he had suffered in childhood as a threat to his specialness. Here, for example, is how he reacted to a book he had picked up on cognitive behavior modification:

It's telling me that I'm not responsible for the bad things that happened to me. It makes things too easy. I know it gets me off the hook, but I can't trust it. I'm afraid I'd be fooling myself if I believed it.

George's model illustrates many of the different sources of error we have talked about: over-valuation of the cortex, a culture that condemns biology, a family structure that has deviated from the norm, and a socioeconomic environment that places people at a disadvantage from birth.

chological distress. It is these models that psychotherapists are generally called on to address.

The cortex as God

Human civilizations glorify the activities of the cortex — logic, calculation, planning, thought, and spirituality. People develop models that, like Plato's theory of ideas, put abstractions at the center of the universe. The rational and the mystical are placed above the concrete and the earthbound. Throughout recorded history — the most recent five or six thousand years of our existence — we find models of human existence that denigrate the body, sensuality, desire, sexuality, feeding, and all the other basic activities that are the province of the older parts of the brain. Our natural functions and tendencies are denigrated as the source of sin. Virtue is thought to consist of rising above nature.

Some religious systems actually maintain that a part of the person, the soul, is independent of the "lower" functions, and will outlive the body. The cortex has become capable of denying the importance of the organism! The servant can elevate itself to the position of master, dividing the organism against itself.

The cortex as prosecutor

In addition to playing at being god, the cortex has become chief prosecutor. Almost every human being in contemporary society is subject to an inner dialogue in which one voice denigrates the person's achievements, while the other engages in self-defense. Many people take the existence of such a dialogue for granted, thinking it "natural" (human) to spend their lives in inner dialogue as if they were on trial. It is difficult to persuade them otherwise. Here is an example:

C: But doesn't everybody assess themselves all the time? I think that's what it is to be human. I have to keep looking for the answer, otherwise I'll go downhill. Are you suggesting that I just let go?

Only after coming to a realization that this inner dialogue is not the hallmark of humanity do clients begin to understand that the cycle of constant self-assessment and denigration is the result of thinking gone wild. Eventually, they realize that the cortex is quite capable of meting out the death penalty, as the statistics on suicide show. When they discover that there is rarely an acquittal in the courtroom of the self, they generally become willing to stop the trial.

The Trial

Here is how Arnold conceived of his life:

C: It's like I'm on trial and everyone's the jury, so you're on the jury too. My father's the prosecutor, but the judge is something like him too, so I can't really trust the judge either. The jury [people in general] has an open mind but they could be swayed by arguments. Maybe you [the therapist] aren't on the jury, maybe you're the defense attorney, but you don't know all the evidence they have against me, so you might back down. You could withdraw from the case.

T: Is that what is really going on here, a trial?

C: I know that's not what's supposed to be going on, but how can I trust that it isn't? People are always saying that they're not being judgmental, but if you took a poll suddenly, everyone would have an opinion.

T: Perhaps. But here, is that what is really going on?

C: Well, you're assessing what's going on, and that's very similar to a trial.

T: You're right, I am assessing what's going on, but are we moving toward a verdict and a sentence?

C: You're asking me to trust that you really are what you say you are, but how can I trust someone else when I can't trust myself?

T: It's a problem.

C: Maybe you're supposed to trust someone else, and then find out that you can trust yourself, but that feels like jumping off a cliff and hoping you'll float to the bottom.

T: That sounds terribly scary . . .

Arnold's model of interaction with humans had been totally skewed by his upbringing. His cortex had taken his experiences and created expectations which made it impossible for him to have successful relationships or a real career. By projecting these expectations onto therapy, he almost succeeded in undermining his chance for recovery. His actions were not motivated by a desire to hurt himself, nor was he under a "compulsion" to repeat his past. He simply structured reality in such as way as to preclude all alternative interpretations.

Confrontation

Our analysis creates a problem. If it is true that people's ideas get them in trouble, does it follow that therapist and client should spend their time arguing about ideas? Obviously, we are not putting forth any such notion. Clients' beliefs have to be respected, and therapists cannot spend much time in therapy on abstractions. But there are many ways to guide and influence people's thinking without arguing with them. Any therapist who offers or withholds an approving nod is doing it. We do believe that therapists must confront their clients in one way or another about their maladaptive ideas, especially where this is necessary to reconcile the conscious mind to the rest of the organism.

The Adaptive Model

Having identified some elements of maladaptive psychological models, we may ask: what *is* an adaptive model in an unnatural environment? What does "adaptive" mean for a citizen of the United States, for example?

To biologists, the meaning of "adaptive" is clear. Whatever promotes survival and inclusive fitness is adaptive. Clearly, this is not meaningful to ordinary people. Most everyone is interested in survival, but most people are not at all bent on maximizing their reproductive success.[2] People rarely come to psychotherapy to get more children. They seek to improve their own lives. If they want to "maximize" anything, it is personal satisfaction.

Most biologists who study human behavior understand this. As University of Michigan professor Richard Alexander puts it,

> to say that we . . . *evolved* to serve the interests of our genes in no way suggests that we are *obliged* to serve them. In today's novelty-filled environments, human activity may often be directed in ways that do not in fact lead to increased success in reproduction.

---

[2]If a biologist reading this is somewhat taken aback, we would point out that inclusive fitness was never a motivation. It was a by-product of proximate mechanisms working on the environment in which they evolved. Hence there never was a time when humans were "striving" to maximize their inclusive fitness. Therefore, despite the claims of authors such as Monique Mulder, it is not necessarily true that "people learn to adopt different behavioral patterns in different ecological and social contexts such that their behavior maximizes inclusive fitness". (Mulder, submitted for publication). People learn to *adjust* their behavior to different conditions, to achieve *various* goals. Whether these adjustments will maximize fitness cannot be predicted.

How then do we bridge the gap between the biological and psychological meanings of "adaptive?" Do we have to abandon the notion of reproductive success entirely? The answer is no. The mechanisms that once maximized inclusive fitness are still alive within us, in the form of impulses and predispositions—the famous "whisperings within." People must be able to hear the whispers, even if they want to move in different directions. To achieve self-acceptance, they need to come to terms with what their bodies and brains were originally *designed* to do. Hence an adaptive model will contain correct information about these predispositions and about biological realities in general.

One can put it this way: to maximize personal satisfaction, people need to avoid conflict between what their inner motivations are pushing them to do and what they have been induced to believe or taught to strive for.

We have said that, even though modern humans don't seek to maximize reproductive success, the machinery that drove us to do so in the natural environment is still in place. What does this mean? Let us take an obvious example, one that we talked about in our chapters on the male. Modern men, like their ancestors, pursue women. This is common knowledge. But, many men now use birth control and are exceedingly concerned that no offspring result from their matings. The cortex has figured out that birth control is a very good idea; by using birth control, men can have sex without the encumbrances of children. They can go from embrace to embrace, without incurring that particular cost.

The impulse to woo is the mechanism that once caused men to fertilize many women. The mechanism doesn't necessarily produce that effect but the drive still exists. Lust lives on, even though it has lost some of its original function.

The tendency to participate in reciprocal relationships is another biological tendency that has been pushed aside. Many people underestimate the need for community. At crucial points in their lives, individualism sways them to give up their attachments. The inclination to participate in reciprocal relationships is not always strong enough to keep people together, but the need for such relationships *is* sufficiently strong to cause misery in those who ignore it.

The principle can be stated as follows: Without knowing it, modern humans often behave in ways that *used to* maximize inclusive fitness. Lacking knowledge of the original function of their behavior, they cannot put it in perspective, making it difficult for them to change behavior that is now maladaptive. One of the tasks of therapy is to help them to gain perspective, to understand their behavior.

The point we are making here is so crucial that we want to present it from

Culture and Reproductive Success

In some Western subcultures, the urge to have sex is still producing reproductive success. Some years ago, a controversial TV documentary showed young black men bragging about the babies they had begotten on their conquests, mainly teenage girls in the welfare morass. These young men were full of pride in their paternity. They took it as a sign of virility, and of course they were right, in a sense. Their naive enthusiasm reflected one of the mechanisms that once led humans to maximize their inclusive fitness. They seemed to have been uninfluenced by the technology of birth control.

Interestingly enough, the older people get, the more likely they are to use birth control effectively. In our view, this is because the older one gets, the wiser one gets, i.e., the more the cortex can override innate behavioral tendencies.

yet another angle. In the natural environment, survival and reproduction are *coupled*; a good hunter and a good gatherer will be able to nourish their kids. Personal satisfaction and reproduction are coupled; people who are well fed will be interested in sex and will end up with kids. Status and reproduction are coupled: a man with status will tend to reproduce more than a man without. In our society, these factors have gotten uncoupled; personal satisfaction, status, satisfaction and wealth can be pursued without getting involved in reproduction.[3] Hence conflict.

To avoid misunderstanding, we want to emphasize these points: Unlike some of the biologists who have attempted to grapple with human behavior, we are NOT saying that people do, or must, or should, behave the way evolution designed humans to behave. We say only that people will profit by understanding what *drives* them to behave that way.

With this principle in mind, we can begin to specify what elements an adaptive model should contain. Our list follows. We welcome improvements. Note that while some of the items on the list are standard staples of psychotherapy, others are not.

[3]Biologists will recognize that the argument here hinges on the distinction between proximate and ultimate causes.

1. A sense of identity and self-worth that is strong enough to enable a person to deal effectively with others. This seems to require that one have an acceptable "story" about oneself, one's family and one's upbringing. Hence therapists will frequently have to address the vicissitudes of childhood. Since children often absorb messages about themselves without being consciously aware of them, some therapeutic attention to unconscious material will probably be necessary.

2. An absence of grandiosity, excessive pride, selfishness and other traits that make gratifying social relationships impossible. When the cortex places a high value on itself, it often places a low value on other people. There is an old saying: "He loves humanity, but he hates people." Such an outlook derives from hubris, from perfectionism, and from the rejection of the self as organism.

3. A reasonably accurate sense of reciprocity. While the basic rules of reciprocity are universal, some details differ from society to society. Each individual must have the flexibility to adjust to the prevailing social standards.

4. An ability to determine the costs and benefits of a social exchange, so as to be able to engage in exchanges that benefit both self and other. This involves the ability to detect cheating, so as not to be exploited, and the ability to give enough so as not to be identified, and punished, as a cheater.

5. An acceptance of one's own aggressive and self-protective impulses.

6. An acceptance of one's gender and the behavioral predispositions that go along with it.

7. An acceptance of one's sexual predilections. Obviously, if these are unacceptable to society (e.g. sadism, exhibitionism), therapists will have to help their clients to go beyond self-acceptance to an acceptance of society's standards.

8. Correct information about the current environment. The current environment includes the overall socio-economic system, plus the client's social network, workplace, ethnic and religious beliefs and ties, current family, and upbringing. Most psychotherapies do pay attention to goodness of fit in the current environment. If the current environment does not match the expectations that are built into the brain, problems with the client's model can be expected. For example, if the environment is set up so that self-development is only possible by discarding social ties, as when an individual must betray family, friends or social class to get ahead, one can expect a great deal of internal conflict. Guilt can be relieved by helping the client to understand that it is natural to be loyal *and* natural to want to get ahead. In

RECIPROCITY AND THE MODEL

It's easy to say that natural selection has shaped how people think, but it's harder to prove it. Leda Cosmides may have proved it. In a remarkable tour de force, Cosmides, then a young graduate student at Harvard, showed that the human brain contains specialized mechanisms designed especially to calculate the costs and benefits of social relationships.

She did it by analyzing the results obtained on a well-known test of logical thinking, the Wason Selection Task. The results obtained on this test had puzzled researchers for years. For no apparent reason, people did better on certain types of problems than on others. Some psychologists tried to explain these results by invoking "familiarity"; cognitive psychologists are in general comfortable with the idea that people do better on problems with which they are familiar.

Cosmides devised a series of experiments, using familiar and unfamiliar situations. Some of the situations involved reciprocity; others didn't. In the ones that did, people had to figure out how to detect whether or not cheating had occurred. The results showed that familiarity had nothing to do with the results. But reciprocity did. People were able to get at the heart of the problems involving reciprocity, even if the situation was unfamiliar.

Logically, the problems were all similar. But logic only got people so far—about 25% correct answers. When the situation involved reciprocal relationships, the percentage of correct answers was much higher. Hence Cosmides' conclusion: the brain has specialized mechanisms designed to track reciprocal relationships and to make sure that cheating does not occur.

What does this mean for clinical practice? Reciprocity is fundamental. People whose models do not include reasonably accurate assumptions about reciprocity will not be able to function well in any society made up of human beings. Therapy must help people to grasp the principles of reciprocity.

Cosmides is about to turn her talents to sexual jealousy. Stay tuned.

this type of situation, clients need to understand that the fault lies not within the self but within the system.

Take for example the case of Elroy. He was from a lower-class family in an urban ghetto. He was smart. He did well in elementary school, but when he got to junior high, his friends started to tease him about his grades. They said he was going over to "the Man," and excluded him from their social

THE INNER DIALOGUE: ADAPTIVE DIMENSIONS?

The inner dialogue that runs inside most people's head generally involves, we believe, two voices (or positions) which are in partial disagreement with each other. At any given time, on any given subject, one voice is generally taking a positive view and one voice is taking the negative view. The pros fight it out with the cons.

There are clearly pathological forms of the dialogue, such as the one described in the box on p. 190. But this raises an interesting question: If there are pathological forms of the inner dialogue, what is the nature of a non-pathological form? What is an adaptive inner dialogue, one that contributes to both the well-being and survival of the organism?

Some glimmer of an answer can be gleaned from the study of people who don't have both voices. We have encountered, in therapy, people who do not seem to have a voice which presents the negative side of things — a voice which warns of drawbacks, disapproval, or danger. Some of these people behave impulsively or compulsively. Others seem to have figured out a way to compensate. They construct explicit rules of behavior. The rules are designed to avoid bad consequences, i.e., punishment or a punishing outcome. The consequences have to be learned by experience, like a rat: "A" leads to "B," "B" is bad, hence avoid "A." Rules constructed in this manner generally have to be rigid in the extreme. Furthermore, people who

(*continued*)

activities. He pushed his studies underground, got back with his friends, all the while managing to keep his grades up enough to get a scholarship to a good college. There, he did well for a year, but in the second year he started to miss classes, whereupon he was recommended to the school counseling office. Fortunately, the counselor understood Elroy's dilemma. Elroy was brought to the realization that he was not going to help his friends any by flunking out. Eventually he was inspired to "help his race." But years later, he still felt guilty about leaving his friends behind. He never came to terms with his success.

At this point, we anticipate an objection: what about a model that enables a particular individual to live harmoniously in a family, ethnic group or subculture, even though the model contains all kinds of misinformation about biology, the real motives of the self, and the relationship between the cortex and the rest of the body? In other words, what if a social consensus

---

THE INNER DIALOGUE: ADAPTIVE DIMENSIONS? *(continued)*

operate this way are always subject to temptation; they live with the idea that if circumstances are right, they can get away with it.

People with an intrinsic negative voice don't have to go through this kind of learning. Since they can avoid (bad) feelings — the feelings that come up when the negative voice is activated — they don't have to avoid consequences. They can stay away from disapproval, and out of danger, by changing direction as soon as they feel guilt, shame, fear, or some other negative emotion.

This would imply that the tendency to avoid certain feelings is useful and possibly adaptive, even in the strict biological sense of the word. The tendency could play a role in keeping the individual out of trouble and in good standing in the community.

We raise a question: is the duality of the inner dialogue a cortical expression of approach/avoidance mechanisms located deeper in the brain? Is the dialogue, in its intact or healthy form, part of a process of evaluating the risks and benefits of any course of action? And any transaction involving reciprocity? These are questions which seem to be worth investigating.

Some therapists might be alarmed at this point. In therapy, one often seeks to put people in touch with their emotions. We are saying that avoiding emotions can be adaptive. Is there a contradiction? We don't think so. If the tendency to avoid certain feelings is working for someone, s/he is probably not in therapy. Only if that tendency has gotten out of hand, to the point of creating symptoms or interfering with social relationships, will a person seek help. Then the therapist will be called upon to restore the mechanism to its proper function.

---

has crystallized around the misinformation? Our answer to this is simple: people who are functioning well in a family and getting along well in a viable group do not generally come to see psychotherapists. We do not seek to change ideas for the sake of change, but only to help people who are in conflict with themselves or with others.

Note that the approach outlined here moves psychotherapy away from the search for hidden meaning. Models do contain elements that lie beneath the threshold of consciousness. They even have elements that have never been expressed in words, because the events (abuse, etc.) that gave rise to them occurred before the child was verbal. But these "unconscious" elements are not terribly mysterious. They are assumptions about reality, about self and about others that are quite understandable. The expectation of clarity contrasts sharply with the tradition of truth being hidden, as in obscure dreams and repressed wishes. Psychotherapists who are accustomed to interpreting mysteries may regard this expectation of clarity as naive.

Models and split self-representation

The model-building capacity of the brain is what allows some people to carry around conflicting or split representations of self and/or other. Suppose that instead of developing one model of "mother," for example, a child developed two models, one of which included all her positive aspects while the other included all her negative aspects. If all further positive experiences were routed to one of the models and all further negative experiences to the other, the individual could oscillate between the two models, depending on circumstances and the state of the brain. This would produce the erratic social and emotional behavior generally associated with borderline personality organization and others syndromes in the borderline spectrum. (It is not that multiplicity of models implies illness, as all humans appear to have multiple models of reality. Illness occurs when barriers between the representations prevent coherent functioning.)

Models of reward and punishment

As British psychologist Jeffrey Gray showed in *The Psychology of Fear and Stress*, the brain constructs models of the world that include expectations of reward and punishment. Because these expectations exist, failure to get an expected reward is sometimes experienced as punishment, and failure to get an expected punishment can be the equivalent of reward. Examples are easy to think of. If you offer a child an ice cream cone every time she comes home at 3 o'clock, the child will feel cheated if, the next time she comes home on time, you fail to reward her.

The adaptive character of these expectations is clear; they are designed to induce animals to repeat approach and avoidance behaviors that are beneficial. Because a reward is expected, the behavior is repeated. When an animal lives in an environment which is relatively predictable, learned expectations of reward and punishment usually don't give rise to problems. They constitute good guides for behavior. For example, the expectation that a rabbit will be found in a rabbit warren will usually serve a hungry ferret well.

In our society, where individuals are exposed in childhood to extremely diverse and complex situations, expectations of reward and punishment can be more problematic. What one learns to expect in childhood may not serve

RIGHT AND WRONG AS ELEMENTS OF THE MODEL

Sara had been complaining about being weak, unable to express herself or get what she wanted, unsure of who she was. The therapist had no idea what the trouble was. Then, out of the blue, Sara suddenly made a very strong statement about herself: "I have a strong sense of right and wrong." The statement turned out to be the thread that led out of the labyrinth.

T: How do you know what is right and wrong if you don't know who you are?

C: I don't know. I've always tried to do what is right.

T: How did you know what was right?

C: I don't know. What my parents thought, I guess. They were religious. I had no use for it, but I pretended, to please them . . .

T: So you're always searching for what is right and wrong, those are your categories. You turn everything into that.

C: Yes. Of course. Doesn't everybody?

T: Well, you see yourself that what you think is right may not really be anything but what you were told.

C: But some things everybody would agree are wrong. Shoplifting, for example.

T: Lots of people think shoplifting is just fine. You are dealing with nothing but categories your mind has created. The categories aren't real.

C: Oh yes they *are* real, I feel emotion around it.

T: Ah, I think I see. I'll bet you don't feel equally strong emotions around other things.

C: You're right.

T: You've taken all your emotions and invested them in this category of yours. You've actually robbed the rest of your life. Now I understand why you feel weak. You have no emotions around what you want. There's your lack of sense of self. You have no strong feelings about what is you, only about what is right and wrong.

C: Yes, and it's horrible. It's such pressure. I have to be perfect. And I fail, and I have such guilt about it.

Until this session, Sara had no idea that her endless search for the right move in every situation was both doomed to fail and a cause of her problems. She had thought the solution to her problems lay in discovering what was right. The tool she was using was part of the problem, not part of the solution. The unexamined premise that lay at the heart of her model was destroying her life.

Childhood and the Model

As this passage indicates, events of early childhood mark the model indelibly. Logan, who was enmeshed with his fairly abusive family of origin, was being asked for his feelings toward the therapist:

C: If you were killed or if people talked badly about you, I would be upset.
T: Yes, but what can you tell me about what you're feeling now.
C: Well, I don't love you like a brother.
T: That's interesting. I've been much better to you than any of your brothers.
C: If you're saying I should love you like a brother, forget it. Those kinds of relationships always backfire on me.
T: So you run away from relationships because of what you learned in the family?
C: I guess so.
T: It sounds as if you have to treat outsiders as if they were nothing to you.
C: I think you're asking me to abandon my family.
T: To have a relationship with someone outside means abandoning the family? Some people do both.
C: Well, that's what it means to me. I can't even imagine what you're talking about.

Therapy subsequently focused on making a distinction between helpless love, which Logan was afraid of falling into, and the friendship, trust, and love that adults sometimes feel for each other. Until he could make this distinction, which his model didn't include, there was no hope of his ever establishing real trust in the therapist or positive relationships with other people.

as a good guide to future action. One can easily develop a defective model of the environment.

Such models are often remarkably persistent. This is due at least in part to another characteristic of the brain. Expectations of punishment can often be extinguished only by direct confrontation with the feared stimulus. But since fear of a stimulus generally leads to avoidance behavior, the stimulus itself may never be confronted, and the model may persist indefinitely.

Models of status (the social environment)

The brains of animals develop models of the social as well as the physical environment. These models have serious effects on biologically-relevant activity, even among animals with smaller brains and less encephelization. For example, among antelope, males who do not become dominant by defeating other males for a place on the *lek* (mating ground), appear to voluntarily give up their mating opportunities. In other words, they act as if they "know" that they are subordinate, and this knowledge determines their behavior.

Among humans, this tendency has become particularly prominent. Humans are, in general, exquisitely aware of how they (think they) stand. Most people carry around in their heads an internalized hierarchy. Everyone else is either above or below self. Perhaps this explains the human obsession with equality. Members of our species do not like to have others over them. When individuals perceive themselves as being low down on their internalized totem pole, serious psychological problems often ensue, whether or not the perception is distorted.

The existence of the brain's model-forming mechanism implies that cognition cannot be excluded from psychotherapy. Therapists informed by the evolutionary perspective will probably find it necessary to engage in some information-sharing and some theoretical discussion with their clients. However, we do not want to give the impression that cognitive interventions represent the exclusive focus of a therapy informed by evolution. On the contrary, we recognize the value of many techniques. Corrective emotional experiences, support, positive regard, the creation of a therapeutic alliance, and many of the other standard methods of psychotherapy are all essential, and are often far more important than purely cognitive interventions. Indeed, as we hope to show in the next chapter, the notion of adaptive model is a natural bridge between cognition, emotion and intrapsychic structure, as well as between individual and multi-person therapy.

CAUSALITY AND LOYALTY: TWO PROPERTIES OF THE BRAIN

One of the strongest tendencies of the human brain is what might be called a hunger for causality. The brain seeks to find explanations, to connect "A" with "B," to find relationships between phenomena. The almost involuntary search for causal explanations helps to explain one of the most common conditions seen in clinical practice: the self-blame of the abused child.

The child who is abused, physically or emotionally, for no good reason, automatically, it seems, creates an explanation for the inexplicable: "I must have done something wrong." More often than not, no wrong thing can be identified, although the person thrashes about endlessly in search of something specific. If something is identified, and the therapist asks: "Do you think that really justified the abuse?" the client may agree that the crime really didn't merit the punishment, but will then go in search of some other putative cause for self-recrimination.

When clients finally begin to face the fact that unjustified abuse occurred, there is often a crisis. They become uncomfortable, resistant, anxious, blocked, etc. When pressed, they admit to feeling guilty about accusing the parents. Here is a characteristic statement:

C: If I blame them, I feel guilty. It's a lot easier to blame myself. Actually, if feels worse to blame them than to blame myself.
T: What does it feel like, exactly?
C: It feels like lying. Treacherous.
T: Disloyal?
C: That's it. Disloyal.

Loyalty to the family, we have seen, became a fundamental value in human life because without family and band no individual could survive in the natural environment. This basic fact of life helps to explain why so many people choose to blame themselves rather than blaming their families.

In the natural environment, people generally do not have to choose between self and family. Parents can't abuse their children, and all members of the band are interdependent. The conflicts that do arise among adults are clear and can be resolved unambiguously. When a choice between self and family has to be made, the brain can't come up with a good solution. It operates according to principles that do not permit it to deal effectively with this situation. This is one further example of the mismatch between genes and environment.

CHAPTER 12

Towards an Evolutionary
Psychotherapy

Our life is frittered away by detail. . . . Simplify,
simplify.

— Henry David Thoreau

SINCE THE APPLICATION OF EVOLUTIONARY CONCEPTS to human behavior is
relatively new, it makes sense to proceed cautiously. In this chapter, we will
limit ourselves to some general remarks about the interface between evolution and contemporary schools of psychotherapy. We will use evolutionary
theory to pick and choose between conflicting theories of human nature and
the specific interventions that are associated with those theories. What
seems to make sense in the light of evolution, and what doesn't? We hope
our remarks will serve as the basis for future discussion.

We can sum up our findings as follows: When it comes to interventions,
no existing school of psychotherapy has all the answers. Almost all schools
have developed *some* interventions that are clearly compatible with what is
known about human evolution. Among these interventions we would include the following:

1. the provision of new information through teaching, coaching and
training;
2. reinterpretation of past experience;
3. uncovering of previously unconscious (unexamined) assumptions;
4. undoing of pathological intrapsychic structures, such as those involved in so-called primitive defenses;

5. encouraging corrective emotional experiences, such as the formation of new relationships;
6. encouraging the experience of success;
7. reinforcing the performance of new behaviors;
8. altering of the systems in which people live;
9. positive reframing of experiences.

In contrast to the clear value of the interventions, the rationales used by the various theorists to justify their approaches are often seriously flawed, and at worst incompatible with what is known about the behavior of living things. In addition, quite a few theories claim to be in exclusive possession of the truth. Psychotherapy is a divided field primarily because of these competing, incomplete theories.

To combine the recognized therapeutic *interventions* into one smooth eclectic blend is relatively easy and very desirable; most of them are perfectly compatible with each other. They serve different functions and are useful in different circumstances. The existing theories, however, *are* incompatible, because each one describes only a circumscribed portion of the truth. For example, behaviorist theory is incompatible with psychoanalytic theory, but the behavioral technique of desensitization is similar to the psychoanalytic process of exploring childhood traumas. As Paul Wachtel showed in *Psychoanalysis and Behavior Therapy*, exploration *is* a form of desensitization. Similarly, some family and couples therapists may base their work on systems theories that are incompatible with the theories used in individual work, but their methods are not at all incompatible. From a practical point of view it makes perfect sense to treat couples *some of the time*, families *some of the time*, and individuals *some of the time*.

In developing our approach to existing theories, we have relied most heavily on four of the themes developed previously: the mismatch between genes and environment; reciprocity; gender; and model-building. We expect an adequate comprehensive theory to take into account the existence of genetic predispositions; the fact that we live in an altered environment; the need for community and reciprocal relationships; biological differences between the genders; and the propensity of the brain to build models of the environment.

Let us give an example of how we apply these themes to the analysis of theory. Some schools of therapy say that one should focus on current functioning. Others say one should focus on early experience. We find that neither of these approaches is correct. Models begin to form early in life, so childhood events can continue to effect current functioning throughout life. Hence it makes good sense to explore the events that formed the model.

Nevertheless, a change in current functioning is the goal, and if it can be achieved directly, without exploration of the past, why not? The past lives in the model, and if the model is changed, the past is transformed. There is no dichotomy, there are only different pathways to change.

The Therapeutic Relationship

The therapeutic relationship has rightly been considered one of the most important aspects of therapy. Evolutionary theory provides a good explanation. Humans are not autonomous; they were designed to live in bands. Our ancestors were living in bands before they were human. To be included in relationships in which one feels known, heard, seen, and understood is a biological necessity. In the current environment, many people are deprived of such relationships, or find the relationships they have somehow insufficient. The therapeutic alliance gives them something they have been missing. Indeed, the alliance might even be usefully considered as a two-person "band." The therapist stands in for the supportive, interdependent friends and relatives that are absent from the client's life. The band is safe in its home base; danger lies outside, in the jungles, savannas, and deserts — now in streets and alleys, and even in families. The therapeutic relationship must become, for the client, a surrogate home base, a place where it is safe to tell the truth, to let go, to be angry without fear of retaliation, and to be crazy.

This requires therapists to have some special qualities. First of all, we cannot demand reciprocity as we expect it from friends and colleagues. We have to teach it without requiring it, because clients may be in therapy precisely because they are unable to manage reciprocity normally. But we also must foster their capacity to move toward normal reciprocity with other people, including the therapist. Second, we must have qualities that inspire trust. We are strangers to our clients — that is a great barrier. We are not related, we do not have a history of reliable interaction. To inspire trust we need faith in ourselves, faith that we can be relied on, and faith that we can understand. We also need faith in our ability to lead people out of at least some of their difficulties. The idea that therapists should, as an article of faith, expect that their clients can find their own way out of their problems is not very convincing. Attentive listening is sometimes, but certainly not always, enough. A sense of participation is the crucial factor.

The need to establish trust should not be taken as an argument for one particular type of therapy. Trust can be won in different ways. One way is to listen quietly while the client slowly discovers that nothing bad is going to happen in the sessions. Other ways are equally successful. Some clients need a mentor, some an advocate, some a partner, some a coach, others a healer. All of these roles can inspire trust.

Whatever role the therapist takes, healing is accomplished through communication and solidarity. Therapists understand and are not repelled. They are "in it" with the client, allies in the mind.

Inclusion

It follows that providing inclusion is one of the therapist's most important tasks. Much of what therapists already do can be understood in this light. Whenever therapists validate a client through understanding, they are providing inclusion. Unconditional positive regard, empathic listening, and positive reinforcement are all methods for providing inclusion, making the client feel part of something—the alliance, the human race, etc.

A less obvious example is the family therapy technique of positive reframing. In this technique, actions are attributed to positive motivations. For example, a father is restricting his son and the son resents it. The therapist reframes the action as a matter not of hostility but of caring. Restriction then may be seen as a positive concern that is misfiring, rather than as oppression. If the reframing works, both father and son will feel part of the family again. Alienation will be replaced by inclusion.

Reframing is also helpful in individual therapy. It comforts people to believe that they have good intentions, and so, by reducing their self-hatred, fosters their ability to enter into relationships with others.

A reframing intervention that derives directly from the evolutionary approach deserves special mention here: the ability to say (when appropriate), "Your way of doing things (being, behavior, tendency, etc.) is fine, it would have worked perfectly well in the natural environment, but it isn't working out for you in today's environment." This intervention allows the therapist to validate a wide range of problematic thoughts and actions, without fear of increasing their frequency.

It is probably worthwhile at this juncture to contrast the view we are presenting with that of psychoanalysis. In the analytic perspective, the potential for conflict of interest between the therapist and the client is so great that therapists must confine themselves to listening and sharing the world of the client, avoiding any attempt to sway the client in any particular direction, for fear of sending the client in a direction that is good for the therapist rather than for the client. The client's inner world is seen as so special, so unique, and so unknowable, that any attempt to influence it or shape it would be more likely to hurt than help. Secondly, many if not all analysts see themselves as treating conflict that is inherent to all human beings. They are treating the human condition, not psychopathology. The client is seen as being isolated because s/he is human. To decrease this essential human isolation, the analyst listens and conveys understanding.

We agree that there is potential for conflict between therapist and client. However, our reading of the evolutionary record indicates that providing inclusion is the most important aspect of therapy. Listening silently and empathizing does not seem, to us at least, to be the best way of doing this.

It is true that some clients are resistant to inclusion. Indeed, kin selection theory (see Chapter 3) would lead us to assume that clients will be somewhat suspicious of all strangers, including therapists, who claim to be on their side. So one should not be surprised when clients are resistant. Suspiciousness will be intense among clients who are convinced that they are inferior. Such people tend to discount praise and encouragement; they assume that anyone who encourages them is either deluded or self-interested. So therapists can't naively proceed on the assumption that praise will be helpful. But resistance to inclusion does not require that the therapist refrain from active intervention, or become a neutral screen on which the client can project fantasies. Direct interventions by the therapist may well interfere with the full blossoming of transference, but fortunately, a good working alliance does not depend on pristine transference. The therapist can afford to appear as a real human being, one who has special competence and effective knowledge.

We also believe, contrary to many psychoanalytical theorists (but perhaps not to Heinz Kohut and his school) that psychological distress is more the product of the changed environment than of the human condition. Distress is largely the product of confusion about what is going on — "Why isn't what I do working out?" Hence, it is worthwhile risking active interventions. Making a mistake — suggesting something that comes out of the therapist's experience rather than that of the client — is more likely if one is active, but is compensated for by other factors: (1) the sense of participation in a joint endeavor; and (2) the sense of having a therapist who can help to solve pressing real-life problems effectively.

Exploration of Childhood

Models are constructed on the basis of experience. The events of infancy and childhood are undeniably among the most significant elements of experience. Each event in a person's lifetime affects all those that come after it; hence, the early events have greatest potential effect. Furthermore, a good deal of early experience occurs before the brain has developed the capacity for analytical thought. This experience is incorporated, uncritically, as raw data. If the information available to a child is particularly flawed, due to problems in upbringing, the models formed by the brain are likely to be inaccurate and incomplete. Children who learn the wrong (idiosyncratic) rules in the family tend to have trouble adjusting to society later in life. Hence, we consider exploration of the past and the recovery of repressed and dissociated experiences to be vital. Psychotherapy must go back far enough, and dig deep enough, to uncover those elements of the client's model that are preventing growth and development.

But what should be explored? This is a complex question. We suggest that investigation of the past should focus on how the environment of a client's childhood deviated from biological norms, as described in Chapters 4 and 5. This will identify the factors which interfered with the development of an adaptive model of self and other. Among the most important things, therefore, are the events, real or imagined, which affected attachment and individuation, or which contributed to low self-esteem, grandiose expectations, lack of a reasonably integrated sense of self, and lack of trust in others.

Cognitive Interventions

There is clearly a cognitive dimension to the therapy we do, since we often focus directly on assumptions, beliefs, and the information-processing mechanisms which maintain them. In this respect, our approach is similar to that of cognitive therapists such as Aaron Beck and Albert Ellis, who have long argued that emotions and behavior are dependent on cognition. The need for a cognitive approach to therapy is clearly supported by the fact that the cerebral cortex has come to play such a powerful role in the life of our species. Since what goes on in the cortex affects virtually all other functions of the human organism, therapy needs to address the thoughts people think. Hence, rational discourse, reasoning, teaching and coaching have their place in therapy.

Where do we differ from the cognitive therapists? Our understanding of how the brain works suggests that cognitive therapists tend to overstate the rational component of behavior. Thinking can certainly affect emotion, but emotion also affects cognition. Some people have deep-seated emotional reactions which control their behavior without cognitive awareness, obscuring any connection between their emotions, their thoughts and their behavior. Only when these feelings are allowed to surface can the cognitions and behaviors associated with them be dealt with effectively.

We also feel that in emphasizing the importance of maladaptive thinking in creating psychological distress, cognitive therapists tend to convey the

DEFENSES

One of the hottest topics among psychologists with an interest in evolution is the question of defenses. Are they "adaptive" or not, i.e., are they strategies that evolved for good reason over the millennia, or are they pathological responses to the current environment?

Malcolm Slavin, a psychoanalytically-oriented psychologist who has worked closely with Robert Trivers, believes that repression is an adaptive response. His argument is as follows: Children need to be able to suppress, temporarily, certain kinds of information, but they also need to be able to recover this information later in life. Repression allows them to do so.

Why do children have to suppress information? The answer, says Slavin, is found in parent-offspring conflict. What parents do isn't always in the best interests of the child. Parents sometimes try to get children to do things that are good for the parents but not so good for the children. Parents generally try to form children according to some desiderata of their own. Furthermore, parents often have more than one child, and have to divide their attention and resources between all the offspring, to the detriment of each one. But since children are totally dependent and helpless, it wouldn't be in their interests to make a fuss. They need to avoid conflict. So they repress the knowledge of their parent's selfishness until later, when they can use it to develop their own sense of self. It follows that repression is a necessary ability, an adaptive response.

(continued)

message that thinking is the most important aspect of human life. We have not found in the texts of cognitive therapy a strong awareness of the realities of gender or a concern with natural predispositions. Cognitive therapists seem to encourage people to use their minds primarily to overcome (transcend) their limitations, rather than to harmonize their impulses with their thoughts. We think the mind must be guided by messages from the rest of the organism. It is flattering to think that human beings have "unlimited potential," but grandiosity lurks in those words. Clients need to come to terms with the limitations that are inherent in any living organism, in order to counteract inflated expectations of self and of other.

A striking example of the implicit elitism that springs from an overemphasis on thought and language can be seen in Leston Havens' *Making Contact: Uses of Language in Psychotherapy*:

DEFENSES (*continued*)

We tend to agree with Slavin on this point. But can the argument be extended to other defenses? Perhaps. Denial might serve to block out negative information of the kind that fosters pessimism, induces depression, and undermines the will to survive.[1] Denial may be one of the mechanisms that helps some people to overcome apparently hopeless odds. It could also help an individual ward off negative attributions and unfavorable interpretations by others. Denial may also help people to fool other people; it's easiest to fool others when one is oneself sincere.

Projection could have arisen to help members of our highly social species interpret the actions of other people. It can help to understand the motives of others, which is useful whether one wishes to outwit them or to empathize.

But what of such "defenses" as splitting, split self-representation, and the fragmentation involved in Multiple Personality Disorder? At the present time, we tend to think that these defenses are not design features but rather design failures, cracks that appear when the organism is subjected to unusual stress, not mechanisms crafted by evolution to serve a purpose. One might speculate that some of these other defenses appear when repression fails—when it isn't enough to protect the organism. Hopefully, researchers will begin to look into this and related questions.

[1] Interestingly enough, Tom Hackett of the Massachusetts General Hospital has shown that heart attack victims who show more denial about their prognosis have an increased survival rate.

It is no coincidence that existential psychiatry should emerge at this time [now]. The growing awareness of the psychological dimension, of the precariousness of human existence, and of the competing and often oppressive demands on human life makes the existential search for human Being and human beings seem, once again, the response of the organism to the demands of its world. This effort can be thought of as *a psychological speciation in which members of the human race are separated into those who are fully human and those who are not* (page viii, italics added).

Cognitive Behavior Modification

Techniques such as thought-stopping and the deliberate repetition of positive statements about the self should be reconsidered in light of the model-building nature of the brain. Such techniques are often helpful, but we don't think that by themselves they constitute the best way to alter maladaptive models. Negative self-defeating ideas are not flotsam and jetsam, floating around in the mind like driftwood; they are generally elements of the client's model. The most effective interventions address the model as a whole, or the relationships between elements of the model.

A word on the role of cognition in the therapeutic alliance: establishing an alliance is one of the most important cognitive experiences imaginable, because it serves to directly correct faulty models of self and other. Through the alliance, clients gradually realize that they are creating many of the reactions that they attribute to others. They discover that, potentially, they have some control over what happens to them, i.e., by changing the way they think and feel about themselves they can change the way others relate to them.

Among the ideas that are corrected through the relationship one might include the following:

> No one will like me.
> I am too horrible to help.
> I have to be perfect to be with people.
> Contact with others is unpleasant.
> Everyone will attack me.
> I have to remain alone.
> I am too complicated to be understood.

The magic of healing takes place when these kinds of ideas are unlearned through relationship and contact.

Stress Reduction

Some form of stress reduction should be an adjunct of virtually every psychotherapeutic endeavor. The stress response — fight or flight — evolved in order to help organisms mobilize energy to meet emergencies. The fight-flight reactions causes the release of cortisol and adrenaline. When that release is followed by intense physical activity the body is able to metabolize the chemicals that are by-products of the stress response. If no physical activity follows an episode of stress, the metabolites released remain in the body where they are harmful. The tendency of such metabolites to accumulate in people who live relatively sedentary lives means they are, in effect, exposed to prolonged, inescapable stress. The stress contributes to a host of psychological problems. Stress reduction reduces the amount of chemicals the body releases.

In addition to having a direct beneficial effects on physical health, relaxation exercises facilitate the exploration process. In the relaxed state, people discover elements of their models that have hitherto been repressed or dissociated. With surprise and sudden recognition, they sometimes are able to encounter the assumptions that had been hidden from them. They discover how they have been bringing misfortune on themselves. Relaxation facilitates insight.

Relaxation also reduces resistance, so people stop defending their actions and beliefs. In the relaxed state, they establish a temporary truce with their therapists, and allow themselves to experience their defenses. Hence, relaxation facilitates the discovery of new solutions.

Hypnosis and Ericksonian Utilization

Milton Erickson's style of hypnosis would seem to be on the opposite end of the spectrum from cognitive therapy, so it isn't surprising that representatives of the two approaches sometimes disparage each other. From the evolutionary perspective, however, the cognitive and Ericksonian techniques are entirely complementary. The key, once again, is model-building. Cognitive therapy addresses elements of the model directly. Ericksonian techniques address models indirectly, if necessary without the knowledge or participation of the client. Hidden assumptions that have controlled behavior are bypassed, and the new behavior serves to change the assumptions.

The Ericksonian techniques are particularly useful as methods of coping with resistance. The conscious mind is sometimes an ally of the change process and sometimes a source of resistance to change. When resistance is significant and/or the ability to profit from insight limited, it makes sense to bypass conscious processing with informal hypnosis and indirect suggestion; reasoning with the client will probably yield poor results. Paradoxical interventions which keep the conscious mind off balance can also facilitate change even in very poorly motivated clients.

The Ericksonian approach is also valuable in that it provides clients with successes. Through Ericksonian "utilization," clients learn that whatever they do will be accepted by the therapist. They can build on this for success in everyday life.

Other Behavioral Interventions

We have often found behavioral interventions such as rehearsal, role-play, image work, systematic exposure, and homework assignments useful in changing a model and the behavior that depends on it. One can explain this in a variety of ways. We will do it by reference to two properties of the brain: (a) extinction and (b) the need for successes.

As is well known, passive avoidance is often remarkably hard to eliminate (extinguish).[2] In many cases, it cannot be extinguished at all unless the organism is forced to experience the feared stimulus. For example, if a puppy is shocked when it eats from a particular bowl, it will avoid the bowl from that point on, and so will never learn whether or not it will be shocked again if it eats from that bowl. The only way to teach the puppy that the bowl is safe is to push its face into the bowl.

The failure of extinction plays a significant role in psychotherapy. Many people unconsciously avoid various situations (options) because they think that some dire consequence will ensue. Unless they actually do the thing that they fear, they can never learn that they have nothing to fear. Here is a clinical example: Marlene came to therapy because she constantly got involved in unsatisfactory relationships. "I never get what I want. Some people get love, support, affection, even attention. Not me." She was always angry about this, but always tried to hide it. "I pretend to be happy." She never expressed her anger, and played at being the perfect woman. In therapy, she reconnected to her deprived childhood and realized the connection between her childhood and her anger. She realized that her anger at other people was really directed at her parents. But she remained angry, and continued to get involved in bad relationships. Why?

Classically, she might have been considered masochistic, or in the grip of the compulsion to reproduce her childhood situation. We don't think this formulation is particularly helpful. The problem was that her low self-esteem rendered her incapable of experiencing the love and support that she wanted. When she was offered love, it felt exceedingly unfamiliar, even bad. She would imagine she had tricked the other person into giving her something she didn't deserve. She couldn't respond wholeheartedly. Obviously, this did not encourage other people to move in her direction with love and affection.

The solution was twofold. One, she had to learn to recognize how inappropriate it is to feel bad when someone does something nice. Two, she had to deliberately expose herself—desensitize herself—to the bad feelings engendered in her by affection. Her avoidance response to relationships had to be extinguished. When, in the arms of a lover, she experienced panic and overcame it, she gained the ability to establish satisfactory relationships.

The failure to do what is necessary to produce extinction is one of the primary causes of the long stalemates that are common in psychodynamic

---

[2]Passive avoidance is the term used to describe a situation in which an animal can avoid a punishment merely by refraining from doing something. In active avoidance, the animal must do something (e.g., jump from one place to another, or peck a particular button) to avoid the punishment.

psychotherapy and is in part responsible for the popularity of the notion that insight doesn't change behavior.

Another important rationale for behavioral interventions is that people have a biological need to experience success. Success builds self-esteem and influences identity—crucial elements in anyone's model of the world. Hence therapists need to help people recognize tasks that can be carried out successfully.

One final word on behavioral techniques. The fact that all individuals have developed models of their environment and their place in it explains why positive reinforcement is often an ineffective therapeutic tool. If the reinforcement is not "believable," i.e., consonant with the model, the individual will discount it. Thus, people with low self-esteem often think that the praise they receive is false, because the giver is self-interested, unworthy of attention, lacking in insight, or "just doing it to help." The human capacity for detecting "cheating" is put to use to reject praise.

Expressive Interventions

While we don't see expressive interventions as central to change in psychotherapy, we do believe that they can play an important ancillary role when combined with other therapeutic techniques.

For one thing, cathartic techniques generally make people feel temporarily better, and this is not a negligible result. In addition, such techniques may smash barriers between bits of information (experiences), thus allowing the information to come to the surface, where it can be recombined into a new model. Cathartic interventions are particularly useful for people who are going through life thinking that they must not express certain emotions, lest something dire happen. This is simply another form of avoidance response. The expression of the emotion is necessary to produce extinction.

Guided imagery or "directed association", as we prefer to call it, is another expressive intervention that we find particularly useful in modifying maladaptive models. We never use imagery or ideas from a standard repertoire. Rather, we take something specific from what the client says, and then ask him/her to focus on it or to use it as a starting point for free association. Very often, this is enough for the client to realize that there is something strange or damaging about his/her thought, feeling or way of doing things. Clients often spontaneously remark on this and develop options on their own. If they don't, we suggest other possible outcomes to the fantasy that they have described. If they can adopt one of these, all is well. If they can't, we begin to look for the reason why.

The effectiveness of the expressive therapies may be in part due to a characteristic of the brain that was not mentioned previously. The brain stores movements as wholes—routines—not as small bits of movement. Memories can evoke these routines. For example, the memory of an embarrassing incident can produce writhing movements indicative of extreme tension and shame. People tend to suppress these movements, perhaps to deceive others, perhaps to avoid feeling unpleasant sensations. Expressing these movements helps bring the sensations to the surface, robbing the memory of its power to cripple.

Any time a new experience is undergone, whether in real life or in fantasy, the cortex can include new data in its model. This new information can improve the model. The correction of the model—not merely the reliving of the original experience, or the learning a new behavior, or the expression of a new emotion—is what provides the basis for permanent change.

Family and Couples Therapy

We see the need for interventions in the couple or family system as flowing naturally from our approach to human nature. Because humans are a social species, designed to live with relatives in small, supportive bands, people depend on satisfying social relationships for their personal happiness. Improving social relationships increases personal satisfaction.

Indeed, our analysis indicates that therapists working with individuals should also pay particular attention to family and other social relationships. As we have argued before, the excessive emphasis on self-development, in both humanistic and psychoanalytic therapy, is a reflection of prevailing cultural values. It would be more appropriate for members of another species—one whose social behavior is not based on reciprocity.

In a sense, individual psychotherapy might be looked upon as family therapy with only one family member present. The therapist both stands in for other family members in the sessions and helps the individual to recreate a network of friends and supportive relationships outside the sessions.

Some individual therapists might be taken aback by a perspective which sees a focus on the family as fundamental. After all, individual therapy preceded family therapy. But that is only an accident of history. Humans are not autonomous psychological entities; they must belong somewhere, or suffer.

Given this obvious rationale for couples and family therapy, we find it surprising that family and couples therapists remain so enamored of systems theory and its epistemological offshoots. A separate rationale for couples and family work was unquestionably important in the early days of family therapy. Back then, individual therapists tended to see the real people in a

ONE-PERSON COUPLES/FAMILY THERAPY

To understand how individual therapy can be seen as one-person couples or family therapy, one need only think back to the model-building capacity of the brain. Maladaptive, repetitive behavior patterns in families are generally based on assumptions about self and other, i.e., on models of the social environment. Therapy, of whatever modality, must seek to correct the assumptions (models) that interfere with good couple and family relationships. Interventions that improve the client's ability to function socially—to derive support from, and provide support to, other people, starting with family members—are particularly powerful, because social success will feed back on the client's model (assessment) of self.

Many different assumptions can underlie faulty patterns of social behavior. To take one example, some people assume that their needs will never be met, even if expressed. Others, convinced that their needs are transparent, wait to have their minds read. Still others assume, without ever making their assumptions explicit, that there is a "right" way to conduct a relationship, regardless of the needs of the individuals involved. Because these assumptions generally don't allow themselves to be "disproved" (extinguished), they tend to be self-perpetuating. People go on relating to each other in the same ways, and go on feeling about themselves in the same ways.

David Kantor, the innovative Cambridge family therapy theorist, has an identical approach to ours, using slightly different terminology. He writes about the interplay of "critical images" and the structure of mental models. By critical image he means the internalized conception of self and other that leads to impasses in current relationships. His solution is to provide therapeutic experiences that transform these images into something positive.

client's life either as obstacles to self-actualization or as shadows of imagined parents. Ideas about how trouble developed in families were incredibly simpleminded and ridden with stereotypes, e.g. "schizophrenogenic mothers," "castrating women," "cold, distant fathers." Systems theory made it possible for therapists to pay attention to real relationships, to actually take a look at what was going on between people.

But today, the situation is different. The need for multi-person, interpersonal interventions is a matter of common sense and good evolutionary theory. The couple is a basic unit of human society; the family is the closest approximation to the enduring, interdependent groups in which we humans were designed to live. The need for family and couples work is rooted in the nature of the individual. Couples and family therapists don't need a philosophy that sets them apart from the rest of the therapeutic community.

Therapists do need a theory that describes interaction between individuals, but such a theory must explicitly incorporate information about the nature of the individuals who are interacting. Hence, an adequate theory has to take into account the male and female reproductive strategies. At a minimum, the theory would have to describe the differing male and female approaches to sex, and the different life cycles of males and females. For example, it would need to include reference to the fact that female sexuality tends to be enhanced by intimacy, while male sexuality tends to be enhanced by novelty.

A couples and family approach does not always mean joint sessions. As we described in Chapters 6 through 10, there are conflicts between the male and female reproductive strategies. Males and females have different interests, yet they often come into therapy with the idea that they have identical needs and should be able to get along perfectly. Furthermore, in the current environment, individual males and females are often confused about their roles. As a result, is sometimes desirable to coach them about the underlying biological predispositions of the genders. This is most easily and effectively done in individual sessions. One can do much the same thing in couples sessions if it involves *muting* gender-typical behavior, e.g., making a man less aggressive, or making a woman more independent. If the opposite course of action seems necessary (getting a man to take the initiative more; inducing a woman to be more seductive), it is better to work separately.

A final word on family work. The family is not the band. As a consequence of the bewildering stresses we described in chapter 5, families can become too violent, too destructive, or otherwise too deviant to be a suitable setting for therapy. Sometimes, people need help in breaking away. One function of therapy is to help people get a new start with new people, so that they can stop trying to square accounts with their relatives. In the language of evolution, we need to wean people from pathological ties of kinship to productive ties of reciprocity.[3]

---

[3]This helps to explain some of the limitations of the psychoanalytic theory of the therapeutic relationship. Psychoanalytic neutrality is designed to allow clients to replay their old *kin* ties (transference). It does little to help them create new ties based on reciprocity.

Still, no matter how pathological, ties of kinship run deep, and we can expect our clients to resist what they perceive as attempts to make them abandon their families. Therefore, in addition to helping people free themselves from destructive ties to their families, therapists must help them find ways of maintaining connection, so that a sense of loyalty can be preserved. Notoriously, the cost of cutting off from the family is the reemergence of detested parental traits within the adult-child who imagines s/he has escaped.

Group Therapy

Neither one of us is primarily a group therapist, so we will confine ourselves to a few very general comments. For obvious reasons, group therapy would seem to be desirable from an evolutionary perspective. We often suggest that our clients participate in groups of various sorts. However, group therapy does seem to have some fundamental limitations.

The individuals who come together for group therapy are generally not related, and the group will not remain together for the lifetime of the participants. Therefore, the group is not a band. It is an artificial entity, held together by the therapist's rules. It can serve to teach people about social relationships, but the members cannot be relied on for future support, and therefore, reciprocity within the group has limitations. Much of the management of groups deals with just these difficulties. There is always (a) a struggle to define a group task so that the group members can have the positive experience of pulling together, and (b) a need to sort out the rules of what they can and cannot do for each other (the boundaries of reciprocity).

In some ways, though, the therapy group does approximate a band. No member's individual interest predominates over that of any other member. There is no property, no money to be accumulated, and no exploitation of one member by another. Group members are free and equal. So groups can be exhilarating. But, alas, since they are not sharing the struggle for survival as would a band, they sometimes have trouble finding a suitable common task.

Repeatedly one sees in groups a struggle by people of good will to make the group a band. They attribute to the group the importance that they would like it to have, when in fact it isn't that important to its members, because of its limitations. But even so, the resemblance between therapy groups and bands makes them a potentially important experience for their members.

Similar considerations apply to the value of such quasi-therapeutic groups as Alcoholics Anonymous, residential communities, milieu therapy, intentional communities, and the like.

Reciprocity as an Integrating Theme

As we described in Chapter 3, a large proportion of the people we have seen in psychotherapy cannot deal effectively with reciprocity. They do not fully grasp what they owe to other people nor what other people owe to them. Some people are burdened by imaginary obligations; others feel enormously entitled. Some people give too much; others take too much and give little in return. Low self-esteem tends to alter the calculation of reciprocity, causing individuals to undervalue their contribution or overvalue the contributions of others. If a compensatory grandiosity develops, individuals can develop an inflated sense of their own contributions, leading to cyclical (oscillating) idealization and devaluation of others. The resulting failures in social relationship tend to feed back onto the self-concept, further distorting the individual's model of the socioeconomic world. These imaginary debits and credits distort the way people see themselves and the way they interact with others.

Virtually all the modalities discussed in this chapter can help people to achieve the satisfaction provided by reciprocal relationships. Each modality's usefulness in this respect could be the subject of an entire chapter, so we will confine ourselves here to the briefest of overviews.

Exploration is particularly useful in uncovering the roots of guilt, suspicion, victimization, chronic resentment, and entitlement. These "pathologies of reciprocity" often develop in childhood. Some people grow up feeling they are permanently burdened with debts they can never pay off; others seem to acquire the notion that the world owes them happiness and a living. Exploration must seek to uncover the hidden assumptions of the client's model with respect to emotional obligations.

Behavioral interventions, especially desensitization and role-playing, are particularly useful in helping clients give, or take, more than they are used to. People are often extremely embarrassed at the thought of taking or giving more. Even when they understand that they are operating according to a false set of books, they have a hard time changing. Paradoxical interventions are useful in helping people overcome their resistance to giving or taking more.

Couples and family therapy is of course a prime ground for interventions relating to reciprocity. One can directly observe the pathologies of reciprocity in the system, and can devise strategies that will force people to change the amount and nature of their giving and taking. We believe that much of the resentment accruing within couple and family systems is due to individuals counting what they owe and what they are owed differently, with each person thinking that they deserve more—or something else—than what they are getting.

The focus on reciprocity allows the therapist to simultaneously address history, meaning, social relationships, and behavior. This makes it possible to use many techniques with only one goal in mind.

The following case material shows how reciprocity can be used as the focus of many different interventions. A chance remark about current functioning leads, with the help of relaxation techniques, to the uncovering of important, long-buried material. A homework exercise is devised, and later, couples interventions are used to improve the client's relationship with a girlfriend.

The client, Jimmy, happened to mention that he had refused a coveted dinner invitation. The therapist asked why. Jimmy replied that he didn't feel comfortable accepting it. The following exchange, edited for brevity, ensued:

T: What is uncomfortable about it?
C: I guess I don't want to owe anyone anything.
T: How does it make you feel to owe someone?
C: It's a horrible feeling. Creepy-crawly. My stomach gets tight, I sort of freeze. It's almost as if my self is collapsing.
T: Do you have any idea why owing someone should make you feel that way?
C: No.
T: (After a brief relaxation exercise) What comes to mind when you think of owing someone?
C: (Laughing wryly) You won't be surprised. It's my mother. If she ever did anything for you, she'd make you pay forever. I'm still paying. I can't afford to get into debt like that.

At a subsequent session, the therapist assigned the following exercise: "Before your friend asks you for another favor, you ask him for one. See what happens." Jimmy reported that he had found the task extremely difficult to do. First, he had experienced self-loathing over what he saw as selfishness. Then he had gotten in touch with fear of losing the friend. When, using relaxation, we explored the latter fear, he discovered a strong fear of abandonment by his parents. After working through these emotions, Jimmy was instructed to continue asking for reciprocity in his relationships. This he was able to do until he got involved with Janine.

His relationship with Janine went along well for a while, but soon foundered because they couldn't agree on who was doing what for whom. Jimmy asked if he could bring her in. The therapist agreed. Their reciprocity battles, it turned out, revolved around apparently trivial issues. Here is an example:

Janine: He's always taking me to these crummy movies. I just go to be with him. I'm always doing things that he wants to do.

Jimmy: What are you talking about? I take you to the movies because you like movies. I thought you loved to go out. I'd rather stay home anytime.

T: So it seems that each of you is trying to do for the other, and neither of you is getting what you want.

Subsequent work revolved around these types of issues. Each discovered that they were carrying a sense of deprivation along with a strong sense of guilt, and each learned how to give what was needed and asked for what was desired.

II
CASE MATERIAL

CHAPTER 13

Facilitating Altruism, Loyalty, and Cooperation

BEFORE GOING ON TO THE reciprocity-related material that is the subject of this chapter, we would like to make a few general statements about the people described in the next three chapters. They had symptoms such as depression, anxiety, guilt, fear of intimacy, sexual dysfunctions, bizarre thinking, alcoholism, failure to live up to potential, violent impulses, obsessiveness, stress-related trembling and cardiac illness, tics, and suicidal ideation. They had personalities that could be described as schizoid, antisocial, avoidant, dependent, histrionic, narcissistic, borderline, dysthymic, and passive-aggressive. But pathology was not primarily the guide to treatment. Rather, each individual was treated as a normal person whose environment, particularly in early childhood, had deviated too drastically from the natural environment.

These cases demonstrate how one can make use of evolutionary perspectives in psychotherapy. We don't claim there are no other ways to deal with these patients. There are many ways to go about therapy. Nor can we prove that our way is better. We have no systematic basis for such a claim. We offer these cases only to demonstrate how an evolutionary-oriented psychotherapy might be done. We have tried to show both how the focus of therapy might be planned and how to use explicit discussions of evolutionary themes.

The clients described in these chapters were viewed as having problems with community, reciprocity, dominance, and adjustment to gender. The restoration or creation of social relations was given high priority. The need for each client to have a cognitive framework based on the principles of reciprocity was addressed as soon as possible. Self-acceptance and acceptance of gender were assumed to be inseparable. Discussion of the male and female reproductive strategies was sometimes used to help clients resolve the confusion resulting from their ambivalences and contradictions.

Some degree of failure to achieve an integrated sense of self was often found. Hence, interventions designed to promote merging of dissociated parts were used liberally. However, these interventions were in general carefully focused on those aspects of intrapsychic structure that were interfering with normal social interaction.

Relaxation exercises and guided imagery were routinely used to facilitate exploration of the past and of intrapsychic structure, as well as to rehearse new behaviors. The content of guided imagery was always selected from material produced by clients during exploration.

Reciprocity: A Look Back

Before going on to case studies, it might be helpful to review the major points we have made concerning reciprocity. The tendency to reciprocate was once a survival mechanism, one of the factors that enabled a weak, vulnerable species of primate to cope, through cooperation, with the vicissitudes of life in a harsh and violent environment. Humans who did not reciprocate did not survive and did not transmit their genes to the next generation. In this way, the tendency to reciprocate became embedded in the genes, right along with such anatomical features as the enlarged brain.

In our society, of course, humans can survive without reciprocity. Nevertheless, there is no evidence to indicate that the tendency has been eliminated from our genes, nor does any model exist suggesting how it might have been eliminated. We therefore feel safe in proceeding on the assumption that reciprocity continues to constitute a biological foundation of human morality, an element that must be present in a person's cognitive model of the world, if that person is to maintain successful social relationships.

The rules of reciprocity in a hunter-gatherer band can be summarized as follows:

1. every adult individual in a band has an obligation to give gifts;
2. gifts must be accepted;
3. within an unspecified amount of time, the receiver of a gift must give a gift to the giver, but the original object must not be returned.

These rules create a network of mutual obligation such that anyone involved in the exchange network can call upon any other participant in time of need. They also provide a mechanism whereby whoever possesses anything significant at any time (e.g., meat) will be sure to share it with others (to pay back debts and create obligations).

From these rules, several principles emerge, and these principles are what everyone, in every culture, must be able to grasp:

1. the exchange of gift and favors creates relationships;
2. these relationships are open-ended, i.e., no exchange puts an end to them;
3. the giving of a gift creates an obligation, something we might call a debt.

These rules transcend cultural boundaries. In no human society is it acceptable not to reciprocate. Reciprocity is part of the operating system of the human species. Consequently, therapists who focus on reciprocity can deal with moral issues without worrying about whether they are imposing their own values on their clients.

Arthur

Arthur was always being played for a sucker. He gave gifts costing more than he could afford to relatives who never remembered his birthday. He spent hours doing favors for acquaintances who cheated him out of money. He had spent his life trying to ingratiate himself with people who ridiculed and mocked him.

This behavior pattern was particularly marked with respect to his mother. At 30, Arthur kept offering her gifts, making himself available to her for errands on a moment's notice, and visiting her as frequently as he could manage. The more attention he lavished on her, the worse she treated him. She complained that he didn't come often enough and reminded him of things she had asked him to do that he hadn't accomplished. She, on the other hand, was unable to find time to come to his commencement ceremony, and she was unable to find money to lend him when he almost had to drop out of school. She was incapable of saying something nice either to him or about him. But she made a show of praising his older sister, who seldom came to visit and never helped out.

Accustomed to abuse, he was often abusive with the few people who tried to be nice to him. He instantly became suspicious. Consequently, he had extreme difficulty establishing a working alliance.

Arthur didn't understand why his relationships didn't work out, but he kept trying. He believed that if only he would be nicer, more generous, and more accepting of abuse, people would come to realize that he was a good guy.

Throughout the work, the therapist struggled to help him understand two principles: first, don't let anyone take advantage of you; second, don't take out on one person what someone else has done to you. Once he began to operate on these principles, his "symptoms" began to disappear. His difficulties with other people began to diminish. He developed some friendships, and generated a very lucrative working arrangement with his boss. His extreme shyness and social withdrawal began to disappear. He began to engage in casual contact with neighbors. His anxiety, which manifested itself in the form of tremors, no longer required medication. Finally, his outbursts of anger, which usually occurred when someone intruded on one of his long bouts of brooding isolation, became less and less frequent.

When the therapist first asked him if he didn't deserve better, he couldn't really deal with the question. It didn't make sense to him and he simply slipped away by changing the subject. We kept coming back to it though, and finally he got angry enough to talk about it.

He started by expressing his behavior in terms of strategy and principle. Tired of hearing the therapist point out that he had once again allowed himself to be abused, he burst forth with the following credo:

> It works for me. When I go to someone and ask them to do something, they always say "sure, I'll do it." People treat me differently than they do other people. They recognize that I'm different. Even guys who are shady with other people, who cheat other people, they don't do it to me, they respect me, they know I'm reliable. If I tell someone that if they cheat me, I'll never have anything to do with them again, it's a real threat to them, they think about it a long time before they stiff me.

Unfortunately, this marvelous statement of the reciprocity system, which Arthur had reinvented for himself, was in his case almost a total fantasy. There may have been some people who respected him for his naivete and his honesty, but they played a negligible role in his life. Arthur's natural sense of justice and morality didn't work to his advantage in the environment he had to cope with.

To validate his principles without increasing the frequency of his maladaptive behavior, the therapist began talking to him about the reciprocity system:

T: Look, I think that the system you just described is the basis of human morality. I really think it's fundamental, and I think it's amazing that you have hit on it by yourself. When human beings lived in little bands in difficult environments, the moral system you just described was essential to keep them alive. If you took care of other people when you had a chance, they took care of you when things weren't going well for you. If you killed an antelope today, and shared it, tomorrow someone else would give you a piece of his giraffe. So everybody benefited.

But you didn't get too many chances to stiff people out there. If you stiffed somebody once, chances are the whole group would turn on you and that would be the end of you.

Now here, you're involved in all these relationships with people, and they're all stiffing you time and again, and you let them. Your principles are good, but you're involved with people who don't play by the same rules. That isn't working out so well for you.

C: Well, how come I keep getting involved with the wrong kind of people? . . .

T: That's a good question. Let's talk about it.

The roots of Arthur's behavior were actually easy to find. He had been a victim of child abuse, both physical and psychological. His father had alternately ignored him and beaten him. His mother, who had never held a paying job, apparently had little or no use for children either. She didn't normally get up to make breakfast for him, was away from the home frequently at mealtimes, and showed no interest in his schoolwork or other activities.

As an adult, Arthur was working on the assumption that if he went back often enough, he might still get what he had never got before.[1] He was involved in a vicious circle. His attempts to find support and affection elsewhere generally failed because somehow he conveyed his expectation of being abused. Thus, the reactions of the outside world continually forced him back to the family, where he had to beg:

C: My mom called me this weekend because she remembered my birthday. When she asked what I wanted I was real pleased, but when I told her, she said it was too expensive.

T: Were you surprised?

---

[1]Note that similar behavior is reproducible in the laboratory. Rats rejected by their mothers return to them more often than normal rats, despite the fact that their behavior is not reinforced.

C: No, not this time.

T: But you still think you might be able to get her love, if you try hard enough.

C: (Projecting an intent that the therapist did not have) I know you're pushing me to abandon my mother, but I don't think you should do that. I don't have a choice. I don't have anybody else . . .

Had deprivation and abuse been the only characteristics of his upbringing, Arthur might conceivably have become a different sort of person, someone who was unable to give, for example. But the landscape of his childhood was more complicated. His mother's personality had another side. She was unpredictably seductive. On occasion, she would play the devoted mother. She would shower him with attention, buy him lavish gifts, take him somewhere that he really wanted to go and make him feel that he was the most special person in the world. (One might think of the mother's behavior as what behaviorists call an erratic reward schedule. Laboratory experiments with animals have shown that under certain conditions, erratic, unpredictable rewards will maintain behavior more successfully than regular reinforcement. Perhaps this dynamic played a role in shaping Arthur's personality.)

The mother's memory for her motherly acts was extraordinary. She never forgot them and she never let anyone else forget them either. When asked to do something, no matter how trivial, she would begin to recite a list of the favors she had already done, and the sacrifices she had made. She portrayed herself as a perfect mother who could not possibly be expected to do more than she was already doing. Very early on in his life, Arthur had swallowed this story whole.

The following interaction certainly owes something to this aspect of his mother's personality:

C: Why is it that I can never allow myself to be in debt to anyone? If I owe even a few cents, I feel panicky.

T: (after a relaxation exercise) Imagine that you are sitting in a room with someone who has given you a thousand dollars. What happens?

C: I just feel very nervous, very withdrawn. I'm watching him.

T: What are you watching for?

C: I just remembered something. I got hurt once, slipping on the ice, and had to be hospitalized with a broken leg. When I called up my mother in New Hampshire and told her what had happened, she sounded really annoyed. She asked me if the hospital was OK and if they were taking care of me and said she would call back the next day to ask about visiting hours. But she didn't call for two days. Then she came down to visit me, but the whole time she was there, she complained about the trip and talked about all the wonderful things she could have been doing at home. She kept telling me how stupid I was to have fallen. She sort of made a joke out of it, but I realize now that she really meant it. All she cared about was getting away from there. I was in the hospital and she was mad. I just wanted her to go home . . .

The two reasons for Arthur's frenzied giving should now be clear. First, having failed in his childhood to get adequate emotional nourishment, his self-esteem was exceedingly low. He did not really think he deserved any better than he was getting and therefore made no demands. Since, as a child, he could not know that his parents were at fault, he blamed himself for the abuse he had suffered. He tried to improve his chances for love by showing that he was actually better—more altruistic—than others. Secondly, since the price he had to pay for getting anything was so high, due to his mother's emotional blackmail, "not getting" was actually preferable to getting. Arthur didn't want anything for himself because he was afraid of what he might have to give if he took it. Naturally, this cut him off from normal human contact and exposed him to the type of people who would have no qualms about exploiting him.

As he gained insight into this dynamic, Arthur began asking questions about the difficult area where survival issues and notions of right and wrong overlap:

C: What do you do about someone who continues to give you less than you give them?

At this point, it seemed possible to begin to lead him towards a more accurate understanding of his giving behavior, so the therapist answered in a way that surprised him:

T: Well, first you have to be sure that they are really giving less than you are. Most people tend to overvalue what they do for others, and undervalue what others do for them. We are all aware of what it costs us to do something or give something, but the other person's effort or sacrifice is not visible to us. That's why there is usually such tension around gift giving and distribution in general. So you have to be sure that you are really weighing what the other person gives you at its true value.

C: But I'm always giving more than I'm getting.

T: That seems to be true. But what is it that you really want in return for your gifts?

C: Friendship, I suppose, or acceptance. I want to be liked.

T: So in a sense, isn't what you want to get really much more valuable than what you are giving?

C: How do you mean?

T: Well, think about it.

C: You mean I'm offering gifts and favors, but I want to get paid in love?

T: Right. You are demanding to be paid in a different currency. I agree that you are getting ripped off, but is it totally the fault of the other people?

C: You mean I'm asking them to give me something that they don't want to give?

T: Well, something that isn't usually given in return for gifts. If you try to buy friendship and acceptance with favors or gifts, you'll end up with people who'll exploit you. You have to find people who like you first, then you can do favors . . .

This principle clearly applies in any society where one has to interact regularly with strangers, a condition which makes the operation of the reciprocity system extremely complicated.

We returned to the theme of emotional exchange at a subsequent session:

C: I've been thinking a lot about trying to buy my way into a family, or some kind of group.

T: Good. Maybe there's something even more vital that you're trying to get.

C: What?

T: Why don't you relax a little and think about how you feel when you do get what you want from people?

C: (after a pause) It feels like it did when I was a kid and my mother was taking me out. Real good.

T: So actually, what you're after when you give something is that feeling. You want to get back to that feeling of being taken care of. You're not really giving to other people, you're trying to give to yourself . . .

After this problem had been brought to the surface and analyzed clearly, the therapist began to nag him gently about staying around people who kept ripping him off. This finally produced the following exchange:

C: I don't fight back because I don't want to be alone. Everybody treats me the same way, and you said that it was because of what I do. So I have to try to change it with the people I do know.

T: Well, now we have a problem we can deal with. You have been doing what you do to avoid being alone. Do you have to keep on doing that?

C: I don't know. Don't I?

T: Well, you do if you are still exactly the same person that you used to be.

C: How am I different?

T: You tell me.

C: The only thing I can see is that I realize what's happening now.

T: Right. You can observe your own behavior, and that makes it possible to change it. I think we can start working on the problem of finding you new people to associate with.

After working on these issues for some time, we finally got around to dealing with his relationship to his mother:

C: OK, I have all the obligations and she does all the taking. How do I change that?

T: Who does she give too?

C: My sister.

T: And how does your sister treat her?

C: She neglects her and bad-mouths her when she's not around.

T: There's your answer, then.

C: (after a pause) How does that work? That doesn't make any sense.

T: Sure it does. Think of giving as an investment. If you're a selfish person, an unhappy person who's been deprived, you don't have a lot to give, so you want your investment to bring you the maximum return. Your mother is already getting as much as she can from you. She's getting very little from your sister. So she invests in the sister, hoping for a big payback. She takes what you give her for granted.

C: So if I stop giving, she'll start trying to hook me back in by giving to me?

T: That's what I would bet. Anyway, how much do you have to lose? . . .

This plan worked fairly well, in that it helped Arthur to break away from her. It did not transform her into the magical mother Arthur had caught glimpses of as a child.

Arthur eventually became much tougher. He learned to defend himself and his interests. As the following exchange shows, he got his tendency to buy respect under tight control:

> C: We went out to my [rich] uncle's house, and everybody was hanging all over him, trying to talk to him, be friendly, all that. I was the only one who stayed aloof. I nodded to him, but I didn't make any effort to talk to him. So he came over to me, and we chatted for a while.
> T: What made you behave that way?
> C: I figured that everyone wants a piece of rich people, they want to get something from them, so they give to them, whatever they can give, friendliness, or compliments, whatever, hoping for a return. But the rich, they don't need anybody, they have nothing to gain, so they're very suspicious. They realize that people are trying to get stuff out of them. I wanted to show that I wasn't like that . . .

Using skills that he gradually attained over a long period of time, Arthur was able to break out of his isolation and establish relationships with non-abusive people. These relationships in turn helped him to gain the validation and human contact that he had been deprived of in childhood. With this base, it was easier for Arthur to explore his childhood relationships and release the anger that he had stored up inside over the years. The entire process ultimately enabled him to overcome the self-rejection that had been at the root of his depression and his anxiety.

Bruce

Bruce was unable to give. He confessed that he hadn't really had a friend since high school, and that he had never had what is called a "best friend." Nor had he ever been able to establish a lasting relationship with a woman. He was not popular with his coworkers, so he didn't spend much time in the casual camaraderie of after-hours sociality. All he had were some drinking buddies, with whom he hung around in local bars. Alcohol made him feel more relaxed, so he tended to drink too much. Had he not come into therapy, he might have ended up with a serious drinking problem.

He came into therapy because he was feeling lost and hopeless. He had no idea why he was alone, no idea how his behavior contributed to his problem. The routine of everyday life had kept him from recognizing his isolation. Simply put, he had no conception of reciprocity. He didn't know what people wanted from him, and he couldn't formulate what he wanted from them.

When we first began talking about friendship, Bruce seemed to confuse the idea of making friends with the idea of manipulating people:

C: Yeah, it would be great. I really admire politicians like Senator Jones. They're so smooth, the way they move around a party making everybody feel good. Everybody likes them and feels good being around them. I'd like to be able to do that, especially at work, you know, make all the guys like me. It would really help me in my job. But I've never been able to do it.
T: So you see friendship as a means of getting ahead?
C: I guess so. I never thought of it that way.
T: Why not relax a little and see if you can discover why you haven't been able to act that way?
C: (after a pause) I guess I feel phony when I'm being friendly. I guess I don't feel friendly at all, I just feel like I'm trying to get something, and I get afraid that everyone will see it. So I don't try it very often.
T: Can you tell me when you last *felt* friendship?
C: I dunno. I guess with Richard, in college. Fifteen years ago. Jesus!

From bits and pieces of stories about his relationships with other people, it became clear that Bruce did not really experience the desire to do anything for anyone in his life. He felt guilty about a lot of things that he did and didn't do—visiting his parents, for example—but he had little sense of what the people he came into contact with needed to maintain normal contact with him. He would tell people that he was going to do something and then not do it, without informing them. He would then let the incident slip from his mind. He would "forget" to return telephone calls. He would never initiate a contact; anyone who might want to associate with him had to take all the responsibility.

Above all, he would never reveal to anyone what he was feeling or display any emotion (except anger). He had never said "I like you" to any man, and though he had said "I love you" to women, he had never meant it. He claimed to believe that such things should be "understood, not said," but it was clear that the thought of saying them aroused in him a strong sense of revulsion.

We spent some time exploring the roots of his behavior. What surfaced was not surprising: a demanding father who left most of the child-rearing to an invasive mother who demanded love and proper behavior as the reward for her affection and care. Bruce grew up knowing that any expression of affection would be used against him. This was one of his "rules." Not surprisingly, he continued to look for the "hook" in anything that was offered to him.

In addition, he learned to be more than cautious about expressing his feelings. He "knew" that if he let people know that he liked them, they would exploit him ruthlessly. The safe thing was to remain cool and detached in all circumstances.

There is a biological basis for this fear. Expressing an emotion can be seen as an implicit demand that the other person share the emotion. "I love you" carries with it the message "and I hope you love me too." The recipient of the message knows this perfectly well. Hence, most people feel embarrassed and guilty when someone they don't love confesses love for them.

The recipient of unrequited love knows that the would-be lover will be hurt and disappointed, and since most people don't like to inflict pain, they suffer in advance from the pain they are going to inflict. This dynamic is probably quasi-universal, but most people don't let it destroy their capacity to feel and express emotion. Bruce had.

We soon were able to agree that what he needed to work on was the ability to establish relationships with other people; that perception guided us through the therapeutic relationship. By a stroke of luck, an opportunity presented itself before much time had elapsed.

On several occasions, a colleague named Wally went out of his way to invite Bruce to parties. When Bruce first mentioned it, he couldn't understand why Wally bothered. His first thought was to look for the hook:

C: The guy is probably looking for something from me. I don't know what it is, but it's there, I know it's there. I know you talk about friendship but I don't trust this guy. He wants something. Or maybe there's something wrong with him. Maybe he's queer. He doesn't look queer but you never know these days. Anyway, something. He better not come on to me, though, I'll beat shit out of him.
T: Well, supposing he's not gay, what do you think he could want from you? A favor? Would that be so terrible?
C: I've always thought that the right way to be was to fend for yourself. I never ask for help from other people. If I have a problem, I take care of it. If other people do the same, everything works out all right.
T: Sure, but that leaves everybody all alone. Is that what you want?
C: No.
T: So let's look at that theory of yours about fending for yourself. Do you think it has something to do with being afraid of having to give something back?
C: Well, that makes sense.

T: What is it that you have to lose? (pause) Think back to your family.

C: I suppose you mean that he could be like my mother. Make me do what she wanted, just because she had fixed dinner or something. Make me feel bad if I didn't want to go to church. Run my damn life for me.

T: That fits, doesn't it. That's something to be afraid of. But this guy?

C: I guess it wouldn't be so terrible if he did rip me off, but I don't want to be played for a fool.

T: You don't want to take a chance on being his friend, because you would be disappointed if he wanted something back — if he wasn't pure, isn't that it? You could only trust him if he was perfectly pure, a disinterested friendship. Otherwise, you'll feel ripped off, you'll feel like you've been fooled.

C: It sounds kind of crazy when you say it.

T: Not crazy, but awfully unrealistic, isn't it? Look, let me tell you something about the evolution of friendship. In the natural environment — you know, before technology and all that, when humans were out there hunting for a living — what we call friendship was a survival mechanism. People shared food when they had it because when they didn't have any, the people they had given to before would share back. People entered into gift-giving relationships that lasted for years. First one would give something, then the other. You always had to accept a gift and you always had to give something back, eventually. The point is that giving is a way of getting. That's natural. It's not a conscious thing with most people, it's emotional. If you give something and somebody doesn't reciprocate, you feel ripped off. So actually, your mother wasn't that far off the mark, only she asked for too much, when you were helpless and couldn't defend yourself . . .

The discussion of this topic took some time and I suggested to Bruce that he read a book on hunter-gatherers. He did so, and when he came back, we had the following exchange:

C: I can see how that works for them, but things are too screwed up now. People are out for themselves, they're into success, they don't behave that way anymore.

T: You're absolutely right. In a lot of ways they don't. And maybe that's one of the reasons our society has so many problems. But between friends and lovers, people who expect to be close to each other, the old rules hold. If you give, you expect to get; you expect to be taken care of when your time of need comes. Now in your case, you don't want to take from anyone, because the price you had to pay as a child was too great, so you set up this ideal of a person who wouldn't want anything from you. But that isn't realistic. We all are just humans. We have to accept each other as we are . . .

Almost as a homework assignment, the therapist encouraged Bruce to get involved with Wally and to develop a friendship if he could. As the two men got closer, Bruce experienced other difficulties:

C: When he started confiding in me about the problem he was having with his fiancée, I felt flattered, honored almost. But as he kept talking about it, I started to get afraid. I didn't know how to react to him, I felt I was going to say the wrong thing, and screw up the whole deal.

T: Look what this friendship is doing to you. It's raising all sorts of doubts about your ability to handle it and about your self-worth. No wonder you haven't sought out opportunities to get close to people.

C: I felt a helluva lot safer when I thought the whole world was out to get me. I was ready for anything. I was way back inside, nobody could hurt me.

T: And now you feel vulnerable. That's natural. When you have a lot to gain, you automatically have a lot to lose. Why don't you relax and see if we can get in touch with what you're afraid of losing.

C: (after a pause) What I'm seeing is myself as a little boy. My mother is holding me and telling me that I shouldn't get angry. I think I was angry at my father for something.

T: The message is that you were angry over something trivial?

C: Yeah. I had the right to be angry, didn't I?

T: Of course. One always has a right to one's feelings. But how does this connect to the friendship?

C: I guess any kind of affection makes me feel small, trivial, like I don't know what I'm doing . . .

At a subsequent session:

T: What is it that you want him to know about you, when you're wondering what to do or say?

C: (after much floundering) I guess I want him to know that I'll be there for him if he needs me.

T: Then it isn't really a problem of knowing what to say or do, is it? It's just a communications problem: how do you get him to know what you feel.

C: It isn't easy to say something like that. I don't know how he'll respond. He may think I'm being sappy.

T: What you're saying is that it's risky. He might reject your offer, laugh at you. Are you strong enough to take the risk? . . .

Bruce did begin taking some risks and he came back with the following insight:

C: It's like a staircase. I give a little of myself, he gives a little of himself, I take a step, he takes a step, and little by little we build something.

T: That's a fantastic image.

C: But it's so hard. It seems like it can go wrong at any time. If I step out there, and he doesn't follow, I get scared right away. I start to think that he's just been trying to trap me, to get me this far so I'll give him something big, and then he'll walk out on me.

T: Right. Here's how I see that process. Inside of everybody's head, there's a running account of what they owe and what they are owed, by everyone they know. If you are my friend, I have an idea of what I can expect of you; if you don't come through, I get mad. But if somebody I hardly know doesn't come through for me, I don't get mad at him because I didn't expect anything of him. So we have this balance sheet going all the time. That's what you're describing with Wally, and I expect that you have an account with everybody you know. People today aren't aware of it, but if you look at the hunter-gatherers, they really know who owes who what, and if somebody doesn't get their proper share of meat, or if someone forgets to give a gift when a gift is due, there's hell to pay.

C: So where's the friendship, where's the generosity?

T: When you've built up a relationship, step by step the way you were talking about, the payoff is that you have built up so much good will that you know you'll be helped, even if you don't have anything to give back. You build up a web with people, and you go beyond the calculations . . .

At a subsequent session:

C: I've come to realize that I've always divided the world into two kinds of people, the manipulators and the losers. The losers were the guys who get manipulated. So I've spent my time making sure that I wasn't a loser. I would never give anything, for fear of being a sucker.

T: Right. And if you can never start a round of giving, you can't ever start one of those staircases, you have to wait until someone else starts one . . .

As Bruce's relationships got more involved, he began to experience the other side of reciprocity: his new friends sometimes made demands on him that he felt he had to meet, even though he didn't want to. Given his past, he couldn't be sure that his reluctance was legitimate. Such situations felt to him like the double binds of his childhood.

For example, when one of his new friends separated from his wife, Bruce invited him to his house to stay for a few days. After several weeks, the man showed no signs of moving on. Bruce felt trapped; he didn't want to lose the friend, but he didn't want to run a hotel either. Now this situation might seem pretty cut and dried to many people, but for Bruce it was a problem. When he thought about asking the friend to leave, the guilt he had felt in childhood resurfaced and prevented him from thinking clearly. In this case, it was necessary to tip the balance back in the other direction:

T: First of all, relax a little, and then we'll get in touch with those old emotions. (pause) Can you see yourself being manipulated? OK. Create a stage in your mind and put that situation on one side. Good. Now put the situation with your friend on the other side of the stage. (pause) What do you see?

C: (after some time) I guess it's putting me back into an old role. What I'm feeling has nothing to do with the situation now, it's all old stuff. The guy is probably in a state of shock. He probably doesn't even realize how long he's been there. If I tell him nicely, he'll start looking for a place right away. He'll probably be embarrassed about the whole thing. Maybe I'll have to tell him it's OK, that I understand . . .

Later on, an occasion arose which made it necessary to warn Bruce of the fact that he might run into people who would be suspicious of him if he were to make overtures in their direction. He immediately replied: "Oh, you mean I'm not the only one . . . "

Bruce's sense of love started in approximately the same place as his sense of friendship. "Love is bait," he said, in one of the early sessions. Quite naturally, he had never swallowed it. As a result, his relationships with women had always remained on a very superficial level. He could not share his feelings, because they were dominated by suspicion and distrust. Nor could he be interested in what a woman might be feeling; he assumed, subconsciously, that he already knew: she was out to trap him.

Being with a woman meant playing the adult version of hide and seek known as "how to have sex without being seen." The rules of the game are simple but demanding: simulate affection, pretend to believe in any affection displayed by the woman, and stay on guard. The game has its rewards, but in the long run it becomes a drag. Bruce had tired of it, and since he knew no other options, he had responded by reducing his contact with women.

The same work that enabled Bruce to establish friendships also made it possible for him to enter into a real relationship with a woman. Once he was able to share his thoughts and feelings with her, his need for therapy began to diminish and the process was terminated.

Zach

Because therapy has shown so little success with antisocial personality traits, we will end this section with some additional material about Zach, whose case was described in Chapter 3. Zach had a history of violence so extreme that the therapist hesitated to take him on. However, there were several mitigating factors. His last conviction dated back more than four years, he had established a good work history since that time, and he expressed a strong desire to do whatever was necessary to overcome his problems.

The therapist set out with the assumption (hope?) that Zach's condition involved learning, i.e., that he had never *learned* to expect decent behavior from others and therefore couldn't see any reason to behave according to the rules of society. The therapist was of course also open to the likelihood that Zach was, genetically, more aggressive and less sensitive to punishment than most men. The therapist was hoping that he was not constitutionally incapable of empathy, and thus proceeded on the assumption that he would respond to the therapeutic situation.

Zach was quite willing to discuss his upbringing, but there was a problem. Whenever the subject of his family came up, he would get angry, and when he got angry, he would begin to talk menacingly about the violence inside him and the possibility that he might hurt someone, including the therapist. The pent-up rage became particularly severe when he talked about his mother. His father had beaten him severely and had sexually abused both him and his younger sister. His mother had known about it and done nothing. His anger at his father was clearly focused, but when he started to talk about his mother's role, he would break off and begin expressing hostility towards whoever was around.

Whenever possible, the therapist tried to lead him to an understanding of the connection between the abuse he had suffered and his current anger, i.e., to the idea that he was paying back the world for what he had undergone. However, initial attempts to link his childhood to his present behavior simply didn't work.

A breakthrough came more or less by accident. The therapist had made some remark about the role of therapists being to help clients with their problems. Zach gave a sour look, hesitated a few seconds and then offered: "You know, part of me thinks that helping stuff is a load of bull." He stared belligerently, apparently expecting some affirmation of therapeutic saintliness. The therapist took the cue:

T: That doesn't surprise me at all. Why should a guy like you believe that anyone would want to help him?
C: (visibly displeased by this response) Why not?
T: Well, who was supposed to help you, in your life?

At first, he couldn't name anyone. Then he came up with a parole officer who had been nice to him, and a public defender who hadn't gotten him off. Only with prompting did he come up with his parents. He had never thought that he, as a human child, was supposed to have had parents who would help him. He had more or less assumed that it was a matter of luck: some children got good parents and some didn't. Even though he was angry about what had happened to him, he didn't know that he had a right to be angry.

This realization didn't help much right away. He got furious and had to be cooled off. However, from that point on, his threatening behavior in the sessions began to taper off. At the very next session, he reported having "more leeway" with people—he didn't feel pushed into a corner so often. He also stopped attacking the therapist when the subject of his mother's failure to protect him came up. From that point on, the therapist took every opportunity to discuss with him what he had been cheated out of, what he was owed, and what he owed others. Rather than trying to convince him that he should give more, the therapist stressed how much he had been deprived of. This made it difficult for him to get angry.

When Zach clearly realized that he had been spending his life trying to get revenge, it dawned on him that trying to get what was coming to him through violence was a losing game—another trick that his abusive parents had played on him. He began to develop a strategic, or calculating, attitude toward getting what he wanted, rather than reacting out of rage.

Zach did not come around easily. We had to work together for a long time. But eventually the focus on reciprocity led him to understand the reason for rules. He had always seen rules as an arbitrary device for protecting the privileges of the rich and the interests of the physically weak. He eventually came to see them much as one looks upon traffic regulations—as a means to maintain order, and as a framework for moving forward.

Once a rationale for following rules had been established, the therapist began to focus Zach on the effect his violent actions had on others, with the intention of bringing out his capacity for guilt. Whatever guilt had existed before had been buried under the rage and entitlement. But when he allowed himself to dwell on his victims, he began to see that they didn't deserve what he had done to them any more than he deserved what had happened to him.

Some important work was done around the therapeutic relationship. Zach frequently complained about having to pay (at all) for therapy, and was paying less than the going rate. The therapist let these remarks pass for a long time, but finally decided the time was ripe for a confrontation:

T: Do you think that I'm ripping you off?

C: (angrily) No I don't think that you personally are ripping me off, but I don't feel that there is any benefit in my paying for therapy. If I could get it free from some clinic or something, I would be perfectly happy with that. I think it's coming to me.

T: Because of what you went through?

C: Right. The community owes me.

T: I think you may be right, but does that mean that I owe you?

C: No, damn it, I'm not stupid, you know that I don't think you owe me.

T: What are you feeling right now?

C: (smiling, as if caught) I'm feeling a little energy, I know that, it gets in my way, whenever I talk about money or have to negotiate. I feel insecure, scared, I feel as if I'm going to be left with nothing and I have to fight.

T: OK, so look what is happening. Your sense that the community owes you is getting in the way of your individual relationships with other people, and it's cutting you off from them. So you're left alone, which makes you miserable. You have got to keep your sense of deprivation and entitlement from contaminating your relationships with individuals . . .

This theme became the focus of several sessions and eventually served to increase the level of trust between Zach and the therapist.

Much of Zach's progress was probably due to the exploration and venting of his anger, an approach which many schools of psychotherapy would recommend. However, we believe that the explicit focus on reciprocity greatly speeded up his recovery. It defused the transference, made an alliance possible, linked the past to the present, and provided a cognitive framework for his anger. It kept us from getting involved in tangential matters, from dwelling too much on the past, and from wasting time blaming others.

Finally, it enabled us to avoid the kind of confrontations that had prevented him from benefiting from his previous therapeutic experiences.

Conclusion: Reciprocity vs. Pure Altruism

With clients who are having trouble relating because they are excessively selfish, self-involved, or egotistical, there is a manifest need for some kind of countervailing emphasis on the values and behaviors that make community living possible. To some, pure altruism might seem like a good alternative, but for many reasons, reciprocity is preferable. First of all, the selfish individual may well be a person who did not receive enough (as a child); asking a deprived person to give more does not address the real issue. Secondly, behaving in a purely altruistic way is impractical in most situations; encouraging an ideal that few people can live up to could conceivably create additional self-criticism.

The reciprocity model is particularly useful with clients who are excessively selfless, martyred or exploited. It provides a useful antidote to any misplaced ideals of perfection — purity, absolute selflessness — that may be helping to maintain the client's self-defeating patterns of behavior.

Since many clients have trouble both giving and taking, and since both are necessary in human life, reciprocity would seem to provide a prudent, cautious and balanced focus for work on interpersonal relationships.

CHAPTER 14

Validating the Female Role: Competence and Fulfillment

BEFORE GOING ON TO CASE MATERIAL, let us briefly review the main points we have made about the problems of women.

1. In the natural environment, women participate fully in the economic life of the group. They raise the children while gathering and doing other vital tasks. There is no conflict between child-rearing and "career."

2. The sexual division of labor in a hunting and gathering band makes males and females dependent on each other for survival. Women compete with each other, sometimes with great intensity, for resources and status, but the social structure minimizes competition with men.

3. Because of the importance of paternal investment in the successful rearing of human offspring, human females, unlike those of most other mammalian species, are adapted to year-round cohabitation with males. One aspect of this adaptation is the desire of a female to be taken care of, a tendency which elicits protective behavior on the part of the male. This interrelated set of behaviors enhances bonding.

4. The dependency needs of the human female coexist in her with the fierceness and strength of all mammalian mothers.

5. Mammalian males tend to compete with each other, but not with females. Females give off signals—visual, auditory and behavioral—

which inhibit male aggression. If a woman suppresses these signals, men are likely to treat her as they would a man, i.e., as a potentially dangerous competitor.

Two major consequences ensue:

1. It is not reasonable to expect that there are very many women who can achieve happiness by spending their entire day doing nothing but raising children; and
2. It is unlikely that harmonious male-female relationships can exist where women are trying to compete directly with men.

In this chapter, we focus on heterosexual women who are dealing with conflicts between career and home or between self-assertion and relationships. The women described here definitely did not want self-affirmation to destroy their chances for love and marriage. None of them looked on the prospect of a life alone without concern. In working with women who have made up their minds to remain single or engage in homosexual relationships, we would suggest a different approach.

Laura

Laura, 36, came into therapy through the recommendation of her case worker, who thought she might benefit from insight therapy. Despite some musical talent and a middle-class background, Laura had led a totally marginal life. After dropping out of college as a freshman, she had become a kind of pseudo-hippie, sleeping in a succession of pads, with a succession of men, and eking out a living with temporary, menial jobs. This had gone on for 15 years, and she was now the object of charity. Obviously, her self-esteem was minimal. She had never known success at anything.

Laura, it turned out, spent most of her time hanging around bars where rock and roll music was played, talking to the musicians and occasionally sitting in with them. Every once in a while, one of them would sleep with her, and several apparently called her up when they felt like it, to spend the night. She had never known anything more solid, and she talked about these men as if she were in relationships with them. She complained that they frequently didn't come when they said they would, that they never took her out, and that they ordered her around. But, she just figured that this was the way men were. She put up with it because she was hoping that one of them would propose. Marriage, she stressed at length, was her impossible dream.

In therapy, she wanted to talk about how horrible her life had been, and what an awful person she was. She could go on about that endlessly: how her mother told her she was violent, like her father, and would eventually kill someone; how her father rejected her and occasionally hit her; how her sister told her that she was emotionally primitive; how the kids in high school teased her about her unusual appearance; how no man would ever love her because she was hideously ugly; how people talked about her and laughed at her behind her back; and how her emotional outbursts always got her fired, no matter how well she did her work.

The therapist listened to her complaints until it became clear that the needle was stuck in the groove in her head. Her medical records indicated that she had played the same tune with a previous therapist for well over a year. An intervention was designed, using the assumptions about behavior outlined in the previous chapters.

It was first necessary to make her understand that the way these men were treating her was abusive. She resisted this interpretation for three reasons: (1) she hadn't experienced any other kind of relationship; (2) she didn't want to give up the only human contact that she had; and (3) she didn't want to admit to herself that these relationships weren't going anywhere. It was emotionally painful for the therapist to make her face these realities. However, she finally realized she had to tell them off.

Next, she was confronted with the fact that she was seeing men who were significantly younger. The therapist asked her if she really wanted to get married, and if so, why she didn't choose a man who was a likely candidate. Her response was amazing: "That's my problem. Part of me wants to get married, but part of me wants to hang out in bars with musicians." After some probing, she offered the following statement: "I'm divided on everything. Can you help me? That's my problem. I feel two ways about everything."

This, combined with her response to psychological testing, strongly indicated that she had a split self-image, with an ideal self that had arisen in response to her negative self. This became the focus of intervention. After a relaxation exercise, she was asked to visualize how she looked when she was feeling ugly and how she looked when she thought she had a great mind. This exercise immediately revealed a grandiose self—a great musician—as well as the familiar horrible self.

When she had realized the fact that she was carrying around these contradictory images of herself, the therapist asked her what they were. She had already somewhat distanced herself from them: "Mental creations, these are just creations of my mind."

Next the therapist asked her who was watching. After a long silence, she replied: "I guess it's me." When asked who she was, she again took a long time to reply, and then answered: "What's left over." This wasn't much of an affirmation, but it was a step forward.

Within two sessions her propensity to repeat the old complaints and suspicions decreased. Presumably, she was beginning to acquire an identity that included both positive and negative aspects of the self.

The next focus of intervention was her presentation of self with men. Because her mother had treated her as a younger version of her alcoholic father, Laura had grown up unsure of her gender and sexual orientation. At one time, she thought she might be a man. Later, she thought she might be a lesbian. She had decided that she wasn't either. But she had never been trained to behave like a girl. She had never been given nice clothes, never taught to dance, never encouraged to date. As we explored these issues, she began to express jealousy of her best friend, who had been brought up with all those advantages.

Obviously, there may have been something about Laura that contributed to the treatment she received from her family. She didn't have a prepossessing appearance, and she did seem to have some odd emotional quirks. But psychological testing did not reveal any particular abnormalities. Whatever genetic dimensions of her personality existed, they did not seem crucial to her treatment.

Her reaction to her psychological test scores was, however, interesting, in light of what came later. She got an average score on the WAIS, which indicated that she could do much better in life than she was doing. But, as mentioned, she was unhappy with this result. She said she felt that she had a better mind than that, and invested a lot in convincing the therapist that anxiety prevented her from doing well.

In the meantime, there was work to do. Laura had to learn how to behave with men, and the therapist seemed to be the only person in a position to teach her. It wasn't easy. She was so eager to enter into a relationship that she found it very hard to accept the need for reticence, distance and aloofness. The idea that men don't respect women who are too easy or who come on too strong was hard for her to grasp and had to be repeated many times, with explanation. She finally agreed to watch women she admired as they handled this aspect of their lives, and her observations eventually convinced her.

Further progress was achieved through training sessions and homework exercises designed to help her get a better job. Getting one provided her with a successful experience, perhaps her first in over 20 years. This fed back into her self-image. Therapy was in progress as of this writing.

Arlene

Arlene was the daughter of a prosperous family. Her father was a businessman, her mother a housewife. She was raised in one of those typically homogeneous suburbs once thought to be ideal places for children to grow up: no dangers, no bad influences, no obstacles to overcome. Nevertheless, Arlene's memories of her school years were dominated by shame and pain.

C: I always had to go out at recess to play some kind of game and everyone made fun of me. They said I threw like a girl. And I knew that meant I threw badly. I knew the boys thought they were better than girls. So I thought I had to learn to throw like a boy to throw well. But this got complicated, because I hated the boys and didn't want to be like them. I thought they were hateful and cruel and best ignored. . . . The boys would say, "You can't do that, you're only a girl, everyone knows girls are too stupid and weak." I used to fight to hold back the tears, but everyone could see that I wanted to cry, so that proved I *was* stupid and weak. . . . I know my father wanted a boy. He joked about making me into a football player when I started to get big. . . . When my brother was born, I thought that my parents had gotten a boy because I wasn't good enough. I felt like a failure. . . .

Arlene's presenting problem was her inability to decide what to do with her life. Her indecisiveness had prevented her from making a commitment to a man or to a career. As a result, she was living in a kind of limbo. Her life was not unpleasant, but it had no direction. She had a respectable job with no future and she lived alone. She visited often with friends. Like an extra on a Hollywood set, she always stayed on the fringes of the action.

Her own definition of her problem was simplistic and confused. On the one hand, she expressed the belief that her failure to have a successful career was due to the fact that society was dominated by men. She felt that the solution would be for her to go out and get a demanding, high-paying job so that she could show what she was worth. She talked sarcastically about advertisements that imply that a woman can only achieve happiness in a relationship with a man.

But there was another side to her: "Sometimes I think that what I really want is for a man to marry me, put me up in a nice house, and give me some children to take care of."

As we explored this, she offered the following statement, which expresses one of the dilemmas of contemporary women: "Every once in a while, I get so tired of trying to do everything on my own. I get this urge to be taken care of. I fight against it because my friends keep telling me that it's just because I was brought up in a society where women are supposed to be passive, so I try to be strong and not burden anyone with my troubles. But the feeling keeps coming back. At this point, I'm so ashamed of not being independent that I can't even talk to anyone."

Therapy began with exploration. The pattern was not very surprising. Her father was aloof, often out of the house, and sparing in his praise. Her mother was an exuberant, hearty woman who was impatient with her shy daughter. Both parents expected her to do well in school; failure was not well received. Arlene suspected that they had wanted a son, but couldn't really explain why she thought so.

Arlene bitterly complained that her parents had raised her to marry a nice man and live in a nice suburb, but this did not jibe with the rest of her story. Whatever their hopes for her, they had given her the kind of education that one needs to make a career, and they had obviously expected her to compete successfully as a child and as a student.

Therapy focused on these contradictions and conflicted motivation.

T: What I don't understand is this: why did you feel you had to compete with boys on their own turf? Boys do throw better than girls. They are anatomically specialized for throwing. It seems to me that the real problem is that you weren't able to be proud of what girls do. You said, awhile back, that boys thought that girls were weak and stupid. What made you accept that definition as true? Weren't there other girls around who looked down on boys and thought *they* were stupid?

C: Well, we had to compete in these sports, there was no way to avoid it. And so that's what we thought was important. And the boys were better at it, so that's what I concluded.

T: You weren't encouraged by anyone to play girl games? Nobody said that was a good thing to do?

C: Not that I can recall.

T: If we look at games from an adult perspective, which is a more stupid activity, baseball, or dolls?

C: What do you mean?

T: Well, what is the relationship of baseball to adult life?

C: Not much, that I can see.

T: Right. Of course, it does prepare you to throw a spear pretty well, which is what men had to do before agriculture was invented. But that's about all. What about dolls?

C: Well, with dolls, I suppose you learn about family, taking care of children. I guess in a way it is a preparation for adult life.

T: Right. Only the way you were brought up, this wasn't considered important. So what has happened? You've accepted a male definition of what's important. You've accepted male values, the values of competition over the values of family, affection, affiliation. You want to be good at what men do because you have somehow been conditioned to believe that what men do is better.

C: That certainly is another way of looking at it.

T: Yes it is. (pause) But it's important, because if you look at it this way, you can stop hating yourself for not being more like a man—not being able to throw as well.

C: But it isn't just throwing, it's competing. At anything.

T: Well, suppose for a moment that you're not really motivated to compete as much. Would that be so terrible?

C: What do you mean?

T: I know you don't like all the manifestations of competition. You've already told me that you hate war.

C: Well, that's true enough. But I don't see how it relates.

T: You can easily see that throwing well is a male value. You can see that it isn't worth trying to imitate. Would you think for a moment about the possibility that the whole idea of competition is a preeminently male value?

C: Why? Don't women have to compete?

T: They do. But I'm asking you to consider the possibility that competition is more important for men.

C: Why should that be?

T: For one thing, females are more valuable than males, because of all the parental investment they provide. (Explanation omitted: see Chapters 7 through 10.) Since females are so valuable, males have to compete for them. They have to show that they are worthy mates—that they have good genes, and that they can help to support the children. Females tend to choose men who win out in competition with other men. It doesn't matter what kind of competition, really. Athletics, business, politics, whatever. Men have to compete with other men in order to be attractive to women. In every species, actually, the less valuable gender has to compete for access to the more valuable gender. Males who win out in competition with other males manage to reproduce more, because they have access to the females.

C: And that's true of humans too?

T: Isn't that what the women's movement is saying, that women bear a disproportionate burden of the costs of raising children?

C: Yes, but they blame this society for it.

T: True, they do. But they don't really understand that the same thing holds true, and even more so, in a whole lot of other species.

C: That's interesting.

T: There's more to it. Since males are obliged to compete with each other in order to be able to mate, their hormonal system is set up in such a way that there is a connection between sex, aggressiveness and competition. (Explanation omitted: see Chapters 9 and 10.)

C: So females aren't competitive at all?

T: Not so. Human females have to compete too, because human males provide so much more parental investment than males of most other species. That makes them valuable. When a gender is valuable, the other gender has to compete for access to it.

C: Aren't you contradicting yourself?

T: Perhaps. But I don't think so. I'm trying to say that females are somewhat competitive, but other values are more important for them.

C: What values?

T: Peace, for example. The much greater importance of child-rearing as compared to silly games. The importance of affiliation and kinship. All kinds of things, in fact, that women lose sight of when they focus on what men do.

C: So you think the part of me that wants a family is really me, not just something that was put in there.

T: (not answering directly) If you keep defining the part of you that wants to marry and take care of children as the "bad" part, or the "conditioned" part, then you have to reject an important part of yourself.

C: You mean to say that I should give up the idea of getting a better job?

T: Why do you say that?

C: You're telling me to accept the part of myself that wants to give up and just be a housewife.

T: You mean that when I tell you to accept yourself as a woman, you hear that you have to give up.

C: I guess so.

T: Then I guess when you think about getting a better job, you must feel that you have to give up being a woman.

C: Hmm. I never thought of it that way.

T: Do you think that might be the reason you haven't really tried all that hard to get ahead? . . .

At a subsequent session:

T: Try to tell me exactly what happens when you get close to someone.

C: Well, for example, the one time I met someone I really liked, I had to leave. I don't think I really wanted to. I remember what I said to him.

T: Can you tell me what you said?

C: "I want to live with you, and be with you, because I think that would make you happy, but in wanting that, I'm acting towards you the way I did with my parents, which is that I do what they want because they want it, without examining what I want."

T: You couldn't tell if you wanted what you wanted for yourself, or if you wanted it just because someone else wanted it.

C: Right. And now that I'm telling you the story, I know that I wanted it too, but being around him, I felt a kind of lack of myself. At the time, I thought that it was because he was so definite, that he was not leaving me any room for myself, but now I see that it had nothing to do with him . . .

At a subsequent session:

C: It makes more sense to me now to get involved with a man. I don't see it as such a threat. But when I think of being a mother, or even a wife, I get depressed. The words themselves just don't fit. They apply to someone else, not me.

T: Why don't you just close your eyes and picture what you see when you hear those words.

C: (after a pause) I see my mother, basically. Just sitting around the house, cleaning up, waiting for my father to come home. Not doing anything.

T: So basically you see a typical suburban house, with a mother who does nothing but cater to the kids all day.

C: Right.

T: I can't think of a social arrangement that is more alien to what women really need. Do you remember what I've told you about hunter-gatherer societies? Look at the women there. They work together all day, collecting food, building huts, talking, sharing, whatever, fooling around too, probably, and while they're doing all this, they take care of the kids. They nurse them, feed them, keep them out of trouble, and everything else that mothers do. But they're never without adult company and they're never *just* watching kids. They're always doing something else that's important too.

C: You mean I'm right about not wanting that kind of marriage?

T: Look, I can't say right or wrong. What I can say is that there's nothing natural about the social arrangements of the American middle class. Human society has always had a division of labor between the sexes, but it isn't the particular division of labor that characterizes this society. So it wouldn't surprise me if a typical suburban marriage didn't feel right to you. . . .

At a subsequent session:

T: Can you think of another reason you might not have wanted to go out and get a better job?
C: Not really.
T: Look back on what you've told me.
C: I don't see anything.
T: Why don't you relax a little then. You're probably getting tense trying to think of things.
C: (after a pause) I suppose I learned that I couldn't compete, that I would lose, that I wasn't any good, so I don't want to try anything for fear of finding out that I was right, that I am no good.
T: (after giving this time to sink in) Now try to imagine yourself actually winning.
C: My god, what I see is all this anger coming out! I'm in a rage and I stamp on everybody, I'm smashing people to bits. I'm screaming at them, "You see, you see, you bastards, I'm not stupid, I'm not weak, you bastards, you bastards." This is terrible.
T: Just let go, don't try to stop it. . . .

When Arlene did enter into a relationship with a man, she had quite a bit of trouble.

C: When I am with him, I am so concerned, interested, motivated, to find out what he wants that I never take note of what I want. I want to make him happy, and give him things, a baby, anything. I feel a kind of lack of myself. When I first realized that I was feeling something like this, I got angry at him, because I thought that he was being selfish and making me do what he wanted. And that's what my friends told me to believe. Then I realized that it was all happening inside of me.
T: You've felt like this before, haven't you?
C: Of course, I felt that way with my parents. I did what they wanted because they wanted it without examining my own wants. I think that I did that to myself, because if I didn't allow myself to realize what I

wanted, I wouldn't feel angry or disappointed. It seemed like a neat trick then, but now that I'm grown up, it's not so good.

Subsequent work focused on helping her to feel in control even when she was feeling affectionate and giving. Significantly enough, she got a better job soon afterwards.

Barbara

An aggressive career woman, Barbara felt she had gotten onto the fast track. But as she rose in the corporate hierarchy, she was finding herself in conflict with superiors and peers with alarming frequency. Until just before she sought help, Barbara had been convinced that the fights occurred only because she was a female. She felt persecuted. She talked constantly about discrimination. She referred to the "old boy network" as a shadowy force that was trying to keep her down.

However, she acknowledged that her friends saw things differently. They told her that the company was trying to promote a woman to improve its image, and that all she had to do to continue her rise was to stop provoking people. She was reluctant to accept this idea but her desire to avoid sabotaging her career had overcome her strong resistance to the idea of therapy.

We began by exploring her past. Barbara's voice trembled with emotion when she began to talk about her family. Her father, a harsh, demanding man, had goaded her to work hard in school but had praised her successes sparingly. He himself was a workaholic who spent little time at home and seemed preoccupied when he was there. Her mother worked part-time, and drank somewhat more frequently. She resented her fate and was not reluctant to let other people know it.

It soon became clear that her anger at the system was a projection of her problems with her parents. It was also clear that she was interpreting normal workplace behavior as persecution. The therapist concluded that she would need a cognitive framework capable of making sense out of her personal experiences in the corporate world.

The early stages of therapy focused on the connection between her upbringing and the conflicts she was experiencing at work:

T: (after a relaxation exercise) Think about the offices and places you have worked in. (pause) Let your mind run over the people you have had fights with. Don't tell me anything about it, just watch whatever scenes come up. (pause) Have you done that?
C: Yes.

T: All of these people are out to get you?

C: It sounds silly when you put it like that.

T: Suppose someone else was telling you the story. What would you say?

C: I suppose I'd say they were paranoid.[1]

T: So the chances are that you are contributing something to the situation?

C: I suppose so.

T: What could it be?

C: You probably think it's my father.

T: Suppose it was. How would that work?

C: I guess I might be seeing my bosses as fathers.

T: And how do you feel about your father?

C: Well, I'm angry at him. I hate him for what he did to my mother. So I guess I would be angry at them before I even started work. I suppose I'm trying to confront them, to get revenge on them for what he did. I'm ready for a fight when I walk into the place. . . .

At a subsequent session:

T: Relax a little and we'll take a different tack. (pause) Imagine a scene where someone is telling you what to do. Don't tell me about, just imagine it. Let me know when you've got one.

C: (after a pause) Got one.

T: Imagine that you just do what you're told, even though you don't think it's the best move.

C: (angrily) I'm not going to let them do that to me. That's what my mother did, and she ended up a drunk. To hell with that shit.

T: (after letting the anger play itself out) So a lot of what you are doing at work is because you are determined not to be like your mother, not to let yourself get pushed around.

C: That's right.

T: But how do you know that you're being pushed around at the office? You're spoiling for a fight when you walk in the door.

C: Well, maybe some of it is my shit, but that doesn't mean they're not out to get me. . . .

---

[1]There was some indication of paranoid thinking here but it did not become the focus of therapy. It seemed to clear up substantially as the realities of the business environment were clarified.

After bringing out into the open the client's carried-over resentments, the focus shifted to workplace realities:

T: Let's look more closely at what goes on in an office. You see the men ganging up on you and acting together to keep you down. Have you looked closely at how the men behave towards each other?

C: What do you mean?

T: Well, if the men in your office are of the species you and I belong to, the chances are that they are all in competition with each other. They are all strangers, in the sense that they are unrelated. Do you think that there is anyone there who would sacrifice himself for a coworker? Give his life? Resign to protect his buddy's job?

C: I guess not.

T: Of course not. There may be a couple of friends there, but on the whole, the men are in competition with each other. They are in competition with you too — and you attribute that to the fact that you are a woman. But they see you like they see each other, as someone who could get ahead of them. They aren't being nice to you, you're right about that, but they probably aren't nice to each other — unless you work in a truly exceptional place.

C: You mean I'm taking it personally, when it really is just the way things are?

T: Did you read *Catch 22*? One of the flyers keeps saying: "They're trying to kill me." His buddies try to reason with him. "They're not trying to kill you. They're just trying to kill anybody on our side. It's just war." Who was right? . . .

At a subsequent session:

C: Look, what is this bullshit? You're confusing me. If all the men are doing is competing, how come they work together? How do they take care of the business of the company?

T: They understand the rules of the game. To get ahead in a corporation you have to be a team player. You have to keep your competitive instincts under control. You have to know when to subordinate your own interests to those of the corporation — and you always have to seem like that's what you're doing! It goes back to the hunter-gatherers. Men had to cooperate to bring down big animals, so they had to be able to keep their competitive drives under control. They had to learn all kinds of rules about competition. That's probably why men love team sports so much.

C: What were women doing?

T: Women were gathering, in their own groups. But women are not as competitive by nature, so they didn't need to develop so many rules to control their fighting. One needs rules when there's something that has to be kept under control.

C: Are you saying that I'm not understanding the rules at work?

T: It's possible, isn't it? You haven't really looked for them, have you? You haven't ever even considered the idea that there might be legitimate rules there. By the way, have you ever thought of yourself as a member of their team?

C: Well, I've never thought they would let me be on their team.

T: Well, let's relax a little and look at that. (pause) Imagine that you're on the team there, whatever the team is.

C: (after a pause) I guess I've hated them much too much to want to be on their team. I've never even considered it really. It makes me nervous to see myself with them. I feel like a hypocrite, like a traitor, really.

T: To who?

C: To women, I guess. Or to my mother. I don't know . . .

At a subsequent session:

C: Maybe you can explain to me why I got into this fight after work yesterday.

T: What happened?

C: Me and Bill (a male colleague who was in line for the same promotion) went out for a beer after work, to talk over a confrontation we had had and smooth things over, only it got worse. I kept trying to put things right, and he kept getting colder and madder.

T: What did you say?

C: I was trying to find out where we stood. I asked him if we were still good friends, and that seemed to annoy him.

T: Can you tell me exactly what you said?

C: I asked him if he still liked me. I guess I asked him if he thought I was a good colleague.

T: It sounds like you were asking him for his approval.

C: No. Well, maybe. I wanted to establish a friendship. At least I thought I did. But I suppose if I was asking for his approval, I was pulling the father bit again.

T: And if he's the father?

C: I'm the little girl.

T: So one moment you're competing with him, provoking him to treat you like a competitor, and the next moment you're acting like a little girl.

C: He must be kind of confused.

T: Either that, or he thinks you're trying to trick him. You're giving him conflicting signals. We've spoken about how males are set up to compete with each other. The next thing to understand is that they *would* compete with females if the females didn't somehow manage to turn off male aggressiveness.

C: You mean by being coy and seductive.

T: That's one very important way, but any signal that says "I'm female" will have some effect.

C: Is that why boys aren't supposed to hit girls?

T: Exactly. In animals, it happens automatically. In humans, we need to reinforce the controls with training and education.

C: That's interesting. Animals are actually better at following the rules than we are.

T: In a sense, that's true. But we're getting away from your fight with Bill.

C: You're saying that I'm setting him up.

T: In a sense. When a female looks coy, or behaves girlishly, the male becomes protective. So if you are being little-girlish with this guy, he is probably feeling a strong impulse to take care of you, which may also turn him on sexually. But he's in a bind. He's afraid to express those feelings. He probably realizes that you don't mean it that way, so he has to suppress what he's feeling. The coldness you see is the effort it's taking him to sort through all that, and perhaps his anger at what he sees as your being manipulative.

C: Huh. What a mess. . . .

As she gained an understanding of her own dynamics and the rules of competition and cooperation, the intensity and frequency of Barbara's clashes with coworkers decreased substantially. Since she was not under pressure to change other aspects of her life, no further work was undertaken.

Catherine

Catherine, a woman of about 35, made a decent living in the corporate environment, but did not consider herself to be a career woman. She was interested in marriage but felt that she had never met the right man. She had begun, however, to put some distance between herself and this interpretation, because she had met, and lived with, all sorts of men, and always found them wanting in one respect or another.

In the past, Catherine might have been diagnosed as a woman who was in love with her father. She was in fact quite familiar with this interpretation of her behavior, and quite willing to accept it. She idealized her father and didn't have much use for her mother. Unfortunately, the insight hadn't done her any good. She still found fault with all the men she met.

Since that area of inquiry didn't hold much hope of bringing about change, it seemed more promising to focus more narrowly on the specific reasons Catherine rejected specific men. This quickly revealed that she criticized some men for being authoritarian, remote, and humorless, and other men for being dependent, weak, and overinvolved.

The problem was that Catherine had no awareness of her conflicting attitudes. When she was with a man who fit type A, she forgot that she had ever wanted to be led. When she was with a man who fit type B, she forgot that she had ever wanted a man who was warm and cuddly. In other words, the only time she wanted to be led and taken care of was when she was with a man who wouldn't do it, and the only time she wanted a man who was open and vulnerable was when she was with a domineering type. She switched back and forth from one state to the other, depending on her perception of the man she was with. Not surprisingly, she felt that all men were either male chauvinist pigs or wimps.

The therapist's assessment was as follows:

1. Catherine suffered from some degree of splitting and compartmentalization; she oscillated between two ego states, to use Otto Kernberg's terminology. This had to be addressed first.
2. The dynamic was playing into, or mapping onto, elements of the female reproductive strategy, as it played itself out in the altered environment.
3. She did not have a framework for interpreting her ambivalence, and would not be able to resolve it until she did.

Therapy proceeded accordingly. The following exchanges took place after her contradictory requirements of men had been identified and related to separate, highly compartmentalized images of self and other.

T: The real issue then is that you won't accept leadership from a man. You're attracted to it, but when you get it, you don't want it. Then you go to a man who won't give it to you, and you don't like that. So you oscillate back and forth, you shuttle from one type to another.
C: I'd have to say that it looks that way. I thought I knew what I wanted, but I guess I don't. But why do I want to be led?

T: I'm not sure that's the right question. We might be better off asking why you are attracted to that kind of a man. And there, the answer is easy. It goes back to good genes, for one thing. To be big and strong, to look competent and seem successful, these are signs, or indicators, of good genes. The signs may be faulty now, but in the course of evolution, those signs have proved reliable enough to be depended on.

C: That makes sense.

T: Another factor is paternal investment. (Discussion omitted: see Chapters 7 through 10.) Women are adapted to select men who seem like good providers. You keep going to the men who give off these signals.

C: So why do I reject them?

T: You tell me.

C: It could be that I'm still faithful to my father, so I don't really want to give in to them.

T: Yes, that's probably part of it. Anything else?

C: I don't see anything.

T: Are you making it on your own now?

C: How does that connect?

T: Think about it.

C: You mean, I don't really need all that now, so I can reject it? If it doesn't fit the rest of me, if I don't want to get led around just to have my children taken care of, I don't have to?

T: Right. Rationally, or economically, you don't really need a man, you don't have to put up with any of his imperfections. You can tell him to stuff it. If he isn't perfect, you do.

C: What about the guys that fall all over me, then? Why does that turn me off so much?

T: What is it that you're thinking when they do that?

C: I think that there's something wrong with them, otherwise why would they be interested in me.[2]

T: And if there's something wrong with them?

C: I wouldn't want to mate with them, right. But it's so stupid! You say this stuff made sense for animals, or even humans, but it doesn't make any sense now.

T: Look, just because something doesn't make sense, or isn't necessary any more, doesn't mean it goes away. Look at the appendix.

C: So I have to live with it.

T: You have to live with it, but you don't have to have your life destroyed

---

[2]This issue had been explored previously.

by it. Now that you can see what's going on, you'll be able to change the behavior in a way that will get you more of what you want. . . .

Subsequent therapy focused on methods for coping with these responses as well as with the parent-child dynamic that was clearly involved in the genesis of the problem. She made steady progress.

Deirdre

Deirdre's case is interesting because it involved helping a woman to consider the possibility that she didn't really need psychotherapy.

Deirdre had been in therapy with someone else for several years when a career decision forced her to move to a new town. In our first interview, she revealed why she had originally sought help. At 40, she had been through three long, intense relationships, none of which had resulted in marriage or a family. She had enjoyed these relationships immensely, but now had second thoughts about her attitude towards them. Although she had wanted each of the relationships to be permanent, they hadn't turned out that way. Had she unconsciously chosen the type of man who was unable to make a commitment? Deirdre now felt that something self-destructive resided in her soul.

In her therapy, she had related her behavior to her father, a charming man who had abandoned his wife and children at the peak of his career. Deirdre had come to believe that she was choosing men like her father—men who would inevitably leave her.

The therapist's sense of it was that Deirdre was a healthy woman who had lived fully and well. The lack of marriage in her life seemed due more to chance than to her "choice" of men. The men she had lived with were each interesting and had given her a lot in the way of unusual experiences— arguably much more than she would have gotten from more stable, career-oriented men. Since Deirdre was not an unusually attractive woman, the therapist wasn't convinced that she could have gotten a man who was both exceptionally interesting and also inclined towards marriage. In other words, the therapist didn't think she had exercised as much choice as she thought she had.

As a result, rather than focusing on the pathological (her presumed fixation on her father), the therapist engaged her in a discussion of the conflicting biological drives that normally inhabit the female psyche. We spoke of reproductive success, and of how behavior has been shaped by evolution to seek it. We discussed the obvious fact that for an individual in modern society, pursuing reproductive success involves many sacrifices and does not, given all the magnificent opportunities available to young Americans, necessarily lead to the most satisfying life possible. In other words, the therapist helped her to see that she shouldn't castigate herself for the life-style decisions that she had made in the past.

The therapist also pointed out that there might be a different logic to her choice of men:

C: There's still got to be something that's driving me to one kind of guy rather than another.

T: Sure. Let's try to get a hold on this by looking at simpler animals. Choosing a mate is easy for most mammal females. Once they have completed the sexual act, they're through with the male. Except in a few species, he isn't going to invest anything in the offspring, he isn't going to be part of a family, he isn't going to take care of her. So what does she need from him?

C: Nothing?

T: Good genes. If her offspring are going to survive — and remember, she invests a lot in them — they've got to be healthy, know all the right moves, have all the right instincts, that kind of thing. So how do males indicate to females that they have good genes?

C: You tell me.

T: Thanks, I will. Let me count the ways. By being big, by being strong, by having all kinds of bright markings, by knowing how to dance. Males get gaudy, they get fancy, they develop muscles. . . .

C: Why do the females respond to this?

T: Natural selection. These signs do indicate good genes. Females who don't respond to the signs have less viable offspring. So the males who have the right signs have more offspring than the others, and the females who don't respond to them get eliminated.

C: How does this relate to me?

T: Think about it.

C: You mean I'm responding to something that some men have, something interesting, something special, something that might be a good trait to have if you're a male?

T: I suspect so.

C: So I'm getting turned on by signs of good genes.

T: It makes sense, doesn't it?

C: I suppose so.

T: And you reproach yourself for not going with males who don't have these signs. So. Let's look at those other males. In the human species, the task of the female isn't so simple. Human females — you, for example —

want a male who will stay around and help raise the kids. Human females want a commitment, that is, they want males who are going to provide a lot of paternal investment. That's a whole new ballgame. Now there are two criteria for choosing males, good genes and paternal investment.

C: And they don't go together.

T: There is no guarantee that they will. It would be nice if you could find a guy who has both, but it doesn't make a whole lot of sense for you to punish yourself for not having pulled off that trick. . . .

After some discussion of these matters, Deirdre decided that she was not disturbed enough to require further psychotherapy.

Ellen

For five difficult years, Ellen had hung in with her husband even though they quarreled incessantly. They stayed together because they had a lot to offer each other; they fought, because they each wanted more from the other than the other could give.

Ellen was younger than Earl by 10 years. Her tremendous energy gave her a vibrant, compelling vivacity. She was in a rush, and she gave the impression that she could accomplish anything, if she set her mind to it. But she had never been able to focus on anything long enough to succeed at it. She was also highly articulate and verbal to a fault. She could outtalk almost anybody, even on subjects she knew nothing about. Her quick wit served her well in social situations, but made her a difficult companion. Being in a conversation with her was like being in a bullfight. You were either the toro or the toreador, and Ellen showed no mercy to men whose shafts could not penetrate her hide.

When Earl had first met her, he was captivated. He had spent many years in a loveless marriage, and he was a quiet, thoughtful, unassuming sort of man. Ellen was his ticket to bliss. He was attracted to many of the traits that turned off other men. She brought excitement into his life, and if it came with some tension, that was all right with him. He felt that all the problems could be worked out if sufficient good will were shown.

There was potential in the partnership. She had too much energy, he was too passive. She fantasized about the impossible, he conducted himself with extreme caution. She had ambition and no skills, he had skills but hesitated to use them. Together, they had the makings of a team.

The team worked well for a while. Earl quit his job and went into business for himself. Ellen involved herself in his new career, and pushed him to promote himself. Hesitantly, he began to move forward. The business they founded proved itself viable.

But Ellen's ambition was not satisfied. No matter how well Earl did, she wanted him to do more. She kept complaining that he wasn't moving fast enough, taking enough risks. Worse, she began to criticize him, in public and in private, precisely for needing and accepting her help. She kept trying to prove that he was inadequate. For him, it was a no-win situation. If he argued, he spent his life arguing. If he tried to conciliate her, she only got angrier. By the time she came into therapy, she was getting angry at him for not stopping her from behaving so badly towards him. Naturally, their sex life had ground to a halt.

The situation seemed clear. Earl did not have the surface attributes of dominance. He gave off signals that indicated subordination. Ellen wanted someone she could look up to, someone who had status and prestige among his fellow men, someone who would make the world safe for her. She vaguely sensed that the man who could do this would be able to control her destructive and self-destructive tendencies, so she took Earl's failure to do so not as a sign of love, but as an indication of weakness.

On the other hand, the therapist suspected that Earl had some hidden strengths. He had made the switch to entrepreneurship at a relatively late age. These strengths were probably what drew her to him in the first place. Unfortunately, she didn't consciously recognize his strength, and had no insight into the reasons for her anger at him.

So she had a problem. Her method of testing the strength of a man was self-defeating. No truly strong man would tolerate it. She couldn't tolerate a weak man. Furthermore, she was not able to define what she wanted from a man, or for that matter, from life. She had no framework for interpreting her behavior.

When someone is using a strategy that makes no biological sense, there are three possibilities: (1) there is some kind of organic or genetic defect; (2) the organism has been subjected to an unnatural environment; (3) some combination of the above. Exploration quickly revealed that Ellen's childhood environment was a prime suspect. Her mother had been the dominant personality in the family. She was the breadwinner, and she ran the house. She was a self-righteous woman who thought she had all the answers. Her children grew up thinking of her as an all-powerful eminence who represented the Truth and the Way. They all took years to free themselves from her domination.

Ellen's father was essentially a failure. His activities in the outside world were shadowy. Around the house, he was also a figure without substance. His feeble attempts at self-assertion were the butt of frequent jokes. He was

totally unable to control his wife or protect the children from her invasive-
ness.

In her dealings with Earl, Ellen was clearly living out this scenario.
Apparently, she tested all the men she met, to see if they were as weak as
Daddy. Most men refused to tolerate this kind of treatment and left; those
who stayed showed in the process that they were indeed men of little worth.
Given the tightness of this bind, it was a wonder that Ellen was able to
connect with any man at all. She was able to make it with Earl because his
needs and hers were complementary. He combined a degree of inner strength
with a strong need to be motivated and led around.

Therapy soon focused on issues of power and control, with special reference to her family of origin. The therapist spent a lot of time trying to help
her see that the models of behavior that she took for normal were really
biologically aberrant. In the following pages, we will restrict ourselves to
excerpts from dialogues in which concepts from evolutionary biology were
actually discussed.

T: Why do you think all those men who refused to tolerate your attacks
just left the scene?
C: Well, I always assumed that they just couldn't handle it, that they
were too weak. That they couldn't handle it.
T: So, if I understand correctly, Earl started out as a man who could
handle it, which caused you to respect him. Then, as he let you tongue-
lash him, and couldn't defeat you in argument, you began to think of him
as just another guy who wasn't tough enough.
C: That's it. He started to disappoint me. I figured he was just like my
father after all.
T: Now you understand that they simply didn't want to put up with all
that hassle?
C: Part of me sees that. Another part of me just looks on them as
wimps and wants to destroy them, like my mother did. Or seemed to. I'm
not so sure now.
T: We'll get back to that. I want you to understand the men a little better
and I think it might help if we discussed male behavior patterns a little.
Men aren't set up to fight *with* women. They're set up to fight *for* women.
In many species, male animals have to fight other males to get access to
females, so they have to be big, and strong, and have good fighting
ability. They then use all this to defend the females and the young. That's
why males tend to be bigger than females. Now what would happen if
these big, dangerous animals were to use their strength and teeth to fight
with females?

C: It wouldn't be good for the species.

T: Probably not, but it wouldn't be good for that male either. Suppose he killed the mother of his infants. How would they survive?

C: They couldn't.

T: Right. So evolution has tended to create males who tend to avoid fights with females.

C: So you're saying that these guys avoided me because they didn't want to fight with me.

T: Right.

C: Why doesn't Earl avoid me?

T: He likes you. He tries to mollify you, to appease you, because he doesn't want to fight with you. And what happens?

C: I take it as weakness.

T: And actually it's strength of a kind. He is strong enough not to retaliate.

C: Why does he put up with it at all?

T: Well, I don't know the answer to that, but I suppose that he is sufficiently attracted to other parts of you to hope that you'll stop attacking him eventually.

C: But he doesn't fight with anybody!

T: That may be part of what's frustrating you. Females tend to be attracted to highly competitive males—males who show that they are strong and can win fights are really showing females they have good genes. That is something we have to explore, but for the moment, can you see any other sources of strength in him? . . .

Subsequent work focused on helping Ellen to see that Earl was strong and competent, even though he didn't show the usual signs by which a male indicates his power. The therapist also suggested that Earl try to find out why he was so reluctant to promote himself and compete openly with other men.

CHAPTER 15

Working with Dominance

LET US START WITH A BRIEF REVIEW of the major points we made in Chapters 9 and 10. Aggression, bluff, and threat played important roles in determining access to females in prehuman, ancestral species. In the evolution toward humanness (hunting and gathering), the role of aggression declined. Dominance became more a matter of prestige, and prestige rested on skill and personal charisma. The role of dominance hierarchies declined. Leadership became fluid, shifting from person to person at different times.

Nevertheless, the capacity and indeed the need for a male to experience himself as dominant remained. Fortunately, in a band, each individual male could think and feel himself powerful, without having to attack other members of the band. People didn't have to defeat each other. As a result, each one could have self-worth and self-esteem.

Modern societies have taken a step backward. The hierarchies of modern organizations bring out in men the atavistic tendency to bluff, threaten, and defeat each other. The fierce competition for status in organizations divides people into winners and losers. Most men are subordinates, and many experience themselves as losers. So once again we primates find ourselves in a situation in which dominance is limited to a small number of individuals. The result is psychological distress.

Some individuals display social subordination, signal their low status, avoid the spotlight, and meekly accept their fate. Other men, refusing to accept their subordinate position, but unable to advance, develop compensatory mechanisms. Some of them turn into martinets who tyrannize their family and friends, while others strike out violently against a society that they don't understand.

The misplaced aggression and the violence displayed by human males — especially towards women — is due, not so much to "socialization for aggression" or to the expression of "typically male" behavior, but more often to the fact that so many individuals fail to achieve an internalized sense of control and power.

Readers should note that the concept of dominance as we are using it here has much in common with what therapists generally call self-esteem or self-worth. Promoting dominance is thus similar to promoting self-esteem. Nevertheless, the two terms are not identical. "Dominance" contains the idea of power, and involves the notion of success at male-male competition. Furthermore, it implies that men (and women) will be happier, and more sexually in tune, if the man plays somewhat of a protective role in his family and is looked upon in this light by his mate. Hence the emphasis on dominance fits in with the notion that male-female relationships should be based on exchange of dissimilar qualities.

Rudolph

Rudolph came into therapy because he wanted his woman back. He was depressed, dangerously thin, and he was about to lose his job for lack of concentration. He was around 40, and had never really loved anyone else. However, each time he had gotten close to marrying her, he had panicked and fled. She had let him come back four or five times. This time, it seemed hopeless.

The therapist was skeptical of Rudolph's motivation, but was eventually won over. Rudolph said that he knew that he had to get his own life together, and he vowed that he would continue in therapy even if it wouldn't bring back the woman he loved.

The problem was that Rudolph had no idea why he had fled, or why his own life wasn't together. He was a high-school dropout, a mechanic by trade, and a man with no sophistication about therapy. He presented himself in a very tentative, sheepish manner, which immediately indicated that he thought of himself as an inferior. Furthermore, he was still living with his aged parents. He had tried several times in the course of his life to get away from them, but had never managed to live on his own for as much as a year.

Given Rudolph's level of commitment to his former lover, the therapist decided that to do whatever was possible to maximize his chances of getting her back. Moreover, it was clear the changes he would need to make to get her back were the same changes he would need to improve the quality of his life. The reasoning was as follows:

1. He lacked a sense of self-worth and a capacity for assertiveness (in our terms, an internalized sense of dominance) which had to have an effect on her attitude towards him.
2. The fact that he lived with his parents was both part of the problem and a symbol of the problem.
3. He had fled in part because he didn't think himself worthy of this woman, in part because he couldn't give up his mother, and in part because he couldn't tolerate closeness without feeling smothered.
4. His repeated flights had finally indicated to her that he was not a man she could count on or trust in any way.

The therapist devised a plan of action that would address all these issues. First, the client was told that he would have to forget about his ex-girlfriend for three months. He was forbidden to contact her, to hang around her, or even to allow her to see him on the street. To ensure his cooperation, the therapist stressed that this was part of a strategy that might win her back if we were lucky. He agreed to the terms and took steps to avoid all contact with her from then on.

Secondly, the therapist did everything possible to make him aware of his presentation of self. It proved necessary to mimic his manner to make him aware of it. He was surprised, but able to work on it. Very soon, he was able to talk without showcasing his assumed inferiority.

The therapist talked to him about the role of the male, and insisted that doing well on his job was a major factor in his campaign. This seemed to enable him to focus on doing his work. Assertive moves with respect to his bosses were practiced, and the client was encouraged to go out an look for a better job. He began to spend less time in the session crying over spilt milk and more time getting his act together.

When we explored his childhood, we discovered that his father, an immigrant, had held two jobs simultaneously and was hardly ever at home. His mother was bitter over her fate and totally unaware of life in America. He could not remember ever being praised. After a few months of arduous exploration, he realized that he was still trying to get the love his parents had never given him, and he began to prepare to move out of their house.

The exploration gave him insight into his own life pattern. He understood why he had such low self-esteem and why he had never been able to marry, live alone, or hold a good job. However, he had a hard time linking any of this up to his inability to tolerate closeness with his lover. But this was a key question, because the therapist was convinced that if she was ever to think about letting this man back into her life, she would want to know if he could understand and control the dynamic.

Consequently, the therapist asked him over and over to link up his problems with his mother to his problems with his lover. He didn't like it, and there were times when he came close to leaving therapy. But, there really was no choice if he was to have a chance at his goal. He finally understood that intimacy was threatening to him because his parents, with whom he wanted to be close, had never made him feel wanted and secure. This realization gave him confidence that he would never have to repeat the pattern again.

After three months, he was in a different place. He understood what had happened to him and why he had lived his life the way he had. He soon moved into an apartment of his own, and shortly afterward got a better job. He also began seeking out leisure activities with friends and organized groups. What was needed was a little bit of luck.

The luck, and the opportunity to use his new skills, came when he passed his lady in the street by accident. Instead of running over to her like a puppy, he kept on walking, waved in a friendly, casual manner, and continued on his way.

The next day, more than a year after they had broken up, she called up a friend of his and asked about him. A week later, they started dating again. She did ask him why he had fled all those times, and he was able to answer her honestly. Within a month, they had (again) agreed to get married. Their subsequent relationship was not without difficulty, nor did all of his problems disappear. But his life did take a long-lived turn for the better.

The Defensive/Aggressive Response: Alan

Alan's style throughout life had been tyrannical: he used coercion on his subordinates, was contemptuous of almost everyone he knew, got into fights in bars, and had a reputation as a male chauvinist. He had no close personal friends.

He came into therapy because this style wasn't working for him anymore. He was confused and becoming progressively unhappy. At work, he was generating too much hostility, and at home, he was having trouble with Ann, his new girlfriend—the first woman in his life that he was "really crazy about." Although he reported that she was quite compliant, he was experiencing difficulty performing sexually.

Exploration revealed that he had grown up without a sense of being wanted and valued by his parents. Harsh arrogance was his manner of coping with his insecurities. The problem was not too much dominance, but too little. This theme recurred both in his private life and at work.

His job-related problems seemed to constitute a perfect opportunity to explore these issues. He was perceived as an egotist who was out only for himself. His superiors were reluctant to entrust him with important tasks because his loyalty to them was suspect. He quarreled with them frequently.

Therapy focused on giving him a sense of his own power.

T: (after a relaxation exercise) What is really causing those fights?
C: I don't know. Oh my god, now I see it. They're bigger than me. I can see myself. I'm little. I'm nobody. I have to defend myself. They're above me. I have to keep them from intimidating me, and because I'm so little, I do it by raising these tantrums. . . .
T: (later in the session) What do you really want from them?
C: I don't know.
T: Think about it. They disappoint you, you get angry, you fight with them. What does that remind you of?
C: I guess maybe they're the adults. So I must be behaving like a little boy. That's it. I want them to pat me on the head. I want to be loved, I guess. When it doesn't happen, I get angry. Yeah, that's it.
T: That's interesting. (pause) How do you think you would feel if they actually responded by treating you like a little boy?
C: Wow, I guess I would resent it a lot, I would wonder why they were treating me like an idiot or something. Hm. No wonder I get into so many hassles. (pause) So what do I do?
T: What do you think?
C: Stop looking for praise, I guess. Just concentrate on doing the job. Establish my own territory, my own self.
T: I think so. What about your expectations of your bosses?
C: I guess I have to realize that they're just human, they make mistakes all the time. They're not going to know what I need and what I want, and there's no point being disappointed or angry about it. Even if I do my job better, I'll still have to say so, and ask for what I deserve, like a raise or a promotion. I can't sit around waiting for them to bring me into the inner circle, or raise me up to their level, like I was doing. . . .
T: There's something else. You have to realize something about competition. You're a fully grown male, and when you fight, you cause the others to fight back. You provoke them. But since you see yourself as a little boy, you don't think you can hurt anybody, so you swing away without restraint.
C: That's why I'm surprised when they attack me, isn't it?

T: I think so.

C: They're just retaliating. Now that I look at it, the people over me must think I'm some kind of raging madman. I keep coming at them all the time. They must think I'm trying to beat them out of their jobs, so no wonder they don't treat me the way I want to be treated. I don't give them a chance to, because I don't realize my strength . . .

With Ann, the pattern was similar. He appeared to be in control, maintained his image as the boss and leader, but was in fact totally lost and helpless. The immediate problem was that his fiancée wanted sex more often than he did. The therapist asked him to describe the situation:

C: Well, there's two things. First of all, when I get home, she's all over me. She wants to hop into bed right away, and I just can't do it. I want to, I've been thinking about it all day, but when I get there, I'm too wound up. I need some time to rest, and even if I had it, I don't think I would be into having sex with her every day. So I'm beginning to feel like I just can't handle her, her needs, you know.

T: It seems to me that you think that a man should always be ready to have sex, any time of the day or night. Am I right?

C: Well, I guess I feel that if I'm not like that, and she wants me to be, then she'll leave me for someone who will be everything she wants.

T: The real issue, then, is that you're not sure that you're good enough for her, right? Why don't we look at that after some relaxation.

C: (after a pause) I guess I think I have to be a superstud in order to make up for my other inadequacies. No one will love me if I'm not the perfect lover. It's like I'm trying to prove myself again to my parents, only this time it's her that I'm trying to convince.

T: Do you think this has anything to do with the violence you spoke about?

C: Sure it does. It's when I'm feeling that I'm not coping with anything that I start to feel violent. That feeling just wears away at me until I don't know where to turn, what else to do.

T: Well, I think it's natural for you to feel anger when you feel threatened. After all, males have to defend themselves and maintain their position against threats from others. That's part of the male role. The problem here is that the threats to you aren't coming from outside, they're coming from inside your own head.

C: Right! That's why I turn the violence against her. It should be turned against some other guy, but no other guy is threatening me, so the anger gets turned against myself—or the person nearest me. . . .

At a later session, we returned to this theme:

C: Look, I'm relaxing now when I come home, and I've told her that I need time to unwind and all, but there's still something there that's bothering me. I don't like it when she comes on to me so strong. I want to feel like I'm the one who takes the initiative, like I'm in control. When she leaves me alone for a while, I get this surge of desire for her, and then when we make out, it's really good. But when I sense her there, just waiting for it, I get turned off. What's wrong? I should feel flattered, but I don't. I feel like I'm being pushed around.

T: I can understand what you're feeling. A man doesn't perform well sexually when he feels that he's being pushed around. And a man can't perform on demand. He isn't able to control his erection. It happens or it doesn't. So the minute he senses that someone else expects him to perform, he's going to experience some anxiety. And the minute that happens, the chances are that he won't be excited anymore. Fear suppresses male sexuality. It has to do with dominance. If you're not feeling powerful and in control, you don't feel like sex.

C: Why the hell are we made that way?

T: There's a good reason for it. It has to do with natural selection. It's nature's way of ensuring that only the genes of strong, competent males get passed along. The sexuality of weak males gets suppressed and they don't mate. So males who are naturally fearful don't reproduce as much as the more daring kind.

C: Are you saying that I'm weak?

T: Not really. But I do think that your upbringing weakened you a little. You learned certain ways of behaving, those ways have had certain effects and now you have to unlearn them . . .

C: In other words, I wasn't born weak, I was made that way. So I guess it's OK to pass along my genes, then?

T: I think so. . . .

Some time later, issues of control arose in the couple relationship. Though Ann had long since graduated from college, she was expected to come home to her parent's house every night. She and the family maintained the fiction that she was a virgin. This meant, for example, that she and Alan couldn't go away for a weekend together, even after they were officially engaged. She categorically refused to do or say anything that would hurt her family.

Alan had expected that her attachment to her parents would weaken over time. When it didn't, he became resentful. He didn't want to pretend that his fiancée was still a virgin. She, on the other hand, wanted to draw him into her family circle. They had quarreled several times and he had been on the verge of hitting her. Though Alan did believe that "it didn't hurt to show a woman who was boss," he was finally frightened by his own violence. He didn't want to do her an irreparable injury.

C: The thing is that we're always getting into arguments over what we're going to do. Last night, she wanted me to drive over to their place after work to have dinner. I didn't want to, but I didn't want to get into another argument over it. I know if I just tell her to shut up and leave me alone, she'll eventually leave me completely. So I went. What a waste of time.

T: Did you ever get around to asking her to go away with you for the weekend?

C: I mentioned it to her and she said that she would like to, but she didn't want to hurt her family. So I got mad, and asked her who she would choose, me or her father. She just got hysterical.

T: Does she do that often?

C: Anytime I want to spend an evening by myself, that's what she does. She gets angry or cries. So either we quarrel, or I end up doing what she wants, which is usually going over to their house.

T: Well, let's review the facts. She's afraid of her father, so she won't do anything that reveals that you are sleeping together. Instead, she plays this elaborate charade with her family. You, on the other hand, go along with it. What's the message you're giving her?

C: I guess that I'm afraid of him too.

T: Right. And then when she cries or gets angry, you do what she wants. So what's the message there?

C: That I'm afraid of her?

T: Must be. So if you're afraid, how is she going to choose you over her father? How is she going to break away from her family? You've got to show her that you're someone she can rely on.

C: So what do I do? Start fighting with him? Push her around and make her do what I say?

T: Not at all. That might be the worst thing you could do. If you fight with him, you'll just generate sympathy for him. You'll look like a clod. And if you push her around, you'll come off as a bully.

C: So what do I do?

T: What you have to do is get more involved with things outside of your relationship. You have to become an independent focus of attention. You have to decide what you want out of your career and leisure time, and you have to go out and get it. If you create a life that is interesting enough, she'll get involved in it, and will move out of her family's orbit. But she'll only do that if you take the lead.

C: How can I take the lead without a fight?

T: Look, the dominant male in a troop is the one that the others look at, the one they watch. If you're watching her father, and hooking yourself into his trip, even as someone who is fighting with him, then you won't be creating a trip of your own. If you spend your time trying to get her to do what you want, the same thing will happen. So you have to generate your own decisions and hope they're interesting enough for her to follow.

C: How do I do that?

T: You decide what you want to do, and you do it. If she doesn't want to do it, you let her do what she wants. If she wants to eat dinner with her family, fine. If you want to go off to Maryland for the weekend, you go. You don't get angry if she does her own thing, you take an interest in it. . . .

Even though Alan eventually developed the capacity for leadership, his relationship with Ann ended. He is currently involved in a relationship which seems to be following a completely new, mutually satisfactory course.

It might also have worked to teach Alan to be more compliant, more understanding, or more willing to have a marriage based on "equality." In fact, it is likely that such a stance is taken more often than not by contemporary therapists who believe they are thereby avoiding sexist attitudes. But we think that in this case the emphasis on leadership was more sensible.

One might note in this context that leadership and reciprocity are not opposites; they are complementary values. A good leader, one who leads with by consent, both gives and takes. Furthermore, it is perfectly legitimate for leadership to shift from one person to another. Problems arise when neither side accepts leadership, or when both sides try to set up a situation in which no leadership can be exercised.

The Defensive/Aggressive Response: Bernard

On the surface, Bernard also seemed like an overly dominant man. He was a successful, aggressive entrepreneur, with opinions to match. As an arch-conservative, politically, economically and socially, he believed in three great rules: government should stay out of business, people should fend for themselves, and woman's place was in the home. Most of the people he knew found him opinionated and offensive.

The reality behind this facade was quite different. He had sought help

because he was having marital troubles. He was madly in love with his wife
and declared that she was the most important thing in the world to him. All
his thoughts revolved around her, and he lived only for the pleasure he could
give her. He catered to her every whim and when he eventually perceived that
she was unhappy, he begged her to invent desires so he could satisfy them. In
short, he was driving her crazy.

It was easy to see what had happened. She had married him because he
seemed like a powerful man, and he turned out to be a fawning little boy.
Exploration focused on this contradiction in his behavior. The usual childhood experiences turned up: he had been raised in a fragmented family and
felt he had received no love from his father or his mother. He had grown up
feeling that he was alone in the world. Consequently, he had to compete
against everyone in order to keep from being destroyed. No quarter could be
expected from anyone.

In this inhospitable world, his wife was his only friend. With her, he
could let down his guard, but when he did, the needy child popped right out.
He had never really established himself as a man in his own mind.

Therapy focused on helping him get in touch with his power. The passages that follow describe some of the work done on his relationship with his
wife:

T: But you can't expect her to love you if you make her the center of
your world.

C: Why not? What more can a woman want? You hear them bitching
all the time about men who are selfish, and now you tell me that they
don't want a man who is devoted to them.

T: You have to take reality into account. Women are attracted to men
who make them feel secure, men who seem to be good providers, healthy,
strong, and all that. In choosing you, she chose a man who seemed
powerful and independent. Now you're asking her to be your mother. If
she wanted to be a mother, would she have chosen you?

C: But she bitches all the time about my being a male chauvinist, so
why do you say she wants a dominant man?

T: Come off it now, we've already talked about your male chauvinism.
Where does that come from?

C: From the need to defend.

T: Why don't we look at that. But let's relax a little first. (pause) So, the
need to defend, is that part of your strength, or part of your weakness?

C: Part of the weakness, I guess. So, it's the weak parts that she doesn't
like. The unnecessary fights, all that.

T: I think you're right.

C: But why are we so fucked up? Why aren't we simple enough to love the people who love us?

T: You might add, why are we turned off by people who are too eager, too emotional, too open in their affections? You know, I don't think your question is just one of those old philosophical chestnuts that people ask rhetorically. There may actually be an answer. We are adapted to life in small, solitary bands that had to fend for themselves in a difficult, dangerous environment.

C: What's that got to do with me now?

T: Well, our emotional reactions were forged in that environment. We respond the way we do because those responses once helped us to survive. We are attracted to people we think we can rely on in a tough spot. Self-reliance is a turn-on. As a businessman, you can understand that. When people come on too soft, we get suspicious. We suspect that they might not be tough enough to survive and pull their weight in the group.

C: You think that's what's happening here?

T: It's worth considering, don't you think?

C: Actually, I can see that what you're saying fits the business world. I just never thought any of that stuff went on in a marriage . . .

Subsequent therapy focused on allowing the little boy in Bernard to receive the affection he had missed. As he internalized his sense of strength and self-worth (dominance), the imbalance that had characterized his personality began to disappear. He became more self-contained at home, and more open and democratic at work.

Social Subordination: Colin

For Colin, avoiding the typical stereotypes of masculinity was a matter of deep conviction. He was a genuine old-style liberal who despised machismo, believed in the unlimited potential of all human beings, passionately advocated government help for the underprivileged, and actively embraced feminist principles. He had developed a life-style which reflected these convictions. He professed to hate competitive games, always tried to be friendly and helpful, and never pushed himself into the limelight.

He had a knack for making himself seem invisible. His gestures and manner of speech were soft and deferential. His quiet monotone was barely audible, and his drawn-in posture made him appear much smaller than he really was.

He had come into therapy because of persistent, albeit mild, depression. He said he was in a dead-end job, and had no friends to speak of. He didn't think people were interested in him. He had, he said, lost his enthusiasm for life. He was also drinking too much. Later he revealed that he was having problems with potency.

My sense was that his style, his beliefs and his symptoms were all linked, with the link being dominance, or rather, the lack of it. This link became the focus of therapy.

Extensive exploration finally turned up a vividly visual internalized hierarchy on which he occupied the bottom spot. We were discussing this hierarchy when the following exchange took place:

C: Sometimes other people give me the one-up position. I can see them do it.

T: How does it make you feel?

C: Very badly. I try to get away from it as quickly as I can.

T: Can you tell me what is going on in your mind when you try to get back to your one-down position?

C: My being one-up isn't real. I know it isn't real, and if it isn't real, I don't want it.

T: I guess you think that you have to earn the right to be one-up. Am I right?

C: Of course. If my business was (sic) going well, if I had my life together, if my kids were growing up to be great, I would have it all together. I'd have a right to the top position with people. This way, I don't.

T: If you earn it, it's real.

C: Right.

T: Well, let's look at your idea of real for a minute. (We got back to the notion of earning the right to feel OK at another time.) I think we have to ask ourselves what is real. You're telling me that there is a real position, and you want it. That tells me that you think the way you're seeing the situation is real. Can you be sure about that?

C: Yes.

T: Well, suppose that there are two people who both think highly of themselves. They both see themselves on top. Which position is real?

C: I suppose you can't tell.

T: Not really. Neither position is real. Each person can define the situation as they like. In fact, the best relationships, or rather, relationships between healthy adults, go on with both people seeing themselves on top. Which in fact does put both of them on top. The way you define the situation has a real effect on the situation. If you take the top position, you really have it.

C: The idea makes me uncomfortable.

T: Well, let's do a relaxation exercise and then you can practice seeing yourself in the superior position. Perhaps you can get used to it. . . .

Some time after this session, we began to work on a very long-standing problem in his marriage. His wife had a much more exciting job than he did and made more money. According to Colin, she owed a lot of her success to him; in the early days of their marriage, he had actively encouraged her career. But now he felt that it was threatening their marriage. She was coming home at 10 or 11 o'clock every night, and working weekends as well. Interestingly enough, he didn't suspect her of having an affair. His complaint was that they had no time to share anything anymore.

Because of his political and social convictions, he did not want to stand in the way of his wife's career, but these convictions did not prevent him from quarreling endlessly with her about her lateness. The conflict was profound; he rejected all of the options we came up with: he wouldn't leave, he wouldn't give her an ultimatum, and he wouldn't make peace with the fact that he had a part-time marriage.

Exploration revealed that Colin had frequently been ridiculed by his alcoholic father. His mother had suffered silently, but visibly. Colin had become her confidant and devoted helper. It had fallen to him to make up for his father's inadequacies.

Eventually, Colin realized that his relationship with his wife bore many similarities to the relationship he had had with his mother. In both, he saw himself as the helper. The woman was the center of his world. Her doings seemed much more important than his. His role was to make things better for her; his own desires seemed less important. Although his style was very different from Alan's, their behavior was strikingly similar in a variety of ways.

Colin's inability to see himself as a man in his own right explained why he neither left nor demanded that his wife find a way to avoid excessive overtime. If she were to quit her job, he would become the center of attention; there would be nothing of interest in his life other than his own activities, an idea which seemed intolerable to him when he first began to think about it. He preferred suffering to leadership.

Working on the assumption that the key to Colin's problem was his inability to assert his power in the world of men, the therapist started to focus him on his own activities:

T: You're angry at her for staying at work late, but you were the one who first encouraged her to seek out more and more demanding jobs. You basked in the attention and excitement that she generated. Now you don't like what she's doing but you don't tell her she has to stop or lose you. Do you see a problem?

C: I guess I'm giving her a double-message.

T: OK, so what to do?

C: (dejectedly) I suppose I have to develop my own life.

T: To do that, you'll have to stop focusing on her activities. You might have to give up being critic and helper—and you love those roles. Are you willing?

C: I suppose so. But do I just stop talking to her about the problem?

T: I don't think that will be enough. You'll have to make yourself an independent center of attention, one that can attract her away from the excitement of her job. What does she have to come home to now? You are depressed over your dead-end job, and you complain about her job. What is there for her in your house?

C: But my life doesn't seem that important.

T: That's the real problem, isn't it?

C: I guess so. (pause) It seems like an awful risk, but it would put an end to the bitching, wouldn't it?

T: Yeah. Is there anything else it might accomplish?

C: Well, I suppose it might help me to find something more interesting to do with my life. . . .

When Colin found a better job, we began to focus on his social skills. He was complaining about his failure to establish a relationship with an admired colleague at work:

T: How did you approach this man and what were you asking for that he didn't give you?

C: I just wanted him to like me.

T: Like you for what?

C: For being me.

T: What part of you did you try to show him?

C: I guess I tried to show him that I was a nice guy, that I liked him, that I was friendly and helpful.

T: So you were being helpful again. This is what you try to show people, how nice and unthreatening you are. But we already know that this helping attitude you take stems from what you call your desire to be your mother's helper.

C: So I'm showing him a friendly puppy dog face, I'm wagging my tail and turning over on my back?

T: My guess is that that's how he's reacting. Look, there's great value in being helpful and nice. These qualities you have are important. They once served the purposes of the hunter-gatherer group (a subject we had discussed before). Each man did his part and helped the others, which contributed to the survival of the group. You would be a great member.

C: Thanks.

T: But you're not *in* a group right now. And you can't get in by wagging your tail. All you're displaying to other people is the fact that you're harmless. That's not what people want in their group, or in their friends.

C: What do they want?

T: Can you guess?

C: People who can take care of themselves?

T: Sure, people who have something to offer, powerful people, self-reliant people. Once you're in, they'll be happy to find out, if a crunch comes, that you're reliable and loyal. But you'll have to wait for an opportunity.

C: So I have to go out there and show all the skills that I have, all the things that I can do? I've been hiding all that, not wanting to be a showoff. . . .

After considerable exploration of this issue, Colin began to display other aspects of his personality. His social life improved and his career advanced. The sexual problems that were secondary to the dominance/maleness/self-esteem issues were eventually resolved with the aid of sex therapy.

Social Subordination: Donald

Despite his powerful build, Donald came across as a weak and confused man. He constantly interrupted himself to criticize his own statements. A nervous tic around the eyes gave him a puzzled, owlish expression. He had not even sought help on his own. His wife had pushed him into it, for reasons he was unable to explain. He himself had no ideas about what he wanted to accomplish.

Donald, it turned out, was a gifted man who took no pride in his own abilities. He was one of those people who could fix anything, but he was acutely aware that society did not hold his mechanical skills in high esteem. He had never thought to challenge this standard of values.

After some discussion, it became clear that part of his gratingly humble manner was intentional. Like Colin, he was a liberal. He never missed an opportunity to proclaim his belief in nonviolence. Equality was dear to him and modesty was his special passion. Blowing one's own horn was one of the cardinal sins in his moral universe. The result was that he seemed to be walking around in a mental and physical strait-jacket. Everything about him was tense, constricted and confined. He wasn't able to express emotion on any subject.

Exploration revealed that in his teens, he had deliberately adopted a set of values to set himself off from his parents and their friends: white, working-class immigrants whom he often referred to as fascists.

Given all this, his work situation was predictable: he was in a job that was beneath him, he had been promised a better job two years before, and he hadn't done anything when the boss failed to come through. Three factors — a childhood without much love, the sense of inferiority he had acquired as a member of a working-class family, and the political philosophy he had used to reject his parents' values — had apparently combined to produce effective social subordination: a man who kept himself eternally in a one-down position.

Since he had come to therapy at the recommendation of his wife, the therapist first tried to find out what she thought was wrong. Donald wasn't sure, but said he thought she wanted him to do more of the chores. This explanation wasn't too persuasive, since he did all the maintenance on the house, shared many of the house cleaning chores, and spent a good deal of time with his two boys, all while holding down a full-time job.

After some probing, he finally admitted his wife wasn't too thrilled with his love-making technique, but he wasn't sure why. "I always try to find out what she wants," he said, proudly. Only after he was repeatedly asked to talk to her about her dissatisfaction was he able to say what she didn't like: "She says I'm very tentative, and never express any strong desires."

As soon as possible, we focused on his lack of expressiveness and assertiveness:

T: If you're so dissatisfied with what's going on at work, why don't you do something about it?

C: Like what? Get into an argument with the boss? Scream and yell like a madman? What good is that going to do? I'm not going to get into a fight over it.

T: It seems to me that this is always happening to you. You don't stand up for yourself, so you end up in a corner. Once you're in a corner, you have to either fight or lose. Since you are against fighting, you choose to lose. You let the others get what they want. It isn't worth fighting over.

C: That's about the way it works, I guess.

T: Well, how do you get into that corner?

C: I don't know. But it would be nice if I didn't get there.

T: Why don't you relax a little and look at it? I think it has to do with the way you present yourself to others.

C: (after the exercise) I guess I keep giving people the idea that I'm not going to stand up for myself, that I have a real low opinion of myself. So they just accept it at face value.

T: I would have to agree. You are giving people signals about your status. In just about any animal society, individuals indicate their status by the way they behave. Animals that won't fight and won't bluff end up as losers, and all the others treat them that way.

C: So that's why people try to push me around.

T: I think so. You're trying to indicate that you're a nice guy and you're really walking around saying that you're worthless.

C: So I end up having to choose between a real fight and not getting what I want. Actually, I'm creating the confrontations that I'm trying to avoid.

T: (after a long pause) There's more. In many species, females won't accept a male who gives off signals like that.

C: Do you think this could have something to do with why Daniela doesn't enjoy sleeping with me anymore?

T: It's possible. What do you do with her that's similar?

C: Well, I told you that she complains that I'm very tentative with her. I haven't been sure what she meant. But now I think maybe I am treating her like a superior, putting myself down, looking to her for what she wants. I'm really sensitive to her moods. If I start to make out with her and she doesn't respond right away, I ask her what's wrong. I guess I always felt I was being considerate and sensitive, but now I'm not so sure.

T: Well, you know, that's one of the things that happens in a marriage. In the early stages, the man is easily aroused. His enthusiasm carries him through the coyness of the woman, which is there because she needs the time to get ready for intercourse. But later, the man doesn't get aroused as easily, so he can be put off by resistance. But the woman doesn't understand this, she still wants to be taken, gently but firmly. So what happens is that the couple makes love less and less often.

C: That about fits it.

T: It's a natural process. Another thing that happens is that the guy will start to wait until the woman really expresses an interest, so sex starts to happen only when she asks for it, which isn't what she really wants. And when that happens, the guy may start feeling that the woman is too demanding—which puts her in a double bind. So it can be quite a mess.

C: So what do you do?

T: The first thing is, get in touch with your feelings. When you are feeling aroused, you've got to know it.
C: If I know it, she will too, is that it?
T: Maybe. But it doesn't hurt to communicate what you're feeling openly.
C: Isn't that like forcing her?
T: If she isn't interested, it's her responsibility to tell you.
C: Turnabout and all.
T: Right. Besides, there are ways to do it without pressure . . .

After extensive exploration, followed by various imaging and rehearsal exercises—and after a career change—the sex life of this couple reached a level which satisfied both partners, and therapy was terminated.

Dominance and Resistance

The need for dominance helps to explain why men don't like to be in one-down positions, and this in turn throws some light on the phenomenon of resistance in therapy. In the following extract, the concept of dominance is used to work with resistance.

After several years of slow, intermittent progress, Frank was functioning better and better in the outside world. On the other hand, in therapy, he began to behave in an arrogant manner and to make sarcastic remarks. The therapist questioned him about it.

C: I guess I'm growing up. Adults are hard. They don't care about other people's troubles, like children do. I feel cold. I'm asking for what I want, and getting it, but I'm cut off from other people. They can't touch me.
T: So when you're feeling strong, you're also feeling isolated.
C: Yeah.
T: What are you feeling now?
C: Distant. I'm in my fuck-you state. Before, when I would come in, I would be feeling like a little boy, so I could explore my weaknesses. Now I don't feel that you're above me anymore. I'm up here and you're down there. You want me to talk about my problems, and that would bring me down. (then, with a crooked grin) How does it feel to be one-down?
T: Is that why you don't want to do any exercises and find it hard to talk?
C: Of course. When you get me to do those things, you put me right into the one-down position.
T: How can you get help in the state you're in now?

C: I can't. That's the problem. Getting help puts you one-down. There's no getting away from it.
T: (after exploring this) Can you think of any situation where helping or learning can be done without going one-down? . . .

Some time later, he was induced to go through a guided fantasy in which he imagined dealing with another man as an equal; he was not even able to fantasize himself in that situation. Not for several months did he discover an internal position in which he could participate in therapy.

From the evolutionary perspective, resistance in therapy appears to be a natural phenomenon. Clients tend to see attempts to change them as attempts to control them. This explains why paradoxical interventions are often so successful.

Losing the Edge

A male's sense of security and power often declines over the course of a marital relationship. Very often, a man feels in control at the outset (after the first sexual encounter), because his sexual interest and the accomplishment of getting a promising romance started make him feel strong and protective. He tolerates all kinds of behaviors that he doesn't really like because he is so delighted, so turned on. As time goes on, he finds himself increasingly unable to sustain his interest. Here is an example:

C: In the beginning, I felt very protective, I took care of her, devoted a lot of attention to her. She's very volatile, very emotional. Actually, she yells a lot. But (smiling) with charm, sensitivity, being a good lover, and caring, I was able to keep her happy. Proving myself over and over was a challenge. It made me feel good to make her feel good. But she's worn me down. Now I anticipate that she will explode even before she does, and I withdraw. I had expected that she would become calmer and less explosive if I was steady and devoted, but it didn't happen. So now I don't have the energy to put into it anymore. I don't have the energy to defuse conflicts, and she is escalating everything. I need space now, and when I withdraw, she takes it as rejection and just gets more hyper.
T: You thought that if you invested all that, she would change, stop being so needy and emotional.
C: Right.
T: And now you've stopped.
C: Right.
T: Well, she's probably disappointed. She thought she had found a guy

who was going to make it possible to stop the acting-out, as you did, and from her perspective, you've changed. You've stopped doing what you used to do, for reasons that she probably doesn't understand.

C: I can't do it anymore.

T: I understand. She's worn you down. Before, when she acted out, you knew it was her. Now, you feel implicated. You think it might be you, something you've done.

C: Right! So I get defensive. It's like she's worn me down, worn down the part that was able to take care of her.

T: Can you describe that more?

C: What she does brings up stuff that happened to me when I was a kid. I feel helpless, weak, angry, out of control . . .

T: You've lost the edge, lost your ability to be a stabilizing force.

C: So what happens now?

T: Well, there are many possible paths and outcomes. . . .

A Couples Therapy Case

As we stated in Chapter 12, it is somewhat difficult to work on differing male and female strategies in couples sessions but in the following case, it worked pretty well.

When Victor, a small, not-too-successful businessman, and Wanda, a homemaker, came into therapy, their marriage was breaking up. The presenting problem was money. He felt that she spent too much. She felt that he was stingy and mean-spirited. They fought frequently and spent a lot of time not talking to each other. Here is Victor's account:

V: We don't have any money because she spends it all. She forgets to pay a bill, then she looks in the checkbook and sees that there's money, so she spends it on something, a rug, curtains, anything.

T: You have no control over this?

V: No. If I say something, she gets angry. She's like a little girl. If she doesn't get her way, she has a tantrum.

T: Here's what I think. You're spending the money. It's your decision.

V: What do you mean? Me, individually? She has access to all the money, I can't stop her. We have joint accounts, joint credit cards, everything.

T: Really? How did that come about?

V: That's what a marriage is all about, isn't it? How can it be otherwise?

T: Many people have different arrangements.

V: I don't believe it. You mean that they have separate accounts? What if the wife wants to buy clothes for the baby and the guy doesn't want to?

T: Doesn't the man have anything to say about spending money on the baby?

V: But what if he doesn't want to? (Note Victor's assumption that a man wouldn't want to pay.)

T: If that were the problem, we'd talk about that, but here the issue is different.

V: So what are you saying? That I should take some of my money and put it into a separate account, for bills?

T: I'm not telling you what to do, I'm just pointing out that you are responsible for the way the money is being spent. You may think that you're not, but that is just a way to avoid responsibility.

After some discussion of this issue, Victor realized that he had developed a nice safe position. He was letting his wife decide, while enjoying the freedom to criticize her decisions.

At a subsequent session, we addressed the quarreling. The key issue turned out to be his "reasonableness" vs. her need for emotional contact.

T: Let's see if we can get an exact sequence of what happens between you. Think back to an actual incident of fighting that you can remember.

W: The last one happened a couple of days ago. I said something nasty about his friends . . . (details omitted). . . .

T: What happened then?

V: I asked her if she really had to be so nasty.

T: So you were reasonable.

V: Yes.

T: How do you feel about that now?

V: Good.

T: Oh, dear. I'm afraid we have a problem.

We'll omit here much of the work that was necessary to tease out of Victor the realization that in being "reasonable" he was actually putting Wanda down for *not* being reasonable and ignoring what her emotions were expressing.

V: So it's a put-down.

Wanda agreed that it was infuriating, and quickly related this style to her feeling of not being heard. What was going on? His excessive considerateness and fear of giving offense caused him not to hear her desire for a decisive man on whom she could rely. From her point of view, he was refusing to take on his role as a man.

At first, Victor was not happy with her reaction:

V: You seem to be asking me for a way to control yourself.

Wanda could not bring herself to accept this interpretation:

W: It has nothing to do with my controlling myself. It's your style that's driving me crazy.

The therapist, suspecting that this might be a place where communication was counterproductive, did not seek to reconcile these points of view. Therapy focused on changing the styles of relating, letting insight fall where it would.

At a subsequent session, Victor reported that he had responded directly, with anger, to a cutting remark she had made.

T: (To Wanda) How did that feel to you?
W: It felt like he was there, like he wasn't trying to evade the issue. Before I felt like I was alone with the anger. I was in a vacuum. It just bounced around in there, and fed on itself. This time, the anger sort of dissipated. I was really surprised when he did it, like he was a new person really.

The reasons for the style of interaction that this couple developed were easily traced to their families of origin. The "systemic" problem was rooted in the failure to assume the roles that each sex unconsciously expects of the other. A clear understanding of reproductive strategies made it relatively easy to sort out what was going on.

A final word. The picture we have painted of the forces that are active in male-female relationships will undoubtedly be controversial in some contemporary circles, but is certainly not new. The literature of our species is filled with examples. Indeed, we feel that one of the great weaknesses of contemporary psychological theorizing is the fact that it so resolutely ignores the obvious. Consider this passage from Emily Brontë's *Wuthering Heights*. After her husband Edgar, a solid, well-meaning, but wimpy man approaches her in an excruciatingly reasonable way about her passionate relationship with Heathcliff, Catherine replies:

Oh, for mercy's sake . . . let us hear no more of it now! Your cold blood cannot be worked into a fever — your veins are full of ice-water; but mine are boiling, and the sight of such chillness makes them dance.

These attitudes may not be admirable. They may not be suitable to our current way of life. But they are in us and we cannot deny reality. Psychotherapists need to develop concepts of human nature that give them a solid foothold when wrestling with the dramas of love and sex in the modern world.

Epilogue

EVOLUTION IS THE STORY of *what happened*, the story of how all beings on Earth got to be the way they are. Every species that exists evolved from an ancestor that was different. The features of every species alive today evolved from features of the first creatures to appear. When we look at the human species in this way, we can see ourselves as one of the latest variations on the age-old theme of life. This view is somewhat unsettling. We are not as grand as we thought we were, and we are unlikely to last forever, but at least we are full participants in an ancient and ongoing saga.

The evolutionary perspective provides a view of human nature that is neither naively optimistic nor depressingly negative. We are bound to struggle and to suffer defeats. In this, we are not different from the thousands of other species that share the planet with us. But by accepting our limitations we can enhance our appreciation of the good things that can be achieved.

The evolutionary perspective has led us to some new ways to assist our clients. Because we can help them to understand the way they are, we are better able to help them become more like what they want to be. Paradoxically, an understanding of biological constraints can often help people overcome their limitations. Evolution, though blind to everything but survival and reproduction, can serve to free those who understand it.

Human behavior is immensely complicated. We humans are often selfish and aggressive, but we are also social and sexual beings who crave companionship, approval, and love. We are capable of deceit and self-deception, but most of us have an innate sense of fairness that will flower if given the right environment. A theory of human nature which embraces all of these contradictory impulses should prove useful to therapists, regardless of theoretical orientation.

Evolutionary interpretations are simple and powerful. They make sense to people who have learned their lessons from the rough give and take of ordinary life. Simple explanations discourage pretentiousness and serve to reduce the barriers between helper and client.

The study of evolution has enabled us to simplify our goals as therapists. People need to participate in the activities of a group, they need to gain sexual gratification, and they need to achieve intimacy. People also need to understand what is going on in their lives, to feel in control of their destiny, and to have status and respect. We may be wrong, but we believe that these values are universal. They are not created from scratch by culture nor are they independent of the genes. They are part of a package of genes and culture that has co-evolved. Cultures that reject these values will be terribly hard on human beings.

Is it really necessary for psychotherapists to become familiar with evolution? Consider this: high school students are now learning the facts of evolution right along with their computer science. Our editor's son wants to go to the Amazon to live like the hunter-gatherers he learned about in school. The 14-year-old daughter of one of the authors is learning that the human cell is a symbiotic aggregation of formerly independent micro-organisms. In the future, cloning a living creature may be a 9th grade biology assignment. As the momentum of contemporary biological findings permeates our society, every aspect of human life will be understood in an evolutionary context.

Psychotherapy cannot stand apart. This book is an early attempt to place it in an evolutionary framework. We are confident that future books will be able to go much farther.

References

Alexander, R. (1987). *The biology of moral systems*. New York: Aldine.

Altmann, S. (1962). A field study of the sociobiology of rhesus monkeys. *Annals of the New York Academy of Sciences* 102(2).

Andreasen, N. (1984). *The broken brain*. New York: Harper & Row.

Andreasen, N. (1988, March). Brain imaging: Application in psychiatry. *Science* 239.

Bailey, R., & Peacock, N. (in press). Efe Pygmies of Northeast Zaire: Subsistence strategies in the Ituri forest. In I. de Garine & G. Harrison (eds.). *Coping with uncertainty in food supply*. Cambridge: Cambridge University Press.

Balikci, A. (1970). *The Netsilik Eskimo*. Garden City: Natural History Press.

Barash, D. (1979). *The whisperings within: Evolution and the origin of human nature*. New York: Harper and Row.

Beck, A. (1976). *Cognitive therapy and the emotional disorders*. New York: New American Library.

Bell, D. (1976). *The cultural contradictions of capitalism*. New York: Basic Books.

Berndt, R., & Berndt, C. (1964). *The world of the first Australians*. Chicago: Chicago University Press.

Bernhard, G. (1988). *Primates in the classroom: An evolutionary perspective on children's learning*. Amherst: University of Massachusetts Press.

Boas, F. (1888). The central Eskimo. *Annual Reports of the Bureau of American Ethnology*, #6, Washington.

Boesch, B., & Boesch, H. (1981). Sex differences in the use of natural hammers by wild chimpanzees: A preliminary report. *J. Hum. Evo.*, 10.

Boszormenyi-Nagy, I., & Spark, G. (1984). *Invisible loyalties*. New York: Brunner/Mazel.

Bowlby, J. (1969). *Attachment*. New York: Basic Books.

Bowlby, J. (1973). *Separation*. New York: Basic Books.

Bowlby, J. (1980). *Loss*. New York: Basic Books.

Briggs, J. (1970). *Never in anger: Portrait of an Eskimo family*. Cambridge: Harvard University Press.

Brown, J. (1970). A note on the division of labor by sex. *Am. Anthro.*, 72.

Carnes, P. (1983). *The sexual addiction*. Minneapolis: CompCare Publications.

Chagnon, N. (1968). *Yanomamo: The fierce people*. New York: Holt, Rinehart, Winston.

Chagnon, N. (1979). Male competition, favoring close kin, and village fissioning among the Yanomamo Indians. In N. Chagnon & W. Irons (eds.). *Evolutionary biology and human social behavior: An anthropological perspective*. North Wadsworth: Duxbury Press.

Chatwin, B. (1987). *The song lines*. New York: Penguin.

Clutton-Brock, T., Guiness, F., & Albon, S. (1982). *Red deer: Behavior and ecology of two sexes*. Chicago: University of Chicago Press.

Cosmides, L. (in press). The logic of social exchange: Has natural selection shaped how humans reason? *Cognition*.

Cosmides, L., & Tooby, J. (1987). From evolution to behavior: Evolutionary psychology as the missing link. In J. Dupre (ed.). *The latest on the best: Essays on evolution and optimality*. Cambridge: Cambridge University Press.

Cucchiara, S. (1981). The gender revolution and the transition from bisexual horde to patrilocal band. In S. Ortner and H. Whitehead (eds.). *Sexual meanings: The cultural construction of gender and sexuality*. Cambridge: Cambridge University Press.

Dahlberg, F. (1981). *Woman the gatherer*. New Haven: Yale University Press.

David, Henry. (1988). *Born unwanted*. New York: Springer.

DeVore, I., & Konner, M. (1974). Infancy in hunter-gatherer life. In N. White (ed.). *Ethology and psychiatry*. Toronto: University of Toronto Press.

de Waal, F. (1982). *Chimpanzee politics: Power and sex among apes*. New York: Harper & Row.

Dowling, C. (1981). *The Cinderella complex*. New York: Pocket Books.

Draper, P. (1976). Social and economic constraints on child life among the !Kung. In R. Lee and I. DeVore (eds.). *Kalahari hunter-gatherers*. Cambridge: Harvard University Press.

Ehrhardt, A., & Meyer-Bahlburg, F. (1981). Effects of pre-natal sex hormones on gender-related behavior. *Science 211*.

Elkin, A.P. (1938/1964). *The Australian aborigines*. New York: Doubleday.

Ellis, A. (1962). *Reason and emotion in psychiatry*. New York: Lyle Stuart.

Erikson, E. (1964). The Golden Rule in the light of new insight. In *Insight and responsibility*. New York: W. W. Norton.

Fallaci, O. (1978). *Letter to a child never born*. Garden City: Anchor Press/Doubleday.

Farley, F. (1986). The big T in personality. *Psychology Today, 5*.

Fisher, H. (1983). *The sex contract*. New York: Quill.

Fisher, H. (1987). The four year itch. *Natural History, 10*.

Forsyth, A. (1986). *A natural history of sex*. New York: Scribners.

Freuchen, P. (1961). *Book of the Eskimos*. New York: Branhall House.

Freud, S. (1913/1950). *Totem and taboo*. New York: W. W. Norton.

Friedan, B. (1981). *The second stage*. New York: Summit Books.

Gallese, L. (1985). *Women like us*. New York: New American Library.

Gilligan, C. (1983). *In a different voice*. Cambridge: Harvard University Press.

Gould, R. (1969). *Yiwara: Foragers of the Australian desert*. New York: Scribners.

Gould, S. J. (1988). Honorable men and women. *Natural History, 3*.

Gould, S. J. (1982). The oddball human male. *Natural History, 7*.

Gray, J. (1971). *The psychology of fear and stress*. New York: McGraw-Hill.

Greenway, J. (1972). *Down among the wild men*. Boston: Little, Brown.

Hackett, T., Cassem, N., & Wishnie, H. (1968). The coronary care unit: An appraisal of its psychological hasards. *N.E. J. Med. 279*:1365.

Hamilton, W. (1964). The genetical evolution of social behavior. *I. J. Theoretical Biology 7*.

Hamilton, W. (1963). The evolution of altruistic behavior. *Amer. Natur. 97*:354–6.

Hardesty, S., & Jacobs, N. (1986). *Success and betrayal: The crisis of women in corporate America*. Danbury, CT: Watts.

Harragan, B. (1977). *Games mother never taught you*. New York: Warner Books.

Hart, C., & Pilling, A. (1979). *The Tiwi of Northern Australia*. New York: Henry Holt.

Havens, L. (1986). *Making contact: The uses of language in psychotherapy*. Cambridge: Harvard University Press.

Hinde, R. (1984). Biological bases of the mother-child relationship. In J. Call, E. Galenson, & R. Tyson (eds.). *Frontiers of infant psychiatry*. New York: Basic Books.

Hinde, R., & Stevenson-Hinde, J. (in press). Perspectives on attachment. In C. Parkes, P. Mavis, & J. Stevenson-Hinde (eds.). *Attachment across the life cycle*.

Holloway, R. (1976). Paleoneurological evidence for language origins. *Ann. N.Y. Acad. Sci. 280*.

Howell, N. (1979). *Demography of the Dobe Kung*. New York: Academic Press.

Hrdy, S. (1977). *The Langurs of Abu*. Cambridge: Harvard University Press.

Inglis, J., & Lawson, J. (1981). Sex differences in the effects of unilateral brain damage on intelligence. *Science 212*.

Isaac, G. (1978). The food sharing behavior of proto-human hominids. *Sci. Am., 5*.

Jenness, J. (1928). *The people of the twilight*. New York: MacMillan.

Jerison, H. (1973). *Evolution of the brain and intelligence*. New York: Academic Press.

Kagan, J. (1984). *The nature of the child*. New York: Basic Books.

Kantor, D. (1980). Critical identity image: A concept linking individual, couple, and family development. In J. Pearce, & L. Friedman. *Family therapy: Combining psychodynamic and family systems approaches*. New York: Grune & Stratton.

Kaplan, H. S. (1988). Intimacy disorders and sexual panic states. *J. Sex and Marital Therapy, 14*(1).

Kernberg, O. (1975). *Borderline conditions and pathological narcissism*. New York: Jason Aronson.

Kimura, D. (1985). Male brain, female brain: The hidden difference. *Psych. Today, 11*.

Kofoed, L., & McMillan, J. (1987). Sociobiology of addiction in adolescence. *Pediatrician 14.*

Kohlberg, L. (1981). *The psychology of moral development.* New York: Harper & Row.

Kohut, H. (1982). Introspection, empathy, and the semi-circle of mental health. *Int. J. Psychoanal. 63.*

Konner, M. (1976). Maternal love, infant behavior and development. In R. Lee & I. DeVore (eds.). *Kalahari hunter-gatherers.* Cambridge: Harvard University Press.

Konner, M. (1982). *The tangled wing.* New York: Holt, Rinehart and Winston.

Kurland, J. (1986). Baboon society. *Nat. Hist.*

Lacoste-Utamsing, C., & Holloway, R. (1982). Sexual dimorphism in the human brain. *Science 216*(7).

Laing, R. D. (1969). *The politics of the family and other essays.* New York: Pantheon Books.

Leblanc, S., & Barnes, E. (1974). On the adaptive significance of the female breast (letter to the editor). *Am. Nat., 7–8.*

Lebra, T. (1976). *Japanese patterns of behavior.* Honolulu: University of Hawaii Press.

Lee, R. (1979). *The !Kung San: Men, women and work in a foraging society.* New York: Cambridge University Press.

Lee, R., & DeVore, I. (eds.). (1976). *Kalahari hunter-gatherers.* Cambridge: Harvard University Press.

Lee, R., & DeVore, I. (eds.). (1968). *Man the hunter.* New York: Aldine.

Lindholm, C. (1982). *Generosity and jealousy: The Swat Pukhtun of Northern Pakistan.* New York: Columbia University Press.

Lorenz, K. (1967). *On aggression.* New York: Bantam.

Lorenz, K. (1973). *Behind the mirror.* New York: Harcourt Brace Jovanovich.

Lovejoy, O. (1981). The origin of Man. *Science 211*(1):4480.

MacLean, P. (1955). The limbic system and emotional behavior. *Arch. Neuro. 73.*

Mahler, M. (1968). *On human symbiosis and the vicissitudes of individuation.* New York: International Universities Press.

Malinowski, B. (1926). *Crime and custom in savage society.* London: Routledge and Keegan Paul.

Marshall, L. (1976). *The Kung of Nyae Nyae.* Cambridge: Harvard University Press.

Masters, W., & Johnson, V. (1986). *Masters and Johnson on human loving.* Boston: Little, Brown.

Masters, W., & Johnson, V. (1974). *The pleasure bond.* Boston: Little, Brown.

McEwen, B. (1981). Sexual differentiation of the brain. *Nature 291*(6).

McMillan, C. (1983). *Women, reason and nature.* Princeton: Princeton University Press.

Meggitt, M. (1962). *Desert people.* Sidney: Angus and Robertson.

Meggitt, M. (1977). *Blood is their argument: Warfare among the Mae Enga tribesmen of the New Guinea Highlands.* Palo Alto: Mayfield.

Miller, J. B. (1976). *Towards a new psychology of women.* Boston: Beacon Press.

Moller, A. (1988). Ejaculate quality, testes size, and sperm competition in primates. *J. Hum. Evo. 17*(479).

Moore, M. (1985). Non-verbal courtship patterns in women. *Ethology and Sociobiology 6.*

Mowat, F. (1951/1977). *People of the deer*. New York: Jove.

Mulder, M. (submitted for publication). Behavioral ecology in traditional societies. *Trends in Ecology and Evolution*.

Murdoch, G. (1957). World ethnographic sample. *Am. Anthro. 59*.

Murdoch, G. (1967). *Ethnographic Atlas*. Pittsburgh: University of Pittsburgh.

Nauta, W., & Feirtag, M. (1979). The organization of the brain. *Sci. Am., 9*.

Perper, T. (1985). *Sex signals: The biology of love*. Philadelphia: I.S.I. Press.

Piaget, J. (1969). *The moral judgement of the child*. New York: Free Press.

Pilbeam, D. (1984). The descent of hominoids and hominids. *Sci. Am., 3*.

Pittman, F. (1985). Children of the rich. *Fam. Proc. 461*.

Price, D., & Brown, J. (1985). *Prehistoric hunter-gatherers: The emergence of cultural complexity*. New York: Academic Press.

Price, J. (1988). Alternative channels for negotiating asymmetry in social relationships. In M.R.A. Chance (ed.). *Social fabrics of the mind*. New York: Lawrence Erlbaum.

Roheim, G. (1974). *Children of the desert*. New York: Harper Torchbooks.

Savage-Rumbaugh, S., & Wilkerson, B. (1978). Socio-sexual behavior in *Pan paniscus* and *Pan troglodytes*: A comparative study. *J. Human Evolution 7*:327–344.

Schacter, S. (1959). *The psychology of affiliation: Experimental studies in the sources of gregariousness*. Palo Alto: Stanford University Press.

Scollard, J. (1985). *No-nonsense management tips for women*. New York: Simon & Schuster.

Sedgewick, J. (1985). *Rich Kids*. New York: William Morrow.

Shostak, M. (1981): *Nisa: The life and words of a !Kung woman*. Cambridge: Harvard University Press.

Siskind, J. (1975). *To hunt in the morning*. Oxford: Oxford University Press.

Slavin, M. (1985). The origins of psychic conflict and the adaptive function of repression. *Psychoanalysis and Contemporary Thought 8*(3).

Smuts, B. (1985). *Sex and friendship in baboons*. New York: Aldine.

Stack, C. (1975). *All our kin: Strategies for survival in a black community*. New York: Harper & Row.

Steffansson, V. (1951). *My life with the Eskimo*. New York: MacMillan.

Strum, S. (1987). *Almost human*. New York: Random House.

Surrey, J. (1984). The "Self-in Relation": A theory of women's development. Work in Progress 11. Stone Center Working Papers, Wellesley College, Wellesley.

Thomas, E. M. (1959). *The harmless people*. New York: Knopf.

Tonkinson, R. (1978). *The Mardudjara aborigines: Living the dream in Australia's desert*. New York: Holt, Rinehart and Winston.

Trevarthen, C. B. (1977). Descriptive analyses of infant communicative behavior. In H. Schaffer (ed.). *Studies in mother-infant interaction*. New York: Academic Press.

Trivers, R. (1971). The evolution of reciprocal altruism. *Quart. Rev. Biol. 46*:35–57.

Trivers, R. (1972). Parental investment and sexual selection. In Campbell, B. (ed.). *Sexual selection and the descent of man, 1871–1971*. New York: Aldine.

Trivers, R. (1974). Parent-offspring conflict. *Amer. Zool. 14*:249–64.

Trivers, R. (1985). *Social evolution*. Menlo Park: Benjamin Cummings Publication.

Trivers, R., & Hare, H. (1976). Haplodiploidy and the evolution of the social insects. *Science, 191*.

Trivers, R., & Willard, D. (1973). Natural selection and parental ability to vary the sex ratio of offspring. *Science 179*:90–2.

Tucker, D., & Williamson P. (1984). Asymmetric neural control systems in human self-regulation. *Psych. Rev. 91*(2).

Turnbull, C. (1962). *The forest people*. New York: Simon & Schuster.

Turnbull, C. (1972). *The mountain people*. New York: Simon & Schuster.

Turnbull, C. (1983). *The human cycle*. New York: Simon & Schuster.

Wachtel, P. (1977). *Psychoanalysis and behavior therapy*. New York: Basic Books.

Wachtel, P. (1982). *Resistance: Psychodynamic and behavioral approaches*. New York: Plenum.

Wachtel, P., & Wachtel, E. (1986). *Family dynamics in individual psychotherapy*. New York: Guilford Press.

Waipuldanya. (1962/1970). *I, the aboriginal*. New York: Meridian.

Weinrich, J. (1987). *Sexual landscapes*.New York: Scribners.

White, N. (1974). *Ethology and psychiatry*. Toronto: University of Toronto Press.

Williams, N., & Hunn, E. (1981). *Resource managers: North American and Australian hunter-gatherers*. AAAS Selected Symposium #67. Boulder: Westview Press.

Williams, W. (1986). *The spirit and the flesh: Sexual diversity in American Indian Culture*. Boston: Beacon Press.

Wilson, E. (1975). *Sociobiology: The new synthesis*. Cambridge: Harvard University Press.

Index